FIDELITY OF HEART

Fidelity of Heart

An Ethic of Christian Virtue

James E. Gilman

OXFORD

UNIVERSITY PRESS

2001

OXFORD
UNIVERSITY PRESS

Oxford   New York
Athens   Auckland   Bangkok   Bogota   Buenos Aires   Calcutta
Cape Town   Chennai   Dar es Salaam   Delhi   Florence   Hong Kong   Istanbul
Karachi   Kuala Lumpur   Madrid   Melbourne   Mexico City   Mumbai
Nairobi   Paris   Shanghai   Singapore   Taipei   Tokyo   Toronto

and associated companies in
Berlin   Ibadan

Copyright © 2001 by James E. Gilman

Published by Oxford University Press, Inc.,
198 Madison Avenue, New York, New York 10016

Oxford is a registered trademark of Oxford University Press

Library of Congress Cataloging-in-Publication Data
Gilman, James Earl.
Fidelity of heart : an ethic of Christian virtue / James E. Gilman.
p. cm.
Includes biblographical references and index.
ISBN 0-19-513662-4
1. Christian ethics. 2. Virtue. I. Title.
BJ1251 .G47 2000
241'.4—dc21   00-062336

9 8 7 6 5 4 3 2 1

Printed in the United States of America
on acid-free paper

To
Ian James and Caitrin Marie Gilman
for their abiding love

Preface

While working on a different book, on the philosophy of religion, I found my attention repeatedly diverted to issues and concerns that form the core of this book. Although these issues were not particularly new to me, they did impress themselves upon me as somewhat urgent, at least urgent for me to address. And so, setting aside work on the philosophy of religion, I embarked on a journey that led me through terrain I never could have imagined traversing at the outset. For some time I have thought that the two dimensions of human experience most neglected by Christian ethicists are the role of the imagination and the role of the emotions in moral life. Some ethicists do take seriously the emotions, of course, and others take seriously the imagination, but few take account of both as central and vital to constructing a unified approach to Christian ethics. That is what I have tried to do in this book.

My greatest personal and intellectual debt is to Vernon C. Grounds, chancellor of Denver Theological Seminary. Years ago, when I was an awkward theological student, Vernon's vision and vitality, along with his prophetic and pastoral ways, challenged me to think critically about ethics and Christian faith. His insistence on the revolutionary character of Christian ethics coupled with his single-minded commitment to the care of each human being still inspire me all these years later. I am deeply indebted as well to Edward Long, Jr., and to Charles Courtney, both of Drew University. Professor Long introduced me through his teaching and writing to the wonders and worries of Christian ethics, and through his patient and personal concern encouraged me in this scholarly endeavor. Whatever capacity for clear, careful, critical analysis that may be demonstrated in this book is largely due to Professor Courtney who not only models such skills but also elicits them from others.

Professor Roger Gilman, brother and philosophical colleague, and I have had many conversations over the years about religious and philosophical ethics. He has graciously read drafts of some of the material in this book and willingly discussed much of it at one time or another, and provided helpful perspectives and comments. I find it remarkable that as brothers and philosophers we share so much in common regarding matters of philosophy and morality. Remarkable also is the supportive and nurturing academic environment in which I find myself at Mary Baldwin College. Especially colleagues in the Department of Philosophy and Religion, Pat Hunt, Roderic Owen, Edward Scott, Annette Evans, Perry Neel, are unsurpassed in their willingness to converse, critique, comment, or encourage. I am also grateful to many other colleagues who through their friendship, criticisms, and conversations have encouraged me in this project, including Bob Everett, David Murchie, Craig Blomburg, Gordon Lewis, David Kling, Jack Hill, Alan Christy, Tom O'Connor, Helen Hamilton, and Margo Leach. In one way or another each has contributed to the process of completing this book.

I am blessed with a publisher and editor, Cynthia A. Read, who not only is skilled at what she does but who treats the work of others with the kind of care she would treat her own work. I am grateful as well to Oxford University Press's reviewers for insightful comments and criticisms that enhance the substance of the book, and to production editor Robert Milks and other anonymous editors at Oxford University Press whose meticulous editing of form and style make this a much better book.

Not least of all, I am eternally grateful for my children, Ian James and Caitrin Marie, to whom this book is dedicated. Their unhindered love and tender care are immeasurable gifts of God's grace. I am also grateful for the encouragement of Maureen Jones, whose dedication to the life of the mind and spirit is for me a constant source of inspiration.

Contents

PART I

Reenfranchising the Heart

So, like children, we begin again
To learn from things
Because they are in God's heart;
They have never left him.

Ranier Marie Rilke, The Book of Hours

Matters of the Heart

THE HEART OF VIRTUE

When a woman of ill repute heard that Jesus was a guest in the house of a Pharisee, she went to the house with a vial of ointment, entered, and "weeping, . . . began to wet his feet with her tears, and wiped them with the hair of her head, and kissed his feet and anointed them with the ointment. Now when the Pharisee who had invited him saw it, he said to himself, 'If this man were a prophet, he would have known who and what sort of woman this is who is touching him, for she is a sinner' " (Luke 7:31–50).[1] In this story are encapsulated two images of commitment, one represented by the Pharisee, and the other by the disreputable woman. For the Pharisee Jesus is an esteemed guest, a teacher and prophet greatly to be respected and admired; yet there is between Pharisee and Jesus a certain distance. The Pharisee's interest in Jesus seems to be largely a matter of intellectual curiosity and critical inquiry; and indeed when the Pharisee subjects Jesus' acceptance of the disreputable woman to the scrutiny of critical inquiry, his role as prophet is called into question. For the woman, in contrast, Jesus is not only teacher and prophet but master and Lord, who calls forth her deepest pain, remorse, longing, devotion, even intimacy. Both Pharisee and woman are attracted to Jesus. The Pharisee's curiosity and admiration inspire him to share with Jesus his home, table, and hospitality. The woman's faith inspires her to share with Jesus her failures, her heart's longing, her life, indeed, herself. Both are compelling images of commitment, but the contrast between them (admiring and following) gives rise to a question: How can we assess the difference in the way the Pharisee and the woman relate to Jesus? How assess the difference between respectful admiration and passionate discipleship? One way of answering this question may certainly be to examine the Pharisee, finding out why he admires Jesus enough to invite him to dinner and why he is scandalized by the woman's behavior and Jesus's solidarity with her. Another way of answering may be to examine the woman, asking why she feels such devotion to Jesus and why she expresses her devotion with such affection and intimacy. The ethic of Christian virtue set forth in this book examines the difference between these two images of commitment and concludes that when fully articulated and practiced, Christian faith will transform a dispassionate, respectful admirer of Jesus into a passionately devoted follower.

The pivotal notion by which I articulate the distinction between the Pharisee's respectful admiration and the woman's passionate devotion is "virtue" or "heart," two words that I use often and interchangeably. Since these words are widely used in philosophical and theological circles today, I shall need to carefully delineate exactly what I mean to refer to when I use them. By virtue or heart I refer to a quality of human character consisting of two dimensions, dispositions or habits on the one hand and emotions on the other. By dispositions I mean those normal or prevailing aspects of a community's character, like courage or humility or kindness, that incline it to live according to a particular moral pattern of life or not. By emotions I mean those affectional powers, like joy or sorrow or anger, that energize and reenergize a community, enabling it to actually practice a moral pattern of life. These two dimensions, dispositions and emotions, together constitute what I mean by "virtue" and metaphorically by "heart." Together they constitute the systole and diastole, two inseparable motions of the beating heart of Christian faith. More specifically, dispositional habits invite or elicit certain emotional attachments that are commensurate with their particular character trait, so that if a given habit is operative, the emotions correlative to it will manifest themselves. Conversely, the presence of a specific emotional attachment presupposes certain habits of character without which it could not arise. If a person gets angry at the unfair distribution of economic and social goods in America, for example, then we may properly suppose he has developed a disposition of fairness that disposes him toward justice; and if a person does not get angry then we may surmise that such a disposition of character is lacking. Corresponding to dispositions and emotions are two modifiers, "obediential" and "empathetic," that denote function. Thus, the term "obediential dispositions" denotes habits of heart that are essential for obeying God's commandments, and the term "empathetic emotions" denotes certain affections elicited by those dispositions. By their very nature I am so situated in relation to God and so empowered as to be able to actually practice moral projects in conformity with God's commandments. Together, in short, obediential dispositions and empathetic emotions entail what I mean by virtue or heart.

I am aware that this use of these two terms is somewhat novel and unconventional and that they are frequently used to distinguish different moral traditions. "Virtue" often refers to a moral tradition that emphasizes the role of character, habit, and even rational commands, while "heart" often refers to a tradition that emphasizes the moral role of emotions. My use of the two terms, as interchangeable is deliberate, an intentional way of encapsulating the aim of this book, which is to insist that the two traditions, virtue and emotions, should properly be seen as two inseparable dimensions of a single moral experience. Irrespective of how the tradition happens to have employed them, in other words, "virtue" properly and normatively should refer to both character habits and empathetic emotions, and "heart" should likewise refer to both. By doing so I am not intending to disregard inherited moral traditions but intend rather to bring them up to date to show how properly and normatively understood they advance beyond themselves to form a more profound, comprehensive, and harmonious manifestation of human moral experience.

These two philosophical-theological trends (obediential dispositions and empathetic emotions) correspond to one or the other of two threads woven into the historical fabric of Christian ethics. One thread (obediential dispositions) weaves into the fabric a tradition of character or virtue ethics while the other thread (empathetic emotions) weaves into it a tradition of moral passions. But as I will show, neither thread is by itself strong enough to bear the weight of moral life. Rather only when they are securely woven together into a single, seamless fabric will the weight of moral life be sufficiently supported and sustained.

The first thread (virtue ethics) woven throughout the history of Western thought has its roots in Plato's *Republic* and his efforts to answer the question, What makes a state and its citizens just or good? His answer inspired Aristotle to develop what is perhaps the most thorough and systematic treatment of an ethics of character to date and what is certainly the theory most influential in the development of some of its most recent philosophical (Alisdair MacIntyre) and theological (Stanley Hauerwas) versions. Aristotle propounds a teleological ethics of character, the belief that each existing thing, including humans, has an end or purpose distinctive to its own nature, which end it is the proper function of its existence to fulfill. The distinctive, peculiar end of humans, according to Aristotle, cannot be mere biological sustenance, since this is clearly shared with vegetables; nor can it be mere sentient life, which humans have in common with animals. Instead, the peculiar end of human life involves the activity of the soul in accordance with a rational principle and in accordance with virtue. While this rational principle of soul ultimately aims at happiness, the soul's moral principle aims at the good, which, as it turns out, is another name or word for happiness. Indeed, happiness results from the soul's activity that aims at excellence or virtue. Moreover, the rational principle according to which a person achieves happiness, argues Aristotle, is the mean between acting excessively or deficiently. Although the passions, without the guidance of reason, are inclined to lead the soul to perform a wide range of actions that achieve neither goodness nor happiness, they must not be shunned or neglected. Indeed, it is by being neglected that the passions are likely to lead the soul astray, to choose excessively or deficiently. Instead, virtue, as the soul's rational principle of morality, must be fundamentally concerned with human passions, for it alone, according to Aristotle, is able to harness the power of the passions and direct them toward the end of happy self-fulfillment. The virtuous soul, then, involves certain virtues (such as courage, gentleness, and self-control) and passions that, under the control and guidance of reason, form habits of character adapted and correlated to the mean between excess and deficit.

Aristotle's treatment of virtue is retrieved and sustained by Aquinas, who expands Aristotle's views by arguing that humans possess not only a natural but a supernatural end and that the ultimate source and end of human happiness lies with the latter. In concert with Aristotle, Aquinas develops an ethic in which certain appropriate virtuous habits of character (such as humility, justice, wisdom, temperance) are essential to the fulfillment of the blessed, supernatural end with which God has endowed humans. Although Aquinas's Christian version of character ethics continues to attract attention, it was largely marginalized, beginning in the eighteenth century, with the rise of Kant's deontological and Bentham's consequentialist approaches to ethics. For these two approaches, the crux of the moral life lies not so much in virtuous character, although that is not unimportant, but in establishing and conforming to universal principles of reason with which one might calculate and exercise rational moral choices. Because versions of these two traditions have tended to dominate moral philosophy and theology in North America, contemporary ethicists, until recently, have made minimal use of character/virtue ethics.[2]

Contemporary moral philosophy and theology, however, have begun to compensate for this tendency. Philosopher Alisdair MacIntyre in *After Virtue* and theologian Stanley Hauerwas in *Character and Christian Life,* for example, insist that moral choice entails a great deal more than finding a suitable rational principle whereby humans might exercise moral choices. Indeed, both argue that the act of making moral choices presupposes already a moral agent whose character, constituted by appropriate habits of virtue, establishes the possibility of that agent making morally right choices. Drawing on Aristotle and Aquinas, they insist that the focus of moral life is a community's development of moral character and the habits of virtue essential to shaping that character. But although MacIntyre and Hauerwas retrieve Aristotle's and Aquinas's focus on character ethics, they generally neglect a significant component of Aristotle's ethics, namely, the vital role of the emotions or passions.

Not surprisingly, then, a second thread woven throughout Western thought tracks the nature and significance of empathetic emotions in practical reasoning. Western thinkers have generally paid a fair amount of attention to human emotions or passions, although the treatment they have received varies widely. Some eighteenth-century philosophers, like Hutcheson, Smith, and Hume, insisted that certain emotions, such as sympathy, should play an important role in public morality. But most thinkers marginalized the emotions in one way or another. Martha Nussbaum, in *Love's Knowledge,* identifies two ways in which the emotions were marginalized in the Western tradition.[3] First, for some thinkers, like Descartes and Kant, emotions tend to be viewed as "blind animal reactions, like or identical with bodily feelings, that are in their nature unmixed with thought, undiscriminating, and impervious to reasoning."[4] The assumption underlying this view is that emotions are irrational (or at best nonrational), noncognitive experiences that cannot and should not contribute to practical reasoning and moral life. A Kantian argument, for example, goes like this: since emotions, such as love, are nonrational they are therefore not commandable, and since they are not commandable they cannot be trusted as reliable guides for moral life. Similarly, Christian ethicists, like Joseph Fletcher, tend to marginalize the role of emotions in moral reason and practice. For although for Fletcher love is central to Christian ethics, for him, as I will show, divine love is not an emotion but a rational principle that can be commanded and thereby trusted as a reliable guide for practical reasoning.[5] A second way some thinkers, like Plato and Spinoza, marginalize the emotions, according to Nussbaum, is to view them as cognitive yet unreliable. Emotions are constituted by a "cognitive dimension," it is admitted, but they still must be banished from the moral life because, as Nussbaum puts it, "the judgments on which the major emotions are based are *all* false. . . . In other words, their dismissal has, in this case, nothing to do with the fact that they are . . . non-cognitive." Instead, they are perceived "as pieces of reasoning that are actually false"[6] and therefore unreliable guides for moral life.

Again, contemporary philosophy and theology have begun to compensate for this peculiar habit of marginalizing the emotions. Philosopher Nussbaum in *Love's Knowledge* and theologian Edward Vacek in *Love, Human and Divine*, for example, not only insist on emotions as cognitive and central to practical reasoning but insist likewise on their reliability as guides for moral life. This is not to apotheosize the moral status of emotions or suggest that they cannot be falsified or unreliable. Indeed, they can. Rather, reenfranchising emotions to their proper status is simply to acknowledge what ordinary persons experience routinely, namely, that emotions are powerful moral forces and very often, when properly cultivated, function as reliable moral guides. And it is to acknowledge what ordinary Christians presuppose, namely, that obeying God's commandments is made possible when by God's grace the faithful are endowed with the power of holy affections.

The particular challenge of this book lies in its attempt to weave into a single cloth virtue's two threads (obediential dispositions and empathetic emotions) and show how together they account for the difference between the two images of commitment (admiring or following) in Luke's story. To argue that neither obediential dispositions (an ethic of virtue) nor empathetic emotions (an ethic of emotions) possess an independent, privileged status in an account of morality, but rather that they are internally interdependent is indeed a challenge. This is to say that partly the challenge of this book lies in its scope. All of the relevant sources and materials from these two moral traditions, diverse and copious as they are, cannot be treated exhaustively. A sampling from each tradition must suffice. Fortunately, there are a few sources in philosophy and theology that manage to integrate to some extent an ethics of character and an ethics of emotions. Aristotle and Jonathan Edwards, both with a measure of success, manage such a merger, and the writings of both, especially Edwards, are important sources for fulfilling the promise of this book. My aim, accordingly, is to weave together into the fabric of ethics the threads of these two traditions. Separately they are frayed and weak, but together they create a fabric so richly designed and durable as to be able to bear the weight of both the complex intricacies and bold simplicities of the Christian community's moral life.

FIDELITY OF HEART

What are we to make, then, of the many theories of ethics that tend to marginalize one or the other of these two traditions, character dispositions or empathetic emotions? First, we can say that such theories fail to faithfully and fully articulate the heart of virtue they claim to analyze, fail to represent conceptually the intricate complexities of moral life as practiced by moral communities. Such theories, in other words, are partial and fragmented. By neglecting obediential dispositions or empathetic emotions, they leave unfulfilled their promises of faithfully explicating the nature of Christian ethics. This book aims to explicate the meaning of "fidelity of heart" by showing how both obediential dispositions and empathetic emotions are essential dimensions of any community devoting itself passionately, intimately, and singlemindedly to following, and not just admiring, Christ.

In a series of contrasts, Kierkegaard distinguishes between being an admirer of Jesus, like the Pharisee in Luke's story, and being a follower, like the disreputable woman. The gist of his argument presupposes that admiring involves an attitude consisting primarily of a kind of detached curiosity and rational inquiry, while following involves a passionate, intimate, and personal devotion of heart. The peculiarity of admiration, Kierkegaard insists, is not just that a subject regards an object with esteem but that between them a personal, emotional distance is maintained much like that between spectator and admired actor. Admirer and follower alike acknowledge that Jesus is a person to be reckoned with. But while "a follower is or strives to be what he admires, an admirer holds himself personally aloof, consciously or unconsciously, he does not discern that the object of his admiration makes a claim upon him to be or strive to be the thing he admires."[7] The follower believes that Jesus came into the world not only to save it but "to be 'the pattern,' to leave behind Him footsteps for those who would attach themselves to Him, who thus might become followers, for 'follower' corresponds to 'footsteps.' "[8] Indeed, fidelity is the activity of imitating Christ, following these footsteps. Conversely, "[i]t is only through imagination," says Kierkegaard, "that admirers are related to the man they admire, to them he is like an actor on stage except that, this being real life, the effect he produces is somewhat stronger." In real life admirers insist on the same exemption they insist on in the theater, namely, "to sit safely and tranquilly, without any relationship to danger, reckoning it, however, to their personal credit that they admire the man, thinking thereby presumably that they have a claim to share . . . in the merit he deserves."⁹ Unlike a follower, the spectator admires, perhaps even envies, the actor but has no intention of singlemindedly and passionately devoting his life to the actor, no intention of following the actor's pattern of life. Thus, while the admirer, the Pharisee, maintains a personal, emotional distance from the esteemed person, the follower, the disreputable woman, devotes herself personally, passionately to Jesus, making herself available and vulnerable to him and his pattern of life.

This is not, however, the end of Kierkegaard's analysis of admiring and following. In typically provocative fashion, Kierkegaard goes on to argue that the peculiar deception of modern Christianity is that it routinely mistakes admiring Christ for following him, falsely believing that in admiring Christ, as did the Pharisee, one is actually faithfully following in his footsteps. Not a great deal of effort would need to be expended, I think, in order to show that Christian churches today are largely populated by admirers of Jesus who falsely believe that they are followers. There are at least two forms of this modern self-deception. One form I refer to as "objectivism" or "faith as amusement." Faith as amusement deceives Christians into believing that because they are interested in and aroused by Jesus, because they are intrigued by his life and ministry, because they attend Sunday services, worship, and faithfully observe holy days, and because they have great respect and even reverence for Jesus, they must be following the pattern of life to which he called disciples. Like spectators or fans at an athletic event, Christianity as amusement provides frequent and ongoing audience participation. At times noise emanating from fans is so deafening that even the athletes fall under the impressions that the fans are in some sense actually contributing to the outcome of the game. Moreover, spectators eagerly and earnestly follow ritual cues from cheerleaders who themselves often act as if they are playing and not merely observing the event. All in all, the fans experience a diverse and intense family of emotions, so much so that sometimes they actually feel they are participating somehow in the event and are crucial to its outcome. And what admiration fans have for the athletes themselves! Often identifying vicariously with the athletes, they feel with them in their successes and failures but never risk success or failure for themselves. Vicarious identification and emotional arousal are two of the powerful magnets drawing and capturing adoring fans. Indeed, the appeal of being an admiring fan is its capacity to provide a cathartic experience in which emotions are aroused and discharged in such a way that, although therapeutic and enjoyable, the experience does not interfere with the practical affairs of everyday life. In short, admiring Jesus in this way provides a therapeutic amusement without requiring Christians to change significantly the pattern of their daily lives.

Although this form of self-deception continues to be suffered by many in the church today, there is another, perhaps even more common, form of self-deception that I refer to as "tribalism" or "faith as magic." This form also is a way of admiring Jesus while falsely believing one is following him. It presupposes that because my religious experiences are genuinely passionate, personal, and inspirational, the pattern of life I am earnestly living amounts to a genuine form of following Jesus. In truth, however, faith as magic is a way in which devotees invoke Jesus to follow their own pattern of life, inviting him to sanction and sanctify the intensely passionate pattern of spirituality they happen to enjoy. Faith as magic is a form of respectful admiration insofar as it invokes the blessing of a respected and revered prophet on one's way of life. These two forms of self-deception are common to Christianity and are the raison d'être of this book's argument. It is a matter of some urgency for Christian communities, and the theologians that service them, to face up to these forms of self deception and undertake to make the transition from merely admiring to actually following Christ's pattern of life.

My impression is that Christian churches are swelling with both forms of admirers, who nevertheless believe they are followers of Jesus. Are there not among us many admirers for whom faith is an earnest form of religious amusement and just as many for whom faith magically sanctifies the earnestness of their personal spiritual journey? Kierkegaard is typically straightforward in attacking these modern forms of Christian self-deception. "Christ constantly uses the expression 'follower'; he never says anything about wanting admirers, admiring worshippers, adherents."[10] Indeed, "Christ's life as Pattern is precisely calculated to put an end to this game of self-deception,"[11] of believing that by admiring Jesus we are somehow faithfully following him. The ethic of Christian virtue set forth in this book insists, with Kierkegaard, that ultimately Jesus calls followers and not merely admirers. Christian ethicists interested in unmasking and overcoming our contemporary forms of religious and moral self-deception, accordingly, need to be about the business of articulating how this transition from admiring to following might be made. One way, I am arguing, is in terms of "fidelity of heart," by weaving into our theories and practice of Christian ethics an understanding of obediential dispositions and empathetic emotions without which moral communities wither and die. If we do not do so, not only will Christian ethicists continue to construct an ethics of amusement or magic, but our churches will continue to be crowded with admiring spectators who falsely believe they are followers. This is to suggest not that those whose theories neglect one thread of virtue or the other are themselves any less followers of Jesus but only that their lives are not constrained by the limitations of their moral theories and that their moral theories fail to reflect and account for the full, passionate depth of their moral lives. It is to suggest that some who more comfortably relate to Jesus in the manner of the Pharisee than in the manner of the woman and who are more comfortable admiring than they are following may, when it comes to religion, prefer the distance of rational discourse to the intimacy of personal, passionate, obediential devotion. I hope in this book to persuade the reader that the distinction between admiring and following is enormously significant and consequential and that for the Christian community, at least, it is a matter of some urgency that it encourage the faithful to make the transition from admiring to following a primary concern.

THE PLAN OF THIS BOOK

A word about the book's plan and organization. It embraces issues that are in nature methodological as well as substantive. Much of my incentive for writing it arises from doubts I have concerning certain assumptions, substantive and methodological, implicit in many recent approaches to Christian ethics. First, I have doubts that theories of ethics marginalizing the role of empathetic emotions or the role of character dispositions bear sufficient substance to account for the complexities of a community's actual moral practice. Second, I have doubts that even those theories incorporating such substance possess a methodology sufficiently developed to embrace and integrate in a coherent way both dimensions (obediential dispositions and empathetic emotions) of a genuinely virtuous heart.

These substantive and methodological issues are critical points of reference throughout the book and are introduced in chapter 2. The question this chapter poses, is How can Christianity, how can Christian ethics, satisfy the scrutiny of critical inquiry and universal comprehensibility and at the same time maintain a distinctive, local particularity? In answering, I first set forth a methodology of sufficient depth to embrace and integrate virtue's two dimensions—its obediential dispositions and empathetic emotions. I show how the one dimension (empathetic emotions) preserves Christianity's relevance to the demands of universal reason, while the other (obediential dispositions) preserves the demand for distinctive particularity. Finally I show how the methodology thus established provides a framework for constructing an ethic of Christian virtue or, as I shall refer to it throughout, a "covenantal ethic."

Applying the idea virtue or heart to fundamental concepts of Christian ethics is the general aim of part II. I employ the substantive and methodological principles introduced in chapter 2 here for the purpose of interpreting certain moral virtues (love, peace, and justice) that are central to any theory of Christian ethics. My procedure in each of the three chapters is similar. First, I place each virtue in the context of contemporary ethical reflection. Second, I interpret each virtue in terms of the two dimensions (obediential dispositions and empathetic emotions) constituting it. Third, I draw out the implications of each virtue for moral practice, showing what it would be like for a covenantal community to actually practice love, peace, and justice. But questions linger unanswered at the completion of part II. Is not the ethic of Christian virtue set forth in parts I and II an entirely sectarian one? Is it not a wholly inward-looking ethic, one so confessional and self-absorbed that it renders itself irrelevant to other communities and incomprehensible to society as a whole? Does it not advocate a wholly private ethic without public relevance short of a kind of triumphalism? What relevance does a covenantal ethic have in public life? Can such an ethic survive the scrutiny of critical reason? Can it assume a role in public life and discourse?

Part III dedicates itself to the task of answering these questions. First, in chapter 6, I show how love, peace, and justice (examined in part II) converge in a practice of compassion on the basis of which a public covenant among diverse moral communities is possible. In the process I am able to show how the idea of compassion is of sufficient moral and theological depth to embrace the strengths and avoid the weaknesses of two competing traditions, liberalism and communitarianism. In chapter 7, I show how the goal of an ethic of public compassion is to educate a populace for global citizenship. I go on to argue that in order to cultivate habits of compassion and global citizenship, public education must place special emphasis on the narrative imagination and community apprenticeships. Narratives are an essential way humans have access to their emotional life and apprenticeships a way to cultivate those emotions into habits of compassion and global citizenship. In part III, in other words, I show that in the practice of compassion there is established at once both the possibility of the convergence of private and public morality in a public covenant and the possibility of global citizenship.

A word about the sources and resources for developing the substantive argument in this book. I am very much influenced by Jonathan Edwards and his assumption that in developing an ethic of Christian virtue the ethicist should maintain continuous contact with three touchstones: the biblical tradition, the concrete experiences of faith communities, and rational reflection/analysis. It is especially important that an equilibrium be maintained among these three criteria in order to avoid certain excesses, such as biblicism or metaphysical speculation. The biblical tradition provides Christian ethics with a record of first-order moral experiences insofar as it records the experiences of those communities especially called of God to practice a life of covenantal virtue. The story of their experiences is authoritative and definitive for any ethic that claims the Christian tradition. Yet these biblical experiences are always interpreted. As Edward Long says in his recent work on Christian ethics, persuasive interpretations of the biblical narrative will "enable our experiences to be read by the biblical narrative even as they involve a reading of the Bible from where we stand."[12] Many pitfalls accompany those who intend to remain faithful to this biblical tradition, however, principally because there is no single, imperious version of that tradition but rather multiple interpretations and versions to be reckoned with. I intend to try to persuade the reader of my particular interpretation; to do so, however, I must venture beyond the biblical tradition itself and draw on the common, ordinary experiences of persons and communities who claim that tradition. These communities provide first-order empirical evidence of what it is like to practice covenantal love, peace, and justice. Although they are not always in agreement regarding their common tradition, they nevertheless provide a rich variety of perspectives from which to draw out and develop a persuasive version of the Christian community's moral life. Yet, given that faith communities frequently absorb beliefs and values of the society in which they find themselves, religious experiences are insufficient in themselves for constructing a version of moral practice that is distinctively Christian and covenantal. Accordingly, continuous, critical use must be made of the biblical tradition on the one hand and philosophical reflection and analysis on the other. Otherwise one's interpretation of Christian ethics is likely to co-opt or be co-opted by the values and beliefs of the interpreter's culture. To negotiate the relationship between a community's experiences and the biblical tradition and to develop an ethic that acknowledges and accounts for this relationship philosophical reflection and analysis is indispensable. I frequently draw on and benefit from the work of philosophers and theologians whose capacities for reflection and analysis far exceed my own. I call on their rich and rewarding insights to assist in interpreting the biblical tradition, the ordinary experiences of covenantal communities, and the nature of the relationship between the two.

Throughout the book I make frequent use of such phrases as "covenantal community," "covenantal ethic," "covenantal virtue," and such. I would be remiss if I do not clarify what I mean when I use "covenantal" in this way. By "covenantal" I mean what the National Conference of Catholic Bishops mean when they refer to "covenantal union" as a "right relationship between people and God"; a union in which a "covenant bound the people to God in fidelity and obedience" and in which "God was also committed in the covenant, to be present with the people, to save them, to lead them to freedom."[13] Accordingly, I use the term "covenantal" to refer first of all to religious traditions and communities that are historical in character in distinction from religions that are natural. Whereas natural religions constitute themselves cosmically, shaping themselves according to the cycle of seasons and natural forces, historical religions constitute themselves narratively, shaping themselves according to certain revelatory events the memory of which establish concrete promises and mutual commitments between the divine and the human. Mountain Sinai in the Jewish tradition and Calvary in the Christian tradition represent such covenantal, historical events. Second, I generally restrict my use of the term "covenant" to refer to communities who understand themselves as practicing a tradition that is somehow continuous with those traditions whose religious life is recorded in the Jewish and Christian Scriptures. Accordingly, by the term "covenantal communities" I also refer to those Christian churches who identify themselves as communities intentionally continuous with the covenantal communities referred to in Scriptures. Such covenantal communities, admittedly, are diverse and at times at odds with each other, yet in their diversities and disagreements they uniformly appeal to common historical, biblical events. Occasionally my use of the term "covenantal" belies the fact that I believe that there may be communities that, although they do not identify themselves in terms of the biblical tradition, may understand their own practice of morality in ways that are compatible with the ethic of virtue based on that tradition.

The question this book addresses, then, is, What does it mean for a covenantal community to practice fidelity of heart? My hope is that this analysis of covenantal virtue will both clarify the distinction between the two images of commitment, admiring and following, and persuade the Christian community of the urgency of making the transition from the former to the latter. Not only does its vitality as a distinct community depend on fidelity of heart, but the moral health of societies will surely be enhanced because of it. No doubt for some this book will seem to be "too edifying" (as Kierkegaard might say) to be a strictly scholarly, academic book, while for others it may seem too academic and scholarly to be edifying. My hope is that, since scholarly expositions and edifying discourses are not mutually exclusive genres, it might graciously be considered by the reader to be both. Furthermore, my hope is that the methodology set forth and applied here might be employed in the service of interpreting the life of other communities, religious or secular, that do not claim the biblical tradition, on the assumption that virtue or heart is a dimension of spirituality common to all human beings. (It is not within the scope of this particular book, however, to try to show how such interpretation might be extended and articulated.)

Reenfranchising the Heart

$\mathbf{N}$EWS THE PROPHET Nathan delivers to King David is not especially good. A wealthy subject of the kingdom, in order to entertain a sojourner, has taken a lamb from the flock of a poor man. King David's feeling of anger is immediate and intense, a feeling initiated by the fact that an injustice was done, anger anyone hearing the story would probably feel. Moreover, David seems to know immediately what punishment his spiritual community will require of the man. Of course, when David discovers, with Nathan's prompting, that he happens to be that offender, his anger is transformed into genuine feelings of guilt and remorse, and the punishment he suffers, although severe, is merciful in the context of what his community would otherwise require of such an offender (2 Samuel 11 and 12). Latent in this biblical story is a critical dilemma characteristically faced by contemporary ethicists and theists. How is it that David's feeling of moral anger (or guilt) toward the rich man is able to bear the weight of a universal moral judgment that anyone facing the same facts would feel, as it seems to? And how, at the same time, is it able to bear meaning that is distinct to the particularity of his local community of faith?

Contemporary theologians pose this dilemma variously. Jeffrey Stout, for example, refers to "the dialectical situation that is the fate of modern theism": How can Christianity "respond to modernity without becoming either incomprehensible to it or so much like it as to sacrifice the claim to distinctiveness?"[1] Or, as Paul Lauritzen puts it, Christianity must either assimilate its beliefs to "the criteria of truthfulness" established by the Enlightenment and in so doing abandon its distinctiveness; or it must "cling to its traditional beliefs" and "the paradoxical nature of [those] beliefs" and in so doing render them "incomprehensible and hence socially irrelevant in the modern world." The Christian is thus "faced with the problem of how to escape this dilemma: indistinctness or irrelevance. To attempt to revise the faith threatens to make it indistinctive; not to revise the faith threatens to make it irrelevant."[2] The same dilemma is often formulated in terms of a tension between truth and meaning. "Is it enough to say that the biblical narratives are meaningful," asks Gary Comstock, "[o]r are Christians also committed to saying that they are true?"[3] How is it possible for biblical narratives to bear meaning for a particular religious community and at the same time bear truth in a way that is universally intelligible? "Does casting the Christian tradition in narrative terms," in other words, "merely make it more meaningful to people who already believe," asks Edward J. Oakes, "or does it actually give access to a form of truth that it could offer to the scrutiny of free inquiry?"[4] The moral version of this dilemma, with which this book ultimately is concerned, can be formulated in several ways. One way is this: How is it possible for the local Christian community to live a holy life according to the particularity of biblical morality and at the same time participate in public life according to the demands of universal moral principles? How can a covenantal community preserve a distinctive ethic of Christian virtue while at the same time promoting an ethic that is somehow relevant and comprehensible publicly, even globally? In meeting the demands of universal law and the scrutiny of critical reason is Christian ethics compelled to relinquish the distinctive particularity of its moral life, and vice versa?

In this chapter, and indeed throughout this book, I propose one way of resolving the various forms of this dilemma by reenfranchising what Martha Nussbaum calls, narrative emotions.[5] While "narrative" and "emotion" as categories of human experience have attracted a great deal of attention, this attention is generally directed toward one of these categories or the other and not often toward both simultaneously. I argue in this chapter that by attending to narratives and emotions as interdependent dimensions of a single human experience, a way is cleared for reconciling both horns of theology's dilemma. My procedure is, first, to outline a theory of emotions on the basis of which I argue that emotions mediate a practical kind of universal truth comprehensible in public life. Second, I set forth a theory of narrative on the basis of which I argue that narratives mediate meanings distinctive to a faith community. Third, I show how emotions and narratives, truth and meaning, are mutually interdependent dimensions of moral life on the basis of which the moral dilemma facing the Christian community might be resolved. My thesis, then, is that the interdependence of the truths of emotion and narrative meanings provides a way of promoting the distinct, local character of Christian ethics while at the same time preserving its relevance and comprehensibility in public life.

RECONCEIVING EMOTIONS

Of all the features of modernity extracted from human experience, perhaps none is more widely known than the contrast between emotion and reason. As anyone familiar with modernity knows, it has greatly favored reason over emotion. It is not surprising then, that most modern versions of Christianity and Christian ethics favor reason over emotion, and like modernity in general, similarly find themselves trapped in a dilemma, between the demands of meaning for particularity and the demands of truth for universality. My aim is to outline a theory that redresses modernity's bias against emotions and lays the groundwork for resolving the dilemma facing it.

Modernity is accustomed to treating emotions, says Nussbaum, in one of two ways, as already noted: either as "blind animal reactions" or as experiences that, although in some way cognitive, must be banished because they "involve value judgments that attach great worth to uncontrolled things outside the agent; they are, then, acknowledgements of the finite and imperfectly controlled character of human life."[6] Both ways of treating emotions, she argues, have been decisively discredited "by cognitive psychology, by anthropology, by psychoanalysis, and even by philosophy—not to speak of our sense of life itself."[7] In what follows I intend to show that emotions are neither "raw natural feelings" nor "cognitive experiences which nevertheless cannot be trusted" but complex activities that are very often trustworthy guides for human thought and life. Henceforth I use the term "emotion" to refer to a single, complex experience that is constituted by three interdependent ingredients: judgments, projects, and energy. Conceiving of emotions in this threefold way is corroborated in a recent study by psychologists Andrew Ortony, Gerald Close, and Allen Collins, who argue that emotions "involve feelings and experiences . . . physiology and behavior, and . . . cognitions and conceptualizations."[8]

Emotion as Judgment

Although modernity long degraded the emotions, its "myth of the passions," as Robert Solomon calls it, is collapsing; emotions are no longer considered to be the "dumb forces beyond our control but judgements we make. As such they have conceptual and intelligent form and a logic that characteristizes them."[9] Aristotle was one of the first to recognize this: "The emotions are all those feelings that so change men as to affect their judgments, and that are also attended by pain and pleasure." In fact, what can be discovered of the cognitive structure of emotions, he insists, includes "(1) what the state of angry people is, (2) who the people are with whom they usually get angry, and (3) and on what grounds they get angry with them."[10] For Aristotle, emotions consist of cognitive structures and dynamics that distinguish them from mere feelings. More recently, Jonathan Edwards and Friedrich Schleiermacher both perceived the Christianity of their day as suffering from a withering dogmatism, for which both prescribed religious emotion as a cure. But Edwards, unlike Schleiermacher, insists that emotions are cognitive; he argues that "true religion in large part consists of holy affections" and that the "proper seat" of these affections is in "the mind, and not the body."[11] Emotions consist of "the sense of heart where the mind is not speculative but experiences and feels."[12] Even more recently, Lauritzen argues against a "noncognitivist" and for a "cognitivist" view that "makes belief or judgment (1) a constitutive feature of the concept of an emotion and (2) necessary for individuating particular emotions."[13]

The specific kind of relation between judgment and emotion is suggested by Nussbaum. Judgment or "[b]elief is sufficient for emotion, emotion necessary for full belief."[14] Consequently, we must conceive of emotions as being constituted by "beliefs or judgments about the world in such a way that the removal of the relevant belief will remove not only the reason for the emotion but also the emotion itself. . . . Anger, for example, is . . . a composite of painful feeling with the belief that I have been wronged."[15] Acknowledging that Nussbaum and Lauritzen incorrectly equate belief and judgment and that judgments and not beliefs are constituents of emotions,[16] they make a compelling case for the view that emotions involve cognitive judgments. Their case, put succinctly, is as follows. All emotions are constituted by intentional objects about which the mind makes judgments. Thus, if I remove the judgment "I have been treated unjustly," my anger concomitantly disappears; and if I am angry, it can only be because of some judgment I have made about the way the world is. Robert C. Roberts makes the same case by arguing that "an emotion is an intrinsically intentional mental state. That means that an emotion's object is constitutive of the emotion; if the object to which the emotion is directed changes, then, while you may have the same type of emotion, you do not have the same emotion."[17]

Consider the biblical narrative of David, Bathseba, and Nathan (2 Samuel 11 and 12). In the first scene (chapter 11) the tragic failure of David's character is embodied in a story of lust, greed, cunning, and envy. The second scenario (chapter 12) reveals the health of David's spirituality, but only after Nathan's parable quite unexpectedly discloses to him who he truly is. Note how Nathan's narrative both embodies and elicits the dynamics of emotional life. When David hears of the rich man who, because he does not want to waste one of his own, takes the only lamb of a poor man to entertain a sojourner, David's "anger was greatly kindled against the man; and he said to Nathan, "As the Lord lives, the man who has done this deserves to die. And he shall restore the lamb fourfold, because he did this thing, and because he had no pity' " (2 Sam. 12:5–6). Nathan's narrative has power to draw David into its plot and engage him emotionally. David's anger toward the rich man and compassion toward the poor is initiated by a judgment he makes about how the world is—that the rich man treated the poor man unjustly. This judgment, in turn, is prompted by David's belief that the covenant God made with Israel includes a call for justice. His anger at minimum includes a judgment about the unjust way the world is. Remove that particular judgment, and David's anger likewise disappears. But this is only the first stage in a painful process of self-discovery for David. For when Nathan points out to him that he is the rich man, David is drawn personally into Nathan's parable, which becomes a story of David's own spiritual journey and mirrors to him his tragic failure. Yet David's spiritual culture, which tutored him in his emotional habits, does not fail him. His acknowledgement that it is him and not another who is the culprit requires a willingness to readjust his original judgment about what the world is like, now making a judgment about his role in that world. His new judgment, that *he* treated the poor man unjustly, now generates an entirely new family of emotions: not only anger toward himself but feelings of guilt, remorse, and repentance. These feelings are habits cultivated in him by his community and are a catalyst for practicing a spirituality of humble repentance instead of arrogant denial. Feeling emotion entails interpreting and making a value judgment about the world as it is.

Emotion as Project

Emotions are constituted, however, not only by value judgments but also by practical activities or projects. There is "an intimate and perhaps inextricable connection," insists Roger Scruton, "between . . . knowing what to feel and knowing what to do." Simultaneously with judgments, emotions involve "recognized patterns of appropriate behavior."[18] or what Ortony and colleagues refer to as "physiology and behavior."[19] Jonathan Edwards recognizes this intentional, active quality of human affections when he says that "the affections are the more vigorous and practical exercises of the inclination and will of the soul."[20] God made the emotions "the basis of human actions"; they are "like springs that set us moving in all the affairs of life and its pursuits." If the emotions were "taken away, the world would be motionless and dead."[21] Throughout *Religious Affections* and *The Nature of True Virtue* Edwards speaks of religious affection as the actual "exercise," "practice," "habit" of a benevolent heart. Similarly, Lauritzen speaks of emotions as "culturally constructed . . . 'social practices organized by stories that we both enact and tell.' "[22]

Emotions as practices or behavior include, of course, physiological projections such as facial contortions, gestures, utterances, changes in location, changes in blood pressure, and so on. But, as Solomon argues, they are typically a great deal more than physiological events; they are "not only [physiological] projections of behavior, they are our projects. They are not only directed toward intentional objects; they are ladened with intentions to act. Emotions are concerned not only with 'the way the world is' [our judgments], but with 'the way the world ought to be,' " our emotional projects.[23] As such they are teleological projects, actualizing the purposeful intention implicit in emotional judgments. Besides value judgments, even backward-looking emotions, like guilt, presuppose certain actions or projects that I undertake in response to that judgment: for example, in David's case, that repentance is appropriate, that forgiveness and restoration are available, and that I must undertake to reform myself and my world according to what it ought to be.

Thus, when his "anger was greatly kindled against the man," David knew immediately the nature of the project to be undertaken: the rich man must "restore the lamb fourfold," and he "deserves to die" (2 Sam. 12:5–6). The project David's emotional judgment triggers is in this case already stipulated by and through the community to which he belongs. David shares a culture, a system of accepted beliefs and practices. Not only has his community's culture educated him in the appropriate emotional judgment to make regarding the rich man's deed but it has educated him regarding the emotional project appropriate to that judgment. The matter becomes more complicated, of course, when Nathan reveals to David that he is the rich man. David's reputation as "a man after God's own heart" is partly due to his willingness to admit, as he does here, his guilt. For his acknowledgment of the truth of Nathan's words generates not only a different family of emotion—not only a different judgment—but a different project. His feelings of guilt and remorse, appropriate now to a new understanding of himself and his world, concomitantly alter the emotional project he must undertake. David and his family must participate in a project, articulated by Nathan, appropriate to his community's conception of sin. What Scruton says of all communities is true of David's: "There is something that the covenant community acknowledges as correct and obligatory in response," in this case, to an offense. "The common culture embraces these complex feelings [judgments] and obligations [projects] and makes them alive together in the single episode."[24] Whatever the emotion or family of emotions, whether fear, joy, reverence, hatred, anxiety, or love, it includes intentional projects as to how the world ought to be. Based on the value judgment that initiates the emotional experience, accordingly, a community is inspired to undertake a moral project that fulfills the promise of that judgment.

Emotion as Energy

By now it should be clear that the modern habit of mind, which reduces emotions to experiences of raw natural feelings or to a kind of irrational energy, is simply misguided. But it would be equally misleading to disown what everyone knows: that emotions are constituted by affectional forces of such raw power as to be able to vitalize and revitalize the lives we live. Edwards accounts for this aspect of emotion when he speaks of affections as "vigorous and sensible exercises" of the faculty that "through all cultures and times . . . has been called the heart." These "exercises," he says, are of "various intensities" and supply an emotional experience with energy to carry out its project. "The liking or inclination of the soul to something, if it is intense and vigorous, is the very thing which we call the affection of love, and the same degree of dislike or disinclination is what we mean by hatred. So it is the degree to which the will is active, either toward or against something, that makes it an affection."[25]

The technical use of the term *energia* in Aristotle's *Metaphysics*[26] suggests a way of clarifying this particular component of emotions. *Energia*, for Aristotle, is not equivalent to *dynamis*, which is the capacity (but not the actualization of the capacity) or potency of a thing for doing or making, although *energia* presupposes such a capacity. Rather, *energia* is the act of making or doing itself, the power by which potency actualizes itself. But neither is *energia*, for Aristotle, merely kinetic motion or feeling, a process belonging entirely to the physical nature of things, although motion includes kinesis. *Energia* is power itself, a force actualizing the emotional project for which a judgment is the catalyst. It is thus not surprising to discover that Aristotle's derivation of *energia* is from *ergon*, function: the actual doing or making for which humans have capacity. Moreover, since for Aristotle function is inevitably related to the notion of a *telos*, or purpose, project as *telos* is not only an embodied response to an emotional judgment but the intentional act whose realization is impossible apart from affective forces (*energia*). Emotional energy, in other words, is the spark that ignites and drives humans to actualize the projects engendered by emotional judgments; it inspires people and communities to live out those projects whereby they make and remake their worlds.

At least two specific functions of *energia* emerge from this analysis. The first, transformative power is, of course, legendary. It drives people to deeds of great virtue and heroism as well as to deeds of malicious savagery. We might say that emotional energy, analogous to physical energy, comprises a system of transference and transformation. Emotional energy is capable of manifesting itself in various forms (anger, fear, love, joy), transferring its power from form to form as the occasion calls for it. Simultaneously with this transference of energy there occurs a transformation of reality. Emotion is an energy possessing "the ability to alter our surreality," as Solomon puts it, "and constitute it and reconstitute it to our personal needs."[27] Initially David's anger toward the rich man, for example, constitutes his reality, but only momentarily; for that reality is suddenly, almost magically, transformed when he recognizes himself as the culprit in Nathan's narrative. The emotional energy previously expressed as righteous anger directed toward an other is converted by his new self-awareness into feelings of guilt, remorse, and repentance—into a project whereby David's experience of guilt is transformed by repentance into feelings of mercy, forgiveness, and joy.

Which is to say, in turn, that the second function of emotional energy is to serve as a kind of dialectical link between judgment and project. The emotional energy constituting David's guilt and remorse establishes an existential matrix without which his judgment (of having wrongfully treated a man) and his project (of repentance and recompense) are quite inconceivable. Between the judgments (the world as it is) and projects (the world as it ought to be) of emotions there obtains a kind of mutuality inconceivable apart from understanding emotions as *energia*. David's judgment, that the rich man treated the poor man unjustly, if truly held, is not and cannot exist as a disembodied abstraction (as can a belief) discontinuous somehow from an experience of anger. His judgment is interdependent with his righteous indignation and is unintelligible without it. If David's judgment no longer holds or is disingenuously held, then the emotion's energy ceases. Conversely, the practical possibility of a project ceases if the emotional spring "that sets us moving," as Edwards describes it, is absent.[28] In short, moral judgments (what the world is like) and projects (what ought to be done) are mediated by the transformative powers of emotional *energia*.

Emotions, so conceived as experiences of moral feelings, I will now argue, are able to bear a kind of universal truth while at the same time preserving in narrative form meanings that possess local, tribal credibility.

EMOTIONS AND TRUTH

Understanding emotions in the threefold way just outlined makes it possible to address more directly the dilemma of how to reconcile demands for universal truth and demands for local, distinctive meaning. How can the particularity of biblical narratives that plot meanings distinctive to the Christian tradition at the same time embrace universally intelligible truths? In response to this dilemma, modernity produced two theological tendencies, "objectivism" and "tribalism,"[29] each of which, instead of reconciling the dilemma, inclined Christianity toward one of its horns at the expense of the other: objectivism toward the demand for universal truth, tribalism toward the demand for local meaning. Narrative emotion, I am proposing, is a complex category of sufficient power to incline Christianity, or any tradition, simultaneously toward both, narrative inclining it toward particular meanings and emotion toward universal truths. To show how one constituent of this complex, emotion, inclines Christianity toward universal moral truths, I argue the premise here that the judgments/projects of emotions embody claims that are universal in two interrelated senses. First, moral or empathetic emotions are universal in that they are universally accessible and comprehensible; they presuppose judgments that can be subjected to the scrutiny of critical inquiry of any tradition whatsoever. Second, moral emotions are universal in that they presuppose judgments that are normative, value judgments by which the behavior of all humans ought to be prescribed. David's feeling of anger toward the injustice done to the poor man is inaugurated, for example, by a moral judgment ("the rich man unjustly took a lamb from the poor man") that has universal force and appeal. It is accessible and comprehensible to people of all traditions, regardless of the particular community or culture to which they belong, and its normative prescription has universal moral appeal. To say that emotion is "intersubjective" is to say that it is universal in these two senses.

In developing versions of Christianity that would satisfy modernity's demand for universal truth, objectivism established a highly technical "strategy of abstraction," to use Steven Crites's term. This strategy seeks to detach "images and qualities ... from experience" and use them as "data for the formation of generalized principles and techniques ... [which give to] experience a new, nonnarrative and atemporal coherence. ... In its more elaborated forms, the strategy of abstraction is the basis for all science,"[30] including the science of modern theology. This objectivist strategy requires that "in reasoning we should aim for one set of standards that are so rigidly fixed as to be completely unaffected by people's [narrative] standpoints."[31] Or, as P. F. Strawson insists, "[t]he bare possibility of understanding diverse cultures requires a massive central core of human thinking which has no history."[32] An objectivist's assumption, then, is that by abstracting from the Christian story a core of universal truths can be distilled "that all reasonable persons," as Bernard V. Lonergan puts it, "whether 'religiously' involved or not, can recognize as reasonable."[33]

The point I wish to make is not that we should suppress the passion for discovering in Christianity universal truths, but that objectivism fails as an acceptable way of doing so largely because its strategy of abstraction requires that we forfeit the legitimate and compelling tribal qualities that endow a faith tradition with distinctive meaning. The problem is not objectivism's quest for universal truth; the problem is finding a strategy capable of embracing both universal truth and local meaning. I propose here to pursue both paths: first, I examine the nature of emotional intersubjectivity that satisfies the demand for universal truth judgments, second, I examine the nature of narrative imagination that satisfies the need for local meaning.

We must first try to answer the question, To what sort of truths do narrative emotions refer? It is more common to answer this question in terms of narrative or, in Paul Ricoeur's words, textual referentiality. But it is possible to answer it, as I do here, in terms of emotional referentiality. Ricoeur, along with other hermeneuticists, argues that besides having "sense" a narrative text also has "reference" and this reference is the possible world the text creates. The truth to which a narrative refers is metaphorical, for it "displays a world only under the condition that the reference of descriptive discourse is suspended." Thus, the discourse of "the literary work sets out its denotation as a second-level denotation, by means of the suspension of the first-level denotation of [descriptive] discourse."[34] The emotional referentiality that I advocate here differs from Ricoeur's textual referentiality as experience differs from reflection on experience. Although Ricoeur does suggest that "poetic feeling itself also develops an experience of reality,"[35] his primary interest is poetics and not feeling—texts as literary works and not emotions as bearers of truth-judgments.

The question of emotional referentiality can be posed at two levels. As first-level denotations, emotions are experienced as actual, concrete, and historical. The emotional judgments belonging to these experiences refer to "the way the world is" as it is experienced by an individual or community. As second-level denotations, emotions are interpreted and expressed in narratives, especially narrative texts. Insofar as these narratives interpret human experiences, they interpret emotional judgments (how the world is) and projects (how the world ought to be) of a community. But narratives themselves do not so much directly refer to

truths about the world as to emotional judgments and projects that are intersubjectively universal in the two ways just identified. In contrast, narrative is (as I
will show) that dimension of emotions that interprets and embodies those truth-
judgments and confers on them distinctive, tribal meanings.

   The truths to which emotions refer are both subjective and objective. That
truth is subjective, and that emotions and truth are somehow related is not entirely unprecedented in modern thought. Kierkegaard perhaps more than any
other recognized and propagated this relation. His familiar formula states that
truth is a matter of subjectivity and subjectivity a matter of passionate inwardness,
a matter of an individual emotionally appropriating truth.[36] But Kierkegaard's
eagerness to distance himself from Hegelian rationalism led him to develop a
conception of passion that requires a paradoxical object, a belief that is absurd,
and an experience that is somehow nonrational. But since emotions are cognitive
experiences and are not nonrational or irrational, they can and should be seen
as bearing truths that are both universally, accessible, comprehensible, and normative. Take the emotional judgment David makes in response to Nathan's parable, for example. It embodies a truth about the world as it is for him, namely,
that the rich man exploited the poor man. This is the world to which David's
anger partly refers; his judgment about the world is appropriated subjectively in
the anger he feels. Furthermore, implicit in his judgment and explicit in his
project are normative assumptions about how David and his community think
the world ought to be. David assumes, for example, that injustice requires repentance on the part of the offender and that recompense must be made to the
offended. Emotional referentiality involves for David, then, both forward- and
backward-looking moments. Embedded in David's anger is a judgment regarding
the existing (dis)order; embodied in his project of repentance and recompense is
an expectant hope for remaking that disorder into the order it can and ought to
be. Of course, emotional judgments about the way the world is may be expressed
abstractly, in propositions. But, as I will show, in order for truth-judgments to
be universally intelligible they must remain anchored to the concrete, emotional
experiences in which they arise, and in order for them to retain distinctive meaning they must remain embedded in the local narrative history and text of origi-
nation.

   Besides referentiality, a second question we must try to answer is, How is it
possible that truths belonging to emotional judgments/projects possess universal
intelligibility and normative appeal, or what I call practical objectivity? Taking
seriously the view of emotions just set forth; my answer is already suggested in
terms of emotional intersubjectivity. In their analyses of emotions, Kierkegaard,
Edwards, and Lauritzen fail to pursue, as I do here, the implications of emotions
being cognitive, namely, that they are not only subjective but intersubjective.
What then is emotional intersubjectivity, and how does it endow truth with practical objectivity and universal intelligibility?

"Emotional intersubjectivity" is simply a way of conceptualizing a rather common human experience, the experience of shared emotions.[37] It implies that a person's or community's emotional experiences are not privileged but universally accessible, intelligible to others, and normative. This is not to say that my experiences of love or fear are exactly the same as yours; they will differ, as I will show, insofar as our narrative communities and biographies differ. Yet our experiences of these emotions may be similar in their judgments about what the world is and their projects about what the world ought to be. Even for people of widely divergent cultural, ethnic, and religious traditions, I am claiming the possibility of emotional intersubjectivity. How so?

Emotional intersubjectivity presupposes human relations that are constituted by a logic of internal relations. Some properties of individuals are internal and essential while others are external and accidental. Rational thought, for example, is an internal property of being human, and pale-colored skin pigment is accidental. "Intersubjectivity" refers to the fact that one property that is internal to a self is its relation to others—that what defines a self essentially involves its relations with other selves. Emotions are a primary way in which relations among humans are internal; they are a way in which what connects individuals to each other is prior to what separates them. Through emotional experiences the self shares itself with others and others share themselves with a self. This common experience is the basis on which Solomon can insist that "[v]irtually all of our emotions . . . involve other people—explicitly as their objects, implicitly in their choice of standards, subjectively in their mutual constitution of our relationships."[38]

For the Christian, the intersubjectivity (or practical objectivity) of emotional relations manifests itself most dramatically in the birth, life, and death of Jesus and in his injunction to "love one another as I have loved you" (John 15:12). Two moments of emotional intersubjectivity are present in the incarnation. First, of the many ways in which the biblical writers understand and interpret the incarnation, one of the most compelling is the way in which God undertakes to establish relations with humans, namely, by sharing emotionally in the human condition. In fact, love, which bridges the abyss between the divine and human, means nothing if not the practical possibility of shared emotional judgments and projects. The writer of Hebrews, by insisting that Jesus participates in the human condition, its suffering and temptations, presupposes that one matrix of the divine and human relation is emotional (Hebrews 2 and 4). Moreover, as Nussbaum insists, Christianity grants that "in order to imagine a god who is truly superior, truly worthy of worship, truly and fully just, we must imagine a god who has actually lived out the nontranscendent life and understands it in the only way it can be understood, by suffering and death"[39]—by sharing in the concrete, emotional life of humans. That is why we instinctively think of this event not only as a model of loving compassion but also as an event that is universally intelligible and normative, transversing even the Christian tradition that propounds it. God undertakes to feel and suffer what humans feel and suffer. God in Jesus shares those emotional judgments and projects of human suffering: his despair in the garden, his sense that his world as it is is void of hope, his desire in his anguish to love and be loved by those closest to him, and his sense of being forsaken by them. These emotional judgments and projects, so common and universal to the human condition and seemingly so alien to the divine, nevertheless become a way in which the divine enters into human experience and redeems it. Conversely, the gospel message presupposes the practical emotional intersubjectivity of God's incarnate life. It presupposes, as Jesus declares, that peoples of all nations, cultures, and races can share in God's love and are to be persuaded by that love to share in the Kingdom of God. The fact of incarnation, accordingly, in a sense perpetually deconstructs and dechristianizes itself. Its true significance lies in the fact of its intersubjectivity (the fact that love involves shared emotions), that it cannot be contained by or restricted to any particular tradition that fancies itself as its chief warden.

A second level on which the incarnation manifests emotional intersubjectivity is suggested by the Apostle Paul, who enjoins us to have in ourselves the same love, joy, affection, sympathy, and humility of mind as is in Christ Jesus (Philippians 2). Not only are the truths to which my emotional judgments and projects refer intersubjective with divine experience, they are intersubjective and thereby universally intelligible in the experience of all humans, regardless of race, religion, or culture. Consider the parable of the good Samaritan. The poignancy of the story partly depends on understanding the putative alienation between Jews and Samaritans. They were estranged by ancient habits of racial, religious, and cultural hatred. The priest and Levite, with every religious and cultural reason for feeling compassion for their fellow traveler, pass by; but the Samaritan, with every reason not to, has compassion for the injured man. The Samaritan's emotional habit of heart persuades him to embrace in his own experience a judgment about the way the world is for the Jew and to undertake a project of how the world ought to be for the Jew. Such compassion defies the curse of racial, religious, and cultural hatred. Moreover, this parable, as William Prior points out, "is not exclusively or even primarily a religious story: the representatives of organized religion are not cast in a favorable light, the hero is a member of a nation of religious outcasts, and he does not justify his actions by appeal to religious principles," although he may well have. Compassion, as indicative of the family of emotions he felt, is a common experience of intersubjectivity in which "people of many religious and cultural backgrounds, including those who profess no religious faith at all,"[40] share in each other's emotional judgments and projects.

Further evidence of the intersubjectivity of emotional judgments and projects abound: interracial, crosscultural marriages are instances in which, despite radical biographical differences, love, fear, anxiety, and joy become shared experiences. International acts of humanitarian concern, although all too rare, demonstrate that the reality to which emotional judgments and projects refer can be borne intersubjectively by a wide diversity of races and cultures. Take the Persian Gulf war of 1991, precipitated by Iraq's incursion into Kuwait. Although I am in disagreement with the policy of warmaking, the allied countries, representing diverse and sometimes conflicting traditions, nevertheless manifested that emotional judgments and projects are universal and intersubjectively accessible. Christians, Jews, Hindus, Buddhists, Muslims, humanists, and Marxists together judged Iraq's action as wrongful. In spite of the diversity of beliefs and values represented by these communities, they managed to share a universal, emotional judgment (anger toward injustice) about how the world is and undertake a joint emotional project about how the world ought to be for those suffering injustice. Although the moral judgments/projects implicit in emotions are universal and normative, they are not acultural and atemporal but rather transcultural; they are emotions that can and are shared by a great diversity of communities whose cultural profiles differ quite remarkably.

Of course, my claim that the truths to which emotions refer are universal does not, and I do not intend it to, meet modernity's criteria of abstract objectivity. My claim does not fancy itself as establishing an ahistorical, acultural, transcendent universality. But it does assert a practical and transcultural universality whereby people of diverse traditions can begin to nurture habits of compassionate intersubjectivity on the basis of which there might emerge a tradition of international cooperation, for example. Recognition of these sorts of shared human experiences leads Solomon to insist that in our emotional relationships "we 'open ourselves' to others, allow ourselves to share their experiences and opinions, [even] their worldviews, and ultimately, their other emotions."[41] Indeed, this human capacity for shared emotions makes possible the kind of covenantal community without which an ethic of Christian virtue is quite impossible. Yet the fact that moral emotions are intersubjectively universal in no way requires us to forfeit our quest that has to do with the other horn of theology's contemporary dilemma, the demand for meaning that is local, distinctive, and particular.

NARRATIVE AND MEANING

Thus far I have addressed questions about the structure of emotions and how emotional judgments/projects intersubjectively mediate universal moral truths. I turn now to narratives and the quality they possess for endowing experience with local, distinctive meaning. Theologians like Edwards and Schleiermacher, for whom emotions are important, generally fail to recognize the full significance of narratives for embodying and expressing emotion, although Schleiermacher's work in hermeneutics lays the groundwork for doing so. Further, they fail to see the interdependence of emotion and narrative and their joint role in resolving the dilemma of truth and meaning.

The question of primary concern is, What is narrative and how do narratives mediate meaning that is distinctively local to a community of faith?[42] "Narrative" refers to a twofold activity by which the imaginative mind, first, discovers in experience a plot constituted by characters, events, human relationships, and temporal sequence. The shape a plot takes may manifest itself in a wide variety of forms—personal experience, history, music, dance, theater, novel. Second, by "narrative" I refer to the susceptibility of plot to interpretation, to a community discovering in it some pattern of meaning. That pattern of meaning may be regarded as highly significant and pivotal for shaping a community's identity or as relatively insignificant and worthy of little attention. A narrative pattern of meaning, therefore, may or may not be recorded and preserved. When it is, it may possess a power to inspire a tradition to which a community commits itself and in terms of which it identifies itself. Plot and meaning are inseparable aspects of narrative and together constitute a peculiar dimension of narrative that is especially relevant to constructing an ethic of Christian virtue. That peculiar dimension of narrative is the capacity of its plot to endow the pattern(s) of meaning with a concrete, local particularity. What is especially pertinent to moral communities is the moral shape conferred on plot and meaning by certain formative dispositions of heart, like humility and patience or pride and impulsiveness. These dispositions give moral shape not only to the characters and events of a narrative's plot but to any community that chooses to conform its character to that plot and its pattern of meaning. So, whereas shared emotions preserve the universality of truth-judgments, narratives preserve the distinctive, local, and particular patterns of life that a community finds meaningful. How so?

Tribalism attempts to satisfy the demand for articulating the distinct particularity that narrative confers on any quest for meaning. In reasoning, tribalists argue, "we should content ourselves with innumerable sets of standards that are so localized as to be completely subservient to people's contingent standpoints. . . . [We can still judge] between true and false, rational and irrational beliefs. But . . . the standards to which one appeals in making these judgements are confined to one's own 'tribe.' " In the final analysis, then, we must acknowledge that "justification will stop at some principle or alleged matter of fact that only has local credibility."[43] George Lindbeck's "cultural-linguistic" antifoundationalism, for example, exhibits tribalistic tendencies in that it restricts the intelligibility of a religion's beliefs to the local language-game of a particular community. A doctrine thus does not refer to "what the world is like" in a way that transcends reliance on a community's distinctive orientation but rather articulates its own identity and the tradition from which that identity emerges. Cultural-linguistic "intelligibility," argues Lindbeck, "comes from skill not theory, and credibility comes from good performance not adherence to independently formulated criteria." Further, "the reasonableness of a religion is largely a function of its assimilative powers, of its ability to provide an intelligible interpretation in its own terms of the varied situations and realities adherents encounter."[44]

But the narrative (cultural-linguistic) articulation of a tradition need not inhibit the quest for universality, although, as John Yoder rightly notes regarding Lindbeck's tribalistic tendencies, a community's "acceptance of [its] own limits may be read as not facing the challenge of universality."[45] But it need not be so. What I try to trace here is a path whereby the distinctiveness of one's tradition can be advanced without forfeiting the legitimate demand for universality, which I have already located in the intersubjectivity of empathetic emotions. The narrative dimension of emotions lends itself to doing just that; for narratives, and the obediential dispositions shaping them, mediate the demand for local, distinctive meaning while at the same time preserving the intersubjectivity of the empathetic emotions they plot.

Whereas emotions function as a mechanism for attaching universal truth-values to our experiences of the world, "[t]he primary mechanism for attaching meaning to particular experiences," Howard Brody insists, "is to tell stories about them."[46] Ricoeur and narrative theologians have drawn attention to the fact that not only words, sentences, and propositions but also narrative texts bear meanings. Their premise is that the meaning of such texts is their plot.[47] Via plot, narrative is especially suited to penetrating the temporality of human emotions and the dramatic history of a community's habits and character development. A plot's strategy, argues Crites, is suited to "containing the full temporality of experience in a unity of form [meaning].... [For just as] the rhythms and melodic lines of music are inherently temporal and drive the music forward," so too does a narrative's plot embody the impulses and patterns of emotional habits that drive human experience. "We do not hear them [the rhythms and melody] all at once, but in a succession of pulses and pitched vibrations; yet we experience them as a unity, a unity [of meaning] through time."[48] What is distinctive about plot, then, is not only the fact that it is constituted by characters and temporal sequence but that it lies open to patterns of meaning, to being interpreted. So, just as "implication" moves strategies of abstraction forward toward certain conclusions, so plot moves "our understanding ... forward by developing or unfolding it"— by gathering it to a point or unity of meaning, even if that meaning is not a resolution or culmination. "Like implication, it [plot] seeks to make explicit what would otherwise remain implicit; unlike implication ... [its] rules of development are not logical rules because narrative connects contingent events."[49] Narrative's strategy is one of concretion, then, rather than abstraction; its responsibility is to plot the specifically temporal, local, and contingent character of human experience and to mediate meaning for those whose lives are shaped by that plot's narrative.

A second question must be answered: Who then has access to meaning in biblical narratives? Although the moral truths to which emotional judgments and projects refer are intersubjectively accessible, comprehensible, and normative, the nature of narratives and the meanings to which they lend themselves possess a local, tribal quality accessible primarily to those whose own particular story is intertwined with those narratives. Biblical narratives become meaningful, in other words, for those who choose to mold their own life to the meaningful pattern of life plotted in those narratives. As Hans Frei suggests, "the shape of the story being mirrored in the shape of our life is the condition of its being meaningful for us."[50] Conceivably one who does not claim the biblical tradition could still find an episode in the biblical narrative meaningful, for example, Gandhi on the Sermon on the Mount. In this cases the story's meaning, is interpreted in terms of the distinctive traditions of the local Hindu community to which Gandhi belongs.

Biblical narratives articulate the condition of a community's soul as it attempts to understand and endow its experiences with meaning. In his confrontation with David, Nathan's parable tells a story that as David soon recognizes, unexpectedly confers upon his own story more or different meaning than at first anticipated. Initially, the meaning of Nathan's parable for David, although significant (he reacts in anger), is somewhat remote, for he has not yet understood how intricately his own story is intertwined with the one Nathan tells. When suddenly he finds himself a participant in the story, a new depth of meaning emerges for him, a meaning quite unthinkable for one who merely listens rather than participates in the story. Although the truth-value of the world as it is to which David's judgment and project refer is universally accessible to any who cares to listen, what the story says, the meaning that David or anyone derives from it, is tradition-dependent. Indeed, the narrative's most profound meaning is perhaps accessible only to David, whose own story line is central to the parable itself.

For Jews or Christians, for whom this story forms a thread in the fabric of their own narrative tradition, the story's meaning is shaped by their participation today in communities whose lives are continuous with that of the ancient Israelite community to which David belonged. People of other traditions may of course derive meaning from this story, but the meaning for them will be in terms of their own tradition and will depend on how well it is able to accommodate and interpret what the story says in images their own community favors. In any case, this or any episode's meaning remains resolutely local, shaped from and by the cultic beliefs and practices of the community to which a person belongs.

REENFRANCHISING THE HEART

The destination toward which I have been somewhat circuitously steering is this: that if they are to reconcile their contemporary dilemma, theology and ethics must devote themselves to reenfranchising the heart (i.e., the category narrative emotions), devote themselves to showing how emotion and narrative are interdependent and how together they resolve the dilemma of truth and meaning.

Lauritzen is one whose recent work attends to both emotion and narrative, but he fails to appreciate the full extent of their interdependence and their value for resolving the dilemma.[51] Kierkegaard, on the other hand, understood perhaps better than any other the profound mutuality of emotion and narrative or, as he put it, of passionate inwardness and indirect communication. His failure to fully acknowledge the intersubjectivity of emotions should not obscure the fact that for him the passionate inwardness of subjective truth must embody itself indirectly in narrative costume.[52] Similarly, Collingwood's distinction between "inner" and "outer" history, which I employ here, goes a long way toward clarifying the inseparability of emotive experience and narrative form.[53] The category narrative emotion both allows us to distinguish conceptually between outer history, or "what a story is about," and inner history, or "what a story says"—between truth and meaning. They are not alternatives between which one can choose; neither are they identical. By the outside or narrative form of an experience is meant its body, or, as R. G. Collingwood says, "everything belonging to it [an experience] which can be described in terms of bodies and their movements." By the inside or content of an experience is meant its emotions or, as Collingwood puts it, "that in it which can only be described in terms of thought."[54] So the cognitive dimension of an emotion, its judgment about how the world is and ought to be, for example, comprises a kind of inner history, whereas narratives mold and shape that history into patterns of tribal meanings consistent with the self-identity of a community.

How does this interdependence of emotion and narrative manifest itself? In at least two ways, which I call socialization and justification. Martha Nussbaum indicates the important pedagogical role narrative emotions play in human social development. Narratives, she argues, manifest

an attitude toward emotions. . . . It is that emotions are not feelings that well up in some natural and untutored way from our natural selves, that they are, in fact, not personal or natural at all, that they are, instead, contrivances, social constructs. We learn how to feel, and we learn our emotional repertoire. We learn our emotions in the same way we learn our beliefs—from our society. But emotions, unlike many of our beliefs, are not taught to us directly through propositional claims about the world, either abstract or concrete. They are taught, above all, through stories. Stories express their structure and teach us their dynamics. These stories are constructed by others and, then, taught and learned. But once internalized, they shape the way life feels and looks.[55]

So a narrative's plot, as a strategy of concretion, is "profoundly committed to the emotions," suggests Nussbaum, and "its interaction with its readers takes place centrally through them."[56] Whereas narratives and the dispositions of character that shape and are shaped by them function as tools by which a community educates and reeducates its emotional habits, emotions function as transformative powers for appropriating and practicing the narrative meanings a community believes the world normatively ought to reflect.

Second, in addition to recognizing the social, pedagogical nature of narrative emotions, we must also recognize the role narratives play in justifying the judgments and projects of emotional life. Objectivist strategies for justifying beliefs are foundational; that is to say, objective conditions for beliefs being justified include their derivation from other beliefs whose rationality is independently grounded, until the process ends in a most abstract, general belief or presupposition for which no further justification can or need be sought. As such, the more particular belief is justified in terms of the more universal belief or principle. But narratives (meaning) and emotions (truth-judgments) lend themselves to a different kind of justification, what I call practical justification. This term refers to the fact that the universal emotional judgments and projects various communities share are justified in terms of the particularity of each community's narrative tradition, in terms of each community's practice of distinctively local, tribal beliefs and values. The universal judgments/projects of shared emotions, in other words, are justified in terms of local, tribal narratives and the particular patterns of meaning a community discovers in them. This peculiar character of practical justification parallels closely Wittgenstein's claim on behalf of rules and rule-following. If indeed rules or emotional judgments are social and socialized, then, as Wittgenstein insists, they are constructed as "customs," things repeated, regular, and communally established.[57] Since, like rules, emotional habits "rest on the agreed and accepted practices of a community, they are, says Wittgenstein, their own justification."[58] In this sense, what Nussbaum refers to as the "cataleptic," self-certifying character of emotions[59] and Patricia Greenspan calls "emotional justification" is self-referential.[60] What emotional judgments and projects are appropriate and justifiable in any given situation is a function of what one's community agrees is acceptable of its members. There is no extrinsic, objective foundational principle to which one can appeal, other than the constraint implicit in a rule that one's emotional judgment/project is inappropriate and unjustifiable if it fails to conform to the community's narrative tradition and habits. Emotions, in other words, do not arise irrationally or magically but arise cognitively and are justified narratively. As cognitive experiences, their mode of justification is tribal and local, established narratively by the community who through its social practice has come to some agreement regarding their appropriateness.

Suppose we accept this premise, that in contrast to objectivist strategies of abstract justification, strategies of practical justification are such that the universal is justified in terms of the particular, the intersubjectivity of emotional judgments/projects is justified in terms of their concrete, narrative context, and transcultural truths are justified in terms of local custom. What follows? One result is that a single judgment of empathetic emotion, like the judgment "Exploitation of the poor by the rich is a damnable travesty of justice," will have as many practical justifications as there are narrative traditions for whom that judgment is deemed appropriate. The Jew might justify it in terms of Jahweh's deliverance of God's people from bondage, the Christian in terms of the power of Jesus' liberating resurrection, the Marxist in terms of class struggle, and so on. In short, a person's narrative tradition of origin endows that person's emotional experiences with a justificatory power that the distinctive tribal culture alone can provide. Yet this local credibility that narratives provide in no way forfeits the intersubjectivity and universal intelligibility that the emotions, embodied by those narratives, bear. For example, Gandhi's local Hindu tradition of origin inspired a family of emotions whose judgment (that apartheid is a travesty of human and divine love) and project (nonviolent protest) are intersubjective with Martin Luther King, Jr.'s judgment and project against apartheid, inspired in his case by his local African-American version of Christianity. The family of emotions these two men experienced as justice is based on intersubjective, normative judgments/projects about what the world is and ought to be like. But the narrative tradition that inspired each judgment/project and supplied it with practical, justificatory power remains particular, local, and distinct. An important aspect of the ethic of Christian virtue set forth in this book is the point that basic Christian values (such as love, peace, and justice), properly understood, are justifiable and compelling by appealing not to objectivist but to practical strategies of justification.

NARRATIVE EMOTIONS AND AN ETHIC OF CHRISTIAN VIRTUE

Consider the implications of the category narrative emotions as the basis for an ethic of Christian virtue in which both particularity and universality are preserved. The most obvious implication is that any fully developed conception of Christian virtue will include among its essential elements the two dimensions of the virtuous heart: narrative habits, or obediential dispositions, and intersubjectivity, or empathetic emotions.

For both the Greeks and many early Christians, virtue, or *arete*, meant, as Hauerwas puts it, "that which causes a thing to perform its function well. *Arete* was an excellence of any kind that denotes the power of anything to fulfill its function." On this account, then, "human virtue would be that which caused us to fulfill our function as humans."[61] Gilbert Meilaender similarly notes that "the virtues are those excellences which enable a human being 'to attain the furthest potentialities of his nature.' "[62] Accordingly, Christian virtue would include those qualities of life that cause Christians to fulfill their function as followers of Christ.

Hauerwas goes on to point out that all classical accounts of virtue "involve some combination of excellence and power" and that "[o]ne cannot exist without the other."[63] I think Hauerwas is correct. Christian virtue consists of two interdependent dimensions, a balanced synthesis of dispositional excellence and emotional power. A careful examination of these two dimensions of Christian virtue is the manifest aim of the remainder of this book; a sketch of them follows.

Lisa Sowle Cahill notes that Christian ethics (in particular Christian pacifism) manifests itself historically as two distinguishable but interrelated traditions: an "obediential or fiduciary" tradition and an "empathetic or compassionate" tradition.[64] Each of these traditions taken separately privileges one dimension of Christian virtue over the other. The obediential tradition, for example, focuses on the excellences or dispositional habits of a community's character that endow its narrative tradition with a distinctive, moral particularity. Cahill identifies Tertullian, Origen, Menno Simons, H. Richard Niebuhr, Yoder, and Hauerwas as theologians who tend to emphasize this obediential or fiduciary tradition of Christian virtue.[65] The central concerns of the obediential tradition correlate with the narrative dimension of Christian theology just set forth. "Obediential dispositions" refers to those excellences that mold and shape the character of that community whose history and life shaped and continues to shape the gospel narrative to which it has committed itself. The plot of the gospel narratives, for example, is shaped by the obediential character of Jesus. The obedient Christian community, in turn, shapes and reshapes its dispositions of character in conformity with the contours of that gospel story. More specifically, obediential character "imitates," as Cahill puts it, "the qualities of God disclosed in Jesus—mercy, forgiveness, inclusiveness—because that is what is commanded by the Sovereign Lord who creates and redeems."[66] An ethic of Christian virtue, then, involves "obediential imitation of Christ's sacrifice"[67] and the dispositions of character that make such sacrificial obedience possible. Meilaender agrees with Cahill. Christian virtue, he says, consists of "dispositions to act in certain ways"; they are "traits of character" that "actually engage the will" and "cannot be acquired apart from grace."[68] The Christian community must cultivate particular dispositions or habits of heart if it is to be equipped with the kind of character that is able to obey the commands of the gospel narratives. As Meilaender suggests, "what we ought to do may depend on the sort of person we are. What duties we perceive may depend upon what virtues shape our vision of the world."[69] Moreover, obediential dispositions not only endow gospel narratives with distinctive plot but also elicit those empathetic emotions essential to empowering a community to actually practice the life of holiness implicit in that plot. For each virtue (love, peace, justice), accordingly, I will examine several obediential dispositions that must constitute the Christian community's character if it is to obey those commandments that shape the gospel story. I examine obediential dispositions such as humility, vulnerability, and intimacy, for example, as excellences or dispositions that are essential if the Christian community is to fulfill Christ's commandment to love God, neighbor, and self.

In addition to obediential dispositions, Christian virtue consists of empathetic emotions, an affectional dimension of moral life that enables a community to bring into existence the life it has committed itself to live. Cahill identifies Erasmus, George Fox, the leaders of the Social Gospel movement, Dorothy Day, and Thomas Merton as theologians who tend to emphasize this dimension of Christian virtue.[70] For them the moral life "is rooted in a sense of compassion for fellow humanity with its gladness and suffering, with all persons for whose sins Christ died and who are promised new life in Christ's resurrection."[71] The family of emotions comprising compassion inspire "empathetic identification with 'the other,' "—strangers and foes, dissenters and persecuted, as well as with "common humanity."[72] Empathetic emotions, like emotions in general, are shared, intersubjective experiences. As such they anchor moral life to universal truth-judgments that are (as I show in chapters 6 and 7) relevant to public life and susceptible to the scrutiny of critical inquiry.

Ordinarily these two traditions (obediential dispositions and empathetic emotions) have remained somewhat polarized throughout the history of ethics. Ethicists favoring obediential habits locate virtues in the narrative tradition of communities and suspect or ignore accounts of ethics that give prominent place to emotions. Emotions appear to them to be too subjective, fractured, immediate, and fleeting to bear the weight of moral thought and practice. Ethicists favoring empathetic emotions locate the moral life in the common experience of shared human emotions that inspire and enable the practice of love, mercy, and compassion as depicted in the life of Jesus; virtue ethics is viewed with some suspicion, as too dependent on the objectivity and mediacy of tradition and too passionless and impotent to inspire a community to actually practice what Christ requires. One purpose of this book is to weave together the threads of these two traditions, to show that properly analyzed they are inseparable and interdependent and properly conceived, a community's obediential habits, shaped and framed by stories and rituals, invite certain empathetic emotions that inspire and empower a community to actually practice a way of moral life continuous with those stories and rituals. The emphases of both traditions are equally vital and compelling and, when isolated, equally warped and weak. While there is no doubt that separately the obediential and empathetic traditions "each give a distinct flavor" to Christian ethics, Cahill insists that "both strands should characterize [moral] life in the concrete." Indeed, the adequacy of a community's moral life "might be tested by the balance achieved between them."[73] Cahill, however, nowhere sets forth a theoretical framework whereby such a balance between the obediential and empathetic strands of virtue might be secured. This chapter's analysis of obediential dispositions (narrative) and empathetic affections (emotions) establishes such a framework, which in the remainder of this book I shall to use to analyze and interpret specific Christian virtues, namely love, peace, and justice. Based on my earlier analysis, I can claim with confidence that the interdependence of narrative's obediential dispositions and intersubjectivity's empathetic emotions manifests itself as socialization and justification.

Two guiding premises can be distilled from this interdependent relationship. First, for covenantal communities, *universals are accessible through particulars*; the universal value judgments and projects of virtue's empathetic emotions are accessible and intelligible through the particularity of certain obediential habits that shape the gospel story. Second, *universals are justified in terms of the particular*; empathetic emotions are normatively justified by the local particularity of the gospel story and the obediential dispositions that shape it. These two premises will guide us in the quest to determine the meaning and implication of each virtue (love, peace, and justice) for covenantal life and practice.

One might ask, Why love, peace, and justice? Why not other Christian virtues such as freedom, patience, mercy, and the like? My focus is on love, peace, and justice because paradoxically they are at one and the same time "elemental" and "holistic" virtues, in a way other values are not. They are elemental in that they are the basic foundation on which all other values in the Christian moral life are erected, but they are also holistic in that they are comprehensive, embracing within themselves the whole range of Christian values, including freedom, patience, and mercy. Love, peace, and justice are not themselves constituted by any single obediential habit or empathetic emotion but rather are more fairly understood as families of obediential habits and empathetic emotions, overlapping and mutually underwriting each other. So I will show that patience is a value that belongs primarily but not exclusively to the family of habits and emotions we call peace, freedom is a value that belongs to justice, and so on.

A second related question arises. I have already made the claim that emotions, as one of two dimensions of virtue, are reliable and trustworthy moral guides. How so? How is this claim defensible? We all know that certain versions of "love," for example, can be manipulative, controlling, and destructive; and so also with "peace" and "justice." How do we know when love, peace, and justice are trustworthy, reliable moral guides and when are they not? If one is looking for a simple criterion for making such a determination—if one is after formulas such as are readily available (e.g., Kant, Bentham) and easily extracted from the history of ethics—then the ethic of Christian virtue set forth here will surely seem unsatisfactory. My sense, however, is that human moral experience is not so simple and reductive and that it cannot and should not be a matter of inventing a single, simple formula that when executed manufactures for us a supposedly reliable course of action. My answer appeals rather to the elemental and holistic nature of virtue itself. The heart's virtues are determined to be trustworthy in two interrelated ways—subjectively and objectively. Subjectively, virtue's reliability is rooted in the obediential dispositions and empathetic emotions that constitute the character of each virtue. Present and essential to the morally trustworthy practice of any virtue (love, peace, and justice), in other words, are certain specific and concrete obediential habits of character and empathetic emotions. So love is reliably trustworthy, for example, when present to and in it are habits of humility, vulnerability, and intimacy that invite empathetic feelings of genuine sorrow and joy. Any practice of justice is trustworthy when present to and in it are dispositions of responsibility and remembrance that elicit empathetic emotions of holy anger, gratitude, and mercy. When these habits and emotions are not present in the practice of a virtue, then we can be confident that, despite what some might claim, that particular practice of the virtue is unreliable, not trustworthy as a guide to Christian virtue. Objectively, virtue's reliability is rooted in the dignity and integrity of human beings, humans created in the divine image. The practice of a virtue is genuinely virtuous if and when it protects, preserves, or promotes the unique dignity and integrity of human beings. So love is reliably trustworthy when the intrinsic value of humans is not infringed—when humans are, as Kant puts it, ends and not means.

PART II

Virtues of the Heart

Sing heart sing
Call and carol clearly
                Louise Bogan, "Chanson un peu naïve"

3

Love as a Christian Virtue

THE NEWS IS UNEXPECTED. "Go, sell what you possess and give to the poor, and you will have treasure in heaven; and come, follow me"(Matthew 19:21).[1] Only minutes before he was filled with confidence, certain that in keeping all of God's commandments life eternal was assured. Now this news from Jesus, that his faith is misguided and his confidence unfounded. "Sell all, follow me?" Must Christian love be so passionate, so intimately personal, so sacrificial? Very often "we deceive ourselves about love," says Nussbaum, "about who; and how; and whether."[2] Like the man of wealth, many are nurtured on stories of love that turn out to be unreliable. My aim in this chapter is to answer the question, Which stories of Christian love are reliable and which are not? The answer to this question turns on the premise, set forth in chapter 2, that any reliable approach to Christian virtue is one in which love is interpreted as covenantal, as a matter of the heart, a matter of both obediential dispositions and empathic emotions.

Contemporary treatments of Christian love tend to divide themselves into what Stephen Pope refers to as "norm-centered and affective-centered approaches." Norm-centered approaches, exemplified by Garth Hallett and Gene Outka, argue "for either moral parity between self and other or for self-subordination." The strength of norm-centered approaches is that they acknowledge the centrality of love's obediential dimension. In contrast, affective-centered approaches, exemplified by Edward Vacek and Stephen Post, "concentrate on love for God as the central context for neighbor love."[3] The strength of these approaches is that they acknowledge the centrality of love's empathic dimension. Another way of describing the difference between these two approaches is to say that norm-centered approaches focus on the rational, legal aspects of what Dana Radcliffe calls "commanded love,"[4] while affective-centered approaches focus on the emotional, compassionate aspects of love. What I argue for is a covenantal approach to love, one in which both stories of love (the norm-centered, obediential approach and the affective-centered, empathic approach) contribute essential elements without which any story of love must be considered deficient and unreliable. A balance between the obediential dimension and the empathetic, in other words, is the measure of any viable theory of Christian love. In what follows, I employ biblical images in order to show that covenantal love is a matter of cultivating certain obediential habits of heart and certain empathetic emotions. First, I examine what is perhaps the dominant approach to Christian love, commanded love and the Kantian orientation that underwrites it. Second, I discuss several obediential dispositions of heart. Third, I show how these dispositions invite certain empathetic emotions that empower a community to live a life of love. Finally, I examine the interdependent relationship between these two dimensions of love. I show what covenantal way of life is implied by practicing love's empathetic emotions and how this practice is justified and inspired by love's obediential habits of heart.

LOVE AND THE KANTIAN TRADITION

Christian love has attracted the attention of a great many philosophers and theologians; Kant's mapping of this terrain is indispensable for finding one's way. Although Kant's focus is on love's status as rational, universal law, he does not neglect entirely love's emotions and their role in moral life.

There is a substantial biblical basis for insisting on love as consisting of laws that can be commanded. It is central to the biblical tradition's summary of ancient Jewish commandments, "Love the Lord your God" and "Love your neighbor as yourself" (see Leviticus 19:17–18; Matthew 22:28–31; Romans 13:8–10). Loving God, self and neighbor is properly conceived, then, as an act of voluntary obedience to a range of laws woven into the fabric of Jewish covenantal history. But there is also substantial biblical basis for insisting that this notion of commanded love, although persuasive as far as it goes, is by itself deficient as a guide to Christian practice. The man of wealth seems to have understood his relation to God and neighbor largely in terms of commanded love and not so much in terms of a personal, passionate, single-minded devotion to God and love of others. Similarly he seems to have understood his relation to his poor neighbor not so much in terms of direct, personal investment in the lives of the poor as in terms of indirect, impersonal commitment, mediated by duties specified for him by law and custom. What he seems unable to accommodate, what is so bewildering for him, is Jesus's insistence that love's power of life eternal is present only for those willing to engage passionately and empathetically in the lives of God and neighbor, only for those willing to "Go, sell all . . . come, follow me." The man of wealth's understanding of love permits him to be a detached admirer of religion but prevents him from being a passionate disciple of Jesus.

This tendency to treat love as primarily a matter of commanded love, I hardly need mention, reflects a pervasive philosophical and theological tradition of which Immanuel Kant is the most widely recognized modern source. In a familiar passage Kant insists that those portions of "Scripture that commands us to love our neighbor and even our enemy" cannot mean that we should have a feeling for them. For love that can be commanded "is practical love, not pathological love; it resides in the will and not in the propensities of feeling, in principles of action and not in tender sympathy; and it alone can be commanded."[5]

"It alone can be commanded." This phase, explains Ronald Green, "expresses the gist of Kant's objection to any ethic based on emotional preferences and any understanding of Christian love which would interpret it in terms of emotional states." For Kant, all morality consists of normative rules that possess rational and imperative power "which we are called on to obey."[6] When it comes to "mandated love of neighbor," Radcliffe similarly argues, the Kantian view excludes "an emotional response to [a person] and his conditions." "What is prescribed must involve solely a determination of the will" and not "inclinations," among which [Kant] counts compassion and other emotions."[7] For Kant, the require-ments of law compel a person (as did the man of wealth who dutifully obeyed God's commandments) to treat with equal regard all neighbors. Intimate, emo-tional engagement with the one loved is not required; indeed, such passionate attachments lend themselves to self-interested inclinations and personal prefer-ences that detract from loving neighbors with equal regard. Kant makes clear his reasons for disengaging love from emotional attachments; by so doing he excludes from practical reason irrational forces that lie beyond human control, beyond our will to command.

Given the prominence of the Kantian interpretation of Christian love, theories promoting love as primarily obedience to God's commandments are not hard to come by. Even Kierkegaard, a thinker who is unashamedly critical of objective, rational Christianity and sympathetic to the passionate inwardness of faith, is sometimes lured into the Kantian lair when treating the nature of Christian love.[8] Two more recent examples are sufficient to indicate the thrust of the Kantian tradition. Fletcher, in his influential *Situation Ethics*, interprets Christian love as primarily duty to love's commandments. Imitating Kant, he insists that *agape*, or what he calls "non-affectionate love," is a matter of attitude and will and not a matter of feeling; it "is discerning and critical; it is not sentimental."[9] Love "is not at all an emotional norm or motive. It is volitional, conative"; it is "disin-terested," "impartial," "inclusive," and "indiscriminate"; it is "disinterested love, because love wills the neighbor's good whether we like him or not."[10] Fletcher appeals to ethicists like C. H. Dodd in bolstering his case. Of Dodd's view of *agape*, for example, he says: "it is not primarily an emotion or affection; it is primarily an active determination of the will. That is why it can be commanded, as feeling cannot."[11] Many recent Christian ethicists, following in the footsteps of Kant, Dodd, and Fletcher, affirm the basic tenets of this tradition; they seem to inform, for example, the work of theologians like David Sanderlin and Preston Williams.[12]

Consider Sanderlin's argument. On the basis of the teaching of Saint John of the Cross, Sanderlin insists that a pure, self-denying, disinterested Christian love "is both desirable and humanly possible."[13]

> Perfect neighbor-love, like perfect love for God, is disinterested and desireless. We should love our neighbors disinterestedly for the sake of God alone, without attaching ourselves to them as a source of our happiness. ... In order to love others charitably, we must empty our will of desirous attachments to them for their attractive qualities, for with these attachments we love them partly for our own sake, insofar as they please us with these qualities.

"Although charity does not require indifference ... to our neighbor," love of neighbor is nevertheless "understood correctly as interior disinterestedness for God alone;"[14] "all desires and desirous interests, even other-regarding ones, are based in need and are therefore incompatible with charity."[15] Love of neighbor must divest itself of all desire, of all emotional attachments and preferences.

Enthusiastic disciples or detractors, however, often traduce the teachings of the master. This seems to be the case with Kant and the tradition he initiated, as least in regard to moral law and love's emotions. Green and Radcliffe convincingly show how Kant's view of the role of emotions in ethics often is ignored or misunderstood.[16] Green argues that for Kant the *basis* of love must be rational law that can be commanded and must therefore exclude irrational, emotional attachments over which we have no control. Yet Kant does not dismiss emotions entirely from moral life,[17] unlike much of the Kantian tradition, he believes that emotions are important for nurturing a character disposed toward carrying out the duties of that life. Kant himself asserts that "[h]elping others to achieve their ends is a duty. If a man practices it often and succeeds in realizing his purpose, he eventually comes to feel love for those he has helped."[18] Again, when speaking of tender sympathies, Kant insists that "[w]hile it is not in itself a duty to experience sadness, and also joy, in sympathy with others, it is a duty to participate actively in the fate of others. Hence we have an indirect duty to cultivate the sympathetic (aesthetic) feelings in us and to use them as so many means to participating from moral principles and from the feelings appropriate to these principles." For Kant then, love as primarily duty to rational law is supplemented and enhanced by an indirect duty to nurture specific emotional preferences. Although for him the *basis* of love remains duty to universal law, love's emotional attachments are nevertheless important enhancements of the life of love. Indeed, Kant suggests that loving emotions may be just the inducement a person needs to accomplish what duty by itself could not fulfill.[19]

Kant goes a fair distance toward acknowledging the importance of emotions in moral life. I want to go even further and insist that commanded love and love's empathetic emotions are inseparable and interdependent dimensions of covenantal love. In his response to the man of wealth, Jesus assumes the interdependence of head and heart, of rational law and emotional attachment. Jesus knows full well that the man has kept God's law, if at all, with his head and not his heart. Here as elsewhere (e.g., in the Sermon on the Mount and the parable of the good Samaritan) Jesus assumes that keeping the love commandment entails not merely adhering to rational laws but feeling loving compassion; not only satisfying certain duties but investing oneself emotionally and personally in the lives of neighbors. Jesus further seems to assume that emotional experiences, like compassion, are under a person's voluntary control and therefore commandable. He commands his disciples to feel compassion, as did the good Samaritan. And he commands the man of wealth to so share compassionately in the experience of the poor that he will come to see that love requires him to give all of himself and his possessions to meet their needs. Instead of presupposing a disjunction between love's rational law and human emotions, Jesus presupposes that love properly understood is an experience in which duty to law and emotional commitment are mutually interdependent. In what follows I show why and how this is so.

My covenantal approach to love acknowledges the seriousness with which Kant invites us to take emotional attachments in moral life. In contrast to Kant however, I argue that emotional attachments are not only important (as indirect duties) but also inseparable from commanded love and indispensable to any satisfactory and practical conception of love. Both Vacek and Radcliffe insist on this view.[20] Radcliffe argues, for example, that

> one has a duty to "cultivate" the dispositions to feel compassion and similar emotions so that one will feel them and act on them as the situation warrants. In a word, one must train oneself to feel compassion for people in need, so that this emotional response will occur spontaneously and, if necessary, combine with one's abstract respect for persons to motivate whatever actions duty demands.[21]

What does it take to "train oneself to feel compassion" for neighbors? What does it take to cultivate emotions appropriate to love's command so that we feel empathetically for others? My thesis is that we must carefully examine love's obediential dispositions and empathetic emotions if we are to do justice to the rich complexity of love as a Christian virtue.

Roberts observes that "[love] is neither a distinct and particular emotion nor, indeed, a distinct virtue . . . [rather] 'love' is a kind of summary term" that invites "virtually the whole range of proper attitudes and [emotions] . . . with respect to God and neighbors."[22] For this reason, love may properly be referred to as "a metavalue"[23] that constitutes a person's character with specific obediential dispositions that, as I will show, invite a wide range of emotions. I will first examine those obediential habits of heart; I will then consider love's empathetic emotions.

Love as Obediential Dispositions

The Christian notion of love is constituted by a story, a narrative of God's passionate love for human beings and of the human struggle to love God, self, and others passionately. "The very nature of human existence," observes Meilaender, "conceived in Christian terms—is best understood within narrative." Narrative provides "some means other than abstract thought to find the 'refreshment of spirit' for which human beings seem to be made."[24] This story of love, for which humans are made, is, in the biblical tradition, the special province of a covenantal community whose dispositions or habits are shaped by and reshape love's narrative pattern. Participating in love's story requires of a covenantal community, in other words, a certain kind of character. Indeed, as Roberta Bondi insists, "love can be our goal only in so far as it is a *disposition*, a whole way of being, feeling, seeing, and understanding. . . . [It] is a deep attitude of heart, or a . . . disposition . . . that wishes for and seeks to provide for [another's] well being in acts of kindness, consideration, and service."[25] I will examine three obediential dispositions—humility, intimacy, and vulnerability—that not only shape love's covenantal story but endow it with a distinctively Christian particularity. In doing so I draw a great deal on the work of Jonathan Edwards, who perhaps as much as any modern theologian understood the central role dispositions and emotions play in Christian life.

Humility

"Humility," says Jonathan Edwards, "is a most essential and distinguishing trait in all true piety. It is the attendant of every grace, and in a peculiar manner tends to the purity of Christian feeling";[26] indeed, it is the cardinal covenantal disposition, most essential to shaping the plot of love's story and guaranteeing its reliability. Anders Nygren notes how, in recalling the lessons he learned from Neoplatonism, Augustine admits that it had pointed him toward the proper goal but that it was deficient of passion and power wherewith one might progress toward it. "Where was that love which builds on the foundation of *humility*, which is Jesus Christ?"[27] Christian love, as Augustine well understood, manifests itself fundamentally neither as law nor as intuition but as humility, and primarily as a story of God's humility in Christ, a humility whereby all who so wish are empowered by God's grace to imitate it. One need not read far in the gospels to discover that these narratives trace the story of a loving God who, in sending his son, "humbled Himself even to the death of the cross." This familiar story of God's incarnate love manifests the *exemplum humilitatis* to which the community of faithful are to conform.[28] Indeed, for the early church and especially early Christian monastics, humility was "the interior beginning of the process of growth in love, more fundamental that any material renunciation . . . the cultivation of a deep Christian attitude of heart that could make love possible."[29]

What, then, is humility? Roberts is correct, I think, to insist that "humility does not name an emotion [but] a complex emotional disposition," a habit of heart that invites certain emotions and excludes others. Roberts is mistaken, however, when he insists that Christian humility is "the disposition not to feel envy upon noticing that a significant other person is superior to oneself, not to feel invidious pride upon noticing that a significant other is inferior." Christian humility is not, as Roberts thinks, "a disposition not to feel envy or invidious pride in situations where persons are being, or might be compared, for their status."[30] Rather, Christian humility renounces altogether the "worldly" criterion of judging the comparative status of persons. Hence humility precludes not only the envy arising from pride but also the attitude that gives rise to the judgment that "a significant other is inferior." That is, humility relinquishes entirely the assumptions on which comparative judgments are made and envy feeds. This is surely the thrust of Saint Paul's comment that Christ Jesus "did not count on equality with God a thing to be grasped" (Philippians 2:6) but took the form of a humble servant. Jonathan Edwards concurs: "The truly humble do not compare themselves favorably at all."[31] Any conception of humility that retains a standard for comparing the status of persons provides the basis for a kind of self-righteousness against which Jesus frequently rails. If anything, true humility causes one to think of others as better than oneself (Philippians 2:3),[32] to think of oneself as a servant in relation to others.

In *Religious Affections* Edwards distinguishes "evangelical" and "legal humiliation." Legal or "natural" humility is common to all humans and benefits from none of God's gracious affections, but "arises from the common influence of the Spirit of God, especially as it is prompted by the natural conscience." In legal humility, people "are made aware that they are small, indeed nothing, before the great and terrible God. . . . But they do not have a responsive frame of heart in true self-abasement nor do they feel that need to exult in God alone." For those disposed to legal humility, "the conscience is convicted, but there is still no spiritual understanding, nor is the will broken, nor is the inclination of the heart altered"; and people "are brought to self-despair in trying to help themselves."[33] Indeed, this is the despair to which the man of wealth, who goes away sorrowful, faces when finally he realizes that what is required of him is not simply duty to God's commandments but humble commitment to and passionate investment in the life of the poor. But evangelical humility, insists Edwards, "is distinctive of true Christians," resulting from "the distinctive influence of the Spirit of God who implants and exercises supernatural and divine principles. . . . A true sense of sin is only found in evangelical humiliation, in seeing for oneself the beauty of God's holiness and moral perfection." True self-abasement, genuine brokeness of will, and conversion of heart can only be accomplished by evangelical humility.[34] In short, true humility acknowledges the need for God's grace in living a life of covenantal love.

Edwards goes on to argue that legal humility has no spiritual value in itself and is "only useful when it leads to evangelical humiliation."[35] Legal humility by itself cultivates a disposition of moralistic legalism and self-righteousness.[36] One modern formulation of Edwards's notion of legal humility, it seems to me, is the Kantian tradition's tendency to favor commanded love while neglecting those dispositions and emotions necessary for the enabling the practice of covenantal love. No doubt in trying to perform one's duty to rational law one will feel inadequate and morally convicted. But to reduce the *basis* of love to duty to commanded love risks unnecessarily, Edwards insists, "a self-righteous spirit about one's own [alleged] humility" and "a self-[confidence] about one's own abasement. It is the nature of spiritual pride to make men conceited and ostentatious about their humility."[37] The man of wealth exemplifies this tendency; he believes that legal humility (submitting to God's commandments) is sufficient to fulfill love's requirement, and he proudly believes he has done so. Jesus' response indicates that the man's conception of love as duty to God's commandment is deficient and self-deceiving. It is deficient insofar as he conceives love primarily in terms of obedience to commandments; it is self-deceiving insofar as he believes that conformity to law secures for him life eternal. In contrast, each moment of love's gospel story, from incarnation to resurrection, is illuminated by something like Edwards's notion of evangelical humility. Indeed, the Sermon of the Mount is an extended discourse on the struggle between love's evangelical and legal humility, between the inwardness of love's passion and the externality of the law's demands.

Consider Jesus's encounter with the woman at the well (John 4). Jesus's loving treatment of the Samaritan woman exemplifies a disposition of humility whereby he is able to renounce worldly standards of comparative status and voluntarily assume the posture of a servant. The first indication of such a disposition, and the one on which I focus here, is evident in the Samaritan woman's question to Jesus: "How is it that you, a Jew, ask a drink of me, a woman of Samaria?" (John 4: 9) The second indication is when his disciples "marveled that he was talking with a woman" (John 4:27). As the text itself suggests, Jews and Samaritans were alienated by ancient hostilities; law and custom forbade any law-abiding Jew to have anything to do with Samaritans. Now if Jesus, a Jew, had conceived of love as primarily a matter of conformity to law, his comparative status with the Samaritan would justify the Jewish custom of having nothing to do with Samaritans. Assuming love as duty to universal law, Jesus would not have questioned the imperative force of this law, nor would he have questioned its universality. But any story of genuine Jewish and Christian love, the woman and the disciples discover, is conditioned by humility: a willingness to forgo worldly standards of comparative worth, voluntarily assume the role of servant, and identify even with the lowliest. Jesus's willingness to embody love's humility, as I will show, establishes with the woman a relation of spiritual intimacy that makes them vulnerable to each other's joys and pains. Unless the Christian community first internalizes humility as a disposition of heart, it is unlikely that it will be able to obey Jesus's command to love God, self, and neighbor.

Intimacy

Humility, as an obediential disposition of covenantal love, cultivates a second disposition, intimacy. We are accustomed to speaking of sexual intimacy as a function of *eros* and of *agape* as a kind of love transcending *eros* and intimacy. Perhaps this is partly due to the influence of Nygren, who, in his monumental *Agape and Eros*, depicts the two as conflicting motifs.[38] Recently, Sanderlin similarly juxtaposes them.[39] I would suggest, however, that *eros* and intimacy are qualities without which love of God, self, and neighbor remains falsely abstract, rationalistic, and relatively impersonal. From the start, the biblical story of human creation gives us a picture of intimacy between God, humans, and even the earth. What could be more intimate than humanity created from the dust of the earth? And, as Bruce Birch argues, "[w]hat could be more intimate than God breathing the divine breath into the nostrils of the earth creature in order to give humanity animation and life?"[40]

Jonathan Edwards is one of a few theologians willing to enfranchise *eros*, or what he calls "appetite," as a quality of Christian love.[41] For him appetite involves, as Paula Cooey suggests, intimacy; and intimacy "names the quality of the closeness that characterizes highly particular human interrelations. It comprehends depth, endurance, and familiarity of human association. Intimacy also suggest privacy, a privacy that can be mistaken for exclusivity." Sexual intimacy includes, of course, sensuality, touching, feeling, passion, intercourse; a sensual, physical desire for closeness. "Intimacy presupposes," in other words, "some concept of *eros* or desire." Edwards, according to Cooey, insists that intimacy and appetite characterize Christian love "in reference both to divine self-love and to human-divine relations."[42] Divine love displays an "appetitive energy in both its creative and redemptive exertions. This love is made available to the saints through Christ so that the saints themselves become participants in divine [appetitive] love."[43] Accordingly, Edwards frequently uses appetite and intimacy between "earthly lovers" as a metaphor for spiritual lovers, with the qualification that the appetite and intimacy of spiritual lovers, unlike earthly lovers, is never exhausted. God's love, and love of God, self, and neighbor, according to Edwards, is "appetite or complacence, which is a disposition to desire or delight in beholding the beauty of another, and a relation to or union with him."[44] For the Christian, this appetite for God and neighbor involves the one-loving in both a fulfilling and inexhaustible intimacy. As Vacek confirms, the heart of Christian love includes *eros*, and "eros can be creative, whether in dreaming up new cuisine or in discovering ever more ways to give itself over to God." The intimacy of *eros* entails appetite for God, self, and neighbor in a way that invites not only benevolent acts that conform to rational law but passionate desires that compel us to sell all and follow Christ. Christian mystics, especially, Vacek says, "often have talked about their relation to God in these terms," that is, in terms of *eros* as "an *emotional* union with the beloved."[45] Too often, however, human relations are characterized not by a desire for love's intimacy but by a desire to control and dominate. No doubt the motivation for such relations of power and domination is to protect the heart against the undeniable risks intimacy invites.

Jesus' ministry frequently demonstrates the way redemptive love involves intimacy and its risks. His humility in loving the Samaritan woman and his willingness to ignore cultural standards of comparative worth disarm the legal, racial, and gender defenses that typically isolate Jew and Samaritan, male and female. But between Jesus and the woman a spontaneous and mutually intimate discourse ensues: the woman's concern for Jesus' physical welfare, for example, and Jesus' concern for the woman's spiritual welfare. Their mutual compassion for one another, invoked by love's humility, draws them into an intimacy that, strictly speaking, could never be "disinterested" but is always "intensely interested," as Sally Purvis puts it.[46] The intimacy of the conversation between Jesus and the Samaritan is really quite remarkable. Their openness to one another draws them progressively into a relation of personal disclosure and emotional fellowship. In response to Jesus' inquiry into her most intimate relations with men, the Samaritan woman feels no offense, no need to defend herself. Instead she is drawn into a relation of self-discovery and creation that leads from a discussion of true worship to a decisive moment at which she is willing to embody in her own life the kind of intimacy characteristic of passionate devotion to God.

Contrast the intimacy Jesus and the Samaritan women risk with the distance the man of wealth maintains with Jesus and the poor. This distance is created on the one hand because of his mistaken notion that love requires little more than duty to commandments and on the other hand because the passionate engagement with the poor that Jesus says love requires is more than he is willing to risk. How strikingly different is the Apostle Paul's experience of God's love when he writes of his passionate desire for and intimacy with the Thessalonians: "But we were gentle among you, like a nurse taking care of her children. So, being *affectionately desirous* of you, we were ready to share with you not only the gospel of God but also our own selves, because you had become very dear to us" (Thessalonians 2:7–8). Paul's emotional intimacy is not restricted to his relationship to God, as Sanderlin suggests Christian love properly should be.[47] His desire for and intimacy with God boils over into a desire for and intimacy with the Thessalonians themselves. In his desirous affection for and intimacy with God, Paul finds a desirous affection for and intimacy with his neighbor. His intimate desire for God manifests itself as an intimate desire for others and makes him vulnerable with them in their joys and sorrows.

Vulnerability

To "desire affectionately" is to desire intimacy, and to desire intimacy is to risk vulnerability. In *Narratives of a Vulnerable God*, William Placher underscores the significance of vulnerability for Christian faith. His argument, in brief, is that since God in Christ loved humanity so as to risk vulnerability, so too must the community of believers be willing to risk vulnerability. Repeatedly Placher speaks of "a God willing to be vulnerable to pain in the freedom of love"[48] and of a church willing to model "the God it knows and worships, the vulnerable God known in the biblical narratives."[49] But Placher's conception of vulnerability tends to be somewhat myopic, focusing largely on vulnerability as risking pain and suffering: "it is God's vulnerability, God's willingness to risk pain and suffering in being open to love, that is good."[50] The freedom of vulnerability, however, risks not only pain and sorrow but risks what humans seek above all, the joyful fellowship that is bestowed on those who love God and neighbor. Often, however, it is as difficult for humans to risk love's joys and blessings as it is to risk love's suffering and pain.

Gabriel Marcel writes forcefully of the vulnerability of those who risk love's intimacy. When I care lovingly for others, he says, they are present with me. "*With* me: note the metaphysical value of this word . . . which corresponds neither to a relationship of inherence or immanence nor to a relationship of exteriority. It is of the essence of *coesse* . . . of genuine intimacy." Marcel goes on to describe *coesse* as "grounded in the realm of total spiritual availability (*disposibilite*)—that is to say, of pure charity."[51] Intimacy requires that I be present with others in a particular way, that I be available to them, at their disposal. Love's humble intimacy disposes me toward others, places me at their disposal and makes me susceptible not only to exploitation and abuse but also to mercy and fulfillment. Disposability, however, should not be mistaken for subservience. Whereas subservience presupposes relations of unequal power, domination, and judgments of comparative worth, vulnerability presupposes love's humility and intimacy. As Bondi argues, humble vulnerability "in the ancient texts nearly always . . . works to set woman or man who embrace it free to escape ordinary internal cultural patterns of dominance and subservience." Humble vulnerability for the Christian is not "a synonym for manipulative self-sacrifice" as it has often been for women. "Real humility brings freedom and love to its recipients, not guilt and resentment."[52] Neither does vulnerable disposability allow the neighbor merely "a temporary loan on our resources,"[53] as was the expectation of the man of wealth. Such "a temporary loan" requires of me only admiration or, as Edwards puts it, legal humility; it does not require the kind of evangelical humility that would inspire me to sell all and follow Jesus. The man of wealth discovered the terrible difference between the two. Through acts of charity he kept all the commandments. But by doing this and no more he actually makes himself unavailable to the poor: by relating himself to his neighbor solely through the exteriority of law, he distances and protects himself from them, makes himself spiritually indisposable to them. Why? Partly because morality as conformity to law retains worldly standards of comparative worth, placing the recipient of my love in my debt and thereby foreclosing on the possibility of love's intimacy and vulnerability. Robert Kysar makes this point with extraordinary clarity: "Charity is the sharing of my excess for the sake of another who has too little while at the same time assuring my continued excess." Charity does not require what love requires, namely, "solidarity with the condition of the other person." Genuine covenantal love requires not merely "the sharing of surplus on the part of a few with the many but the total redistribution of all the resources of society,"[54] including my own. Jesus informs the man of wealth that charity was not enough, that he must make himself disposable and vulnerable to the suffering poor. The community that nurtured him has failed him, for although it taught him the rigors of love as law, it did not cultivate in him a disposition of intimate vulnerability without which duty to love's law is dry and empty. The risk Jesus and the Samaritan take in making themselves vulnerable to each other is rewarded; their disposability to each other results not only in the sorrow of shared suffering but in a fellowship of shared joy for those who discover "that this is indeed the Savior of the world" (John 4:42). Often, however, Jesus' habit of risking intimacy with society's dispossessed (e.g., publicans, prostitutes, and irreligious) exposes him to criticism and hostility, and ultimately to torture and death. Jesus understood, and eventually his disciples did as well, that painful, as well as joyful, vulnerability is the price paid by those whose hearts beat with the humble intimacy of covenantal love.

For Edwards, the incarnation is the paradigmatic act not only of humility but of spiritual intimacy and vulnerability as well. As Cooey notes, "Edwards wrote that God's love was not passion as human beings experience it except by the Incarnation. . . . The Incarnation, by making the deity visible to redeemed humanity, effects a reciprocal relationship of passionate love shared between God and the redeemed, in short a relationship of intimacy"[55] and vulnerability. In Jesus God experiences not only the joys and delights but also, as the writer of Hebrews suggests, the weakness, temptations, and sufferings of human existence (see Hebrews 2 and 4). To the woman at the well, to the woman caught in adultery, he offers his presence, makes himself disposable and vulnerable to their pain, to their struggle to survive.

Regrettably the Christian community has generally been unwilling to take significant risks. Birch asks Christians to

> [t]hink of some of the tasks to which we are called, and imagine that we could pursue them without risking our own woundedness: seeking peace

in a nuclear age, feeding the hungry in a [world of limited resources], bringing hope and focus to families fragmented by social pressures, fostering community in a day still plagued by economic and racial divisions, nourishing the spirit in an age of materialism, recovering the wholeness of our human sexuality in an age that exploits sexual imagery. These are long-term tasks that the church cannot pursue if its image of itself is invulnerability, success, and minimal risk.[56]

What a community does, perceives, and feels depends a great deal on what kind of character it cultivates. And the kind of character that is indispensable for practicing the costly demands of Christian faith is one shaped most fundamentally by humility, intimacy, and vulnerability. But these obediential habits of heart do not exhaust the essential nature of love as a Christian virtue, for these habits simultaneously invite certain empathetic emotions without which covenantal love cannot flourish.

LOVE AS EMPATHETIC EMOTIONS

For ordinary persons the view that love, even love of God, involves passionate, emotional attachments is generally taken as self-evident. Love, we rightly assume, requires of us significant emotional investment, otherwise it falls short of genuine love. If ordinary persons were to read somewhere that they are simply deceived, that love of God and neighbor does not and should not involve emotional attachments, they would have every right to think that they were reading the script of some science fiction movie written by heartless, alien creatures about a society of mechanical robots. Daily and empirically ordinary humans demonstrate that loving God and self and neighbor calls forth profoundly intense desires and emotional investments. The Synoptic Gospels, Radcliffe points out, assume "that possessing the virtue of *agape* includes being disposed to feel compassion for others in distress and to be motivated by it to help. Further evidence that the Love Commandment prescribes empathetic feeling is the fact that the Synoptic Gospels often portray Jesus himself as moved to feel loving compassion toward people in need."[57] Radcliffe refers to James Gustafson, who insists that the ways in which the gospels portray Jesus

> appear to be grounds for claiming that not only did Jesus follow the command to do acts of love, but there was an affective sensibility which made him identify with the needy, the immoral person, the victim of prejudice. There was a coherence between his affections and his belief that it is fitting to speak of the ultimate power bearing down on man as having the quality of love.[58]

The reluctance of many ethicists to account for this emotional dimension of love is partly due, no doubt, to the influence of the Kantian view set forth earlier. As noted, this tradition insists that love as a moral experience must be commandable, that what is commandable must be rational, and that emotions, as nonrational, are not commandable. But if we presuppose, as I think we must, that emotions are not simple, raw, natural experience and irrational, psychic energy but cognitive experiences, then we must treat emotions as indispensable to any notion of love that is relevant and compelling. My own view, as noted in chapter 2, is that moral emotions consist of three essential, interdependent features—judgment, project, and energy; these features will guide my discussion of love's empathetic emotions.

   The range of emotions constituting love is so vast and diverse, one cannot hope to treat them all. Accordingly, I have chosen to examine two emotions—joy and sorrow—that embrace between them the entire range of love's emotions. Joy and sorrow, insists David Steere, "stand at the foundation of man's response to love—to 'en-joy' one another. Sadness is our basic response to loss of those we love—to grieve our separation from them. So sadness and joy necessitate one another for each to be authentic,"[59] and as authentic make possible the reliability of love's story. The apostle Paul enjoins Christians, "to rejoice with those who rejoice, weep with those who weep" (Rms. 12:15). Similarly, the true Christian, states Edwards, both sorrows for others and rejoices with them.[60]

Joy

Joy is what humans experience when the way the world is and the way the world ought to be converge. For Christians, joy is love's delight in God and God's promised kingdom, when the way the world is and the way God wills the world converge. It is an empathetic feeling of gladness, elation, even bliss that arises when a community experiences the love of God—when it is bestower or recipient of God's love. It may seem odd, then, to discover biblical writers issuing commands to rejoice and be glad in the Lord (Leviticus 23:40; Philippians 3:1 and 4: 4). "Rejoice with those who rejoice" commands Paul (Romans 12:15), as if joy and rejoicing are commandable experiences and experiences a community might readily shun or neglect or forget. Perhaps these commands to rejoice are to remind the covenantal community that in the midst of the world's sorrow and despair there is hope, hope that the way God wills the world to be is the way the world by God's grace someday soon will be. Christian joy is thus distinguishable from pleasure (sensory delight) and happiness (self-realization) with which it may or may not overlap. Pleasure and happiness are experiences in which the way the world is and the way I will the world to be converge. But joy is unique in that it is inspired and sustained by the presence of God's will and love and not by the presence of my personal pleasure and happiness. It is love's joy and rejoicing in the promise of God's kingdom, then, that is commanded of the covenantal community; and such joy, as Johanna Metz puts it, "cannot be worked out from theory, nor, in the long run, can it be simulated. Christian joy is merely natural optimism about existence"[61] about the promise of God's kingdom of love.

Two forms of love's joy can be distinguished: existential and eschatological. Existential joy refers, first of all, to specific feelings of delight and gladness that arise when a community of faith makes the judgment that divine love and human reality converge, when God's kingdom of love is perceived as present in the life and history of the covenantal community. Accordingly, the psalmist invites his community to "Make a joyful noise to the Lord" and praise and give thanks to the Lord, because the "Lord is good" and his "steadfast love endures forever" (Psalms 100, 106). But joy entails not simply the judgment that God's love is present in the world but a project in which love's joy is manifest in and vital to the life of a covenantal community. Such a project involves the community in activities of praise, devotion, and worship of the One whose presence among it is the occasion for love's joy in the first place. Worship partly aims at articulating liturgically, through songs and dances and rituals, a community's joy over the presence of God's Kingdom in its midst. The Israelites, upon crossing the Red Sea, experienced such joy. When "Israel saw the great work which the Lord did against the Egyptians" (Exodus 14:31), it expressed its joy through projects of song and dance in praise to God. Or consider the joy experienced by father and prodigal son. Surprised by love's joy, by the son's humble repentance and return, by the convergence of their world with the world God desires for them, father and son promptly undertake an elaborate, festive project of merrymaking to express love's gratitude and joy. "It was fitting to make merry and be glad, for this your brother was dead, and is alive; he was lost, and is found" (Luke 15:32). The elder brother's arrogance, in contrast, invites anger and defensiveness. Pride disables him, precluding him from love's joyful celebration. But God's Spirit is "love, joy, and peace" (Galatians 5:22), as Paul puts it. Existential joy is a community's empathetic response to the presence of God's Spirit of love in its life.

Eschatological joy is a function of a community's confession of hope that "he who promises is faithful" (Hebrews 10:23). Covenantal love includes the expectant anticipation that ultimately the evil and painful way the world is will be finally and joyously overcome. The Christian's eschatological sensibility is that love's joy persists somehow even in the face of the world's sometimes savage evil and profound suffering. The writer of James has in mind this kind of joy when he enjoins his community to "Count it all joy . . . when you meet various trials, for you know that the testing of your faith produces steadfastness," a quality that is indispensable to perfecting Christian love (James 1:2–4). The Apostle Paul says that he endures suffering with joy because of the hope he has of sharing "in the inheritance of the saints in light" (Colossians 1:11–12, 24–25). Of course, loaded into the meaning of Jesus's life, death, and resurrection is God's promise that love will sustain the weary, redeem the world, and finally establish a kingdom of peace and justice. In this regard, Francis Fiorenza refers to the "predication of joy to God," quoting the prophet Isaiah: "I will rejoice in Jerusalem and be glad in my people; no more shall be heard in it the sound of weeping and the cry of distress." The joy predicated of God here and in Psalms 96 and 97 "has eschatological significance. The suffering and distress of the earth is not explained away." It is not made a part of some unimaginable future. Love's eschatological joy is the belief that former troubles will be forgotten (Isaiah 65:16) and humans shall share in the joy of God.[62] Even though faced with great suffering and sorrow, the Christian's expectant transformation is expressed even in John's gospel, whose orientation is largely a realized eschatology. "So you have sorrow now, but I will see you again and your hearts will rejoice, and no one will take your joy away form you" (John 16:22). Not surprisingly, eschatological joy is expressed through many of the "sorrow songs," or spirituals. These songs of sorrow and survival are often also songs of hope and joy, a profound assurance that from the rich soil of God's love springs hope and joy for those who otherwise are without hope in the world. Although sorrow may be our present lot, the Christian's hope is that joy will persist as a promise of God's covenantal love.

Sorrow

Joy, of course, is not the only emotion constituting covenantal love; sorrow is another. Psychologists "generally agree that the prime cause of sorrow is the experience of loss. The loss may be temporary (separation) or permanent (death), real or imagined, physical or psychological."[63] Sorrow, in other words, is constituted by a judgment I make about the world; that the world as it is has lost something of what it was or should be and thus is not the desirable world it ought to be. Perhaps most profoundly, sorrow involves spiritual loss, the loss of meaning and hope. No doubt the man of wealth felt so deep a sorrow when, choosing wealth over life eternal, he went away sad, apparently in full realization of what he had done and what he had lost. Or recall Jesus's sorrow in the garden, at trial, and on the cross. Is a more profound sense of love's loss and sorrow possible—forsaken by friends and God and life, without hope in the world?

There are two levels on which a person may experience sorrow. On a primary level, sorrow involves direct and immediate feelings of sadness and misery over the involuntary loss of someone for whom or something for which I care. However, a great deal of the sorrow experienced by Christians entails a kind of compassionate sorrow in which I make a voluntary judgment that the way the world is for another has lost something (e.g., freedom, fairness, shelter) of what God wills it to be for them. On the basis of such a judgment, love enables me to feel for them in their sorrow and calls forth in me emotional energy needed to undertake projects that help overcome loss and alleviate sorrow.[64] Isaiah's suffering servant, as "a man of sorrows" who surely "has borne our griefs and carried our sorrows" (Isaiah 53), embodies this empathetic voluntary dimension of covenantal love. Because of the human capacity for shared emotions and for sharing in the life of God's suffering servant, the covenantal community is especially equipped to bear in its own life the pain and loss of others. Sorrow's successful projects, accordingly, aim at alleviating as far as possible all involuntary suffering and loss. They may involve healing the sick, setting at liberty the oppressed, feeding and clothing the poor, comforting those in distress, welcoming the foreigner, and so on. But at times the involuntary suffering of others may be intractable and their sorrow inconsolable. The project of a covenantal community in cases such as these, then, is to be present with those who suffer in their sorrow even as God in Christ is with me in mine. Love as empathetic emotion inspires us to bear in our life the sorrow of those who suffer loss. The Apostle Paul writes, "we know that as you share in our sufferings, you will also share in our comfort" (2 Corinthians 1:7). By joining in the sorrow of loss, the faithful sustain and comfort their neighbor so that the sorrowing neighbor can in turn share the joy that inspires love's empathy in the first place. Love understood primarily as duty to rational law is unable to elicit, as the man of wealth learned from Jesus, this kind of passionate intimacy and care. Indeed, love as primarily norm-centered distances us from the poor's suffering and excuses us from the intimate vulnerability of a love that is genuine. It leaves one with the impression, as it did the man of wealth, that love entails primarily dutiful obedience to God's commandments and not personal, intimate emotional investment in the sorrow of the poor. Although he was apparently prepared to give charitably to the poor, the man of wealth was not prepared to bear their sorrow, suffering with them in their loss, as covenantal love requires. Jesus asks that he so lovingly feel with them in their sorrow that he would come to realize what it would be like to be poor, and through love's sorrow rejoice in making himself neighbor to and not merely benefactor of the poor.

These two empathetic emotions, joy and sorrow, are of course essentially interrelated when love's story is faithfully told. Peter, for example, writes of the way Christian love links sorrow and joy. "But rejoice insofar as you share Christ's suffering, that you may also rejoice and be glad when his glory is revealed" (1 Peter 4:13). Rejoice in sharing the sorrow of Christian suffering? Peter's injunction to share the intimacy of Christ's emotional life presupposes a heart of humble vulnerability without which the Christian story of love is impossible. Love transforms occasions of sorrow into projects of eschatological hope and joy, projects in which "sorrow will turn into joy" (John 16:20). Maya Angelou, in *All God's Children Need Traveling Shoes*, similarly discovers this fundamental relation between sorrow and joy. She visits the Ewe tribe in eastern Ghana, a region from which centuries earlier many of her ancestors were taken as slaves. The ancestors of the Ewe witnessed the desperation of a people threatened with slavery. "They saw mothers and fathers take infants by the feet and bash their heads against tree trunks rather then see them sold into slavery. What they saw they remembered and all that they remembered they told over and over." The descendants of those who survived recognized in Maya one of their own ancestors who had been enslaved. "And you, Sister, you look so much like them, even the tone of your voice is like theirs. They are sure you are descended from those stolen fathers and mothers. That is why they mourn, not for you but for their lost people. . . . [D]escendants of a pillaged past saw their history in my face and heard their ancestors speak through my voice." So the Ewe

> women wept and I wept. I too cried for the lost people, their ancestors and mine. But I was also weeping with a curious joy. Despite the murders, rapes, and suicides, we had survived. The middle passage and the auction block had not erased us. . . . There was much to cry for, much to mourn, but in my heart I felt exalted knowing there was much to celebrate. . . . Through the centuries of despair and dislocation, we had been creative, because we faced down death by daring to hope.[65] For Angelou and for the Ewe women, love is the link that joins joy and sorrow.

Likewise for the Christian, love is the catalyst whereby resurrection joy confers on Calvary's dark sorrow hope for peace and justice.

PRACTICING COVENANTAL LOVE

Suppose, then, that a community understands itself as committed to practicing covenantal versions of love; suppose that its character is shaped by habits of humility, intimacy, and vulnerability; and suppose that these obediantial habits inspire in it empathetic feelings of joy and sorrow. What practice of love is implied? Recall the two premises discussed in chapter 2 that encapsulate the two ways in which virtues, like love, are interrelated. First, universals are a function of particulars: universal moral judgments/projects of love's joy and sorrow are accessible and intelligible because they are inspired by the local particularity of obediential habits of heart, like Christian humility, intimacy, and vulnerability. Second, universals are justifiable in terms of the particular: practicing love's empathetic emotions is justified by the tribal particularity of the gospel story and the obediential habits shaping that story. Hence the normative, universal judgments of love's empathetic emotions are accessible and justifiable to a community through the particular form in which the Spirit of God manifests itself, the life and teaching of Jesus. Specifically, love's feelings of sorrow and joy, although universal and universally shared by devotees of diverse communities, are accessible and justifiable through the particularity of obediential habits (like humility, intimacy, and vulnerability) that shape each community's distinct narrative tradition.

Suppose the community of the man of wealth nurtures in him obediential habits of humility, intimacy, and vulnerability. Suppose that his character so formed inspires in him empathetic feelings of sorrow and joy. Would he then not be so situated that he is actually able to obey Jesus' command to "Go, sell what you possess and give to the poor, and you will have treasure in heaven, and come follow me"? Would he not be so situated that obedience becomes a practical possibility? In feeling love's sorrow and joy, would he not experience a fellowship with the poor, a fellowship so profound that he would probably choose nothing other than obedience? It is precisely this feeling of loving fellowship that the rich man lacks and whose lack prevents him from selling all, following Jesus, and securing eternal life.

Here we can see most clearly the significance of covenantal love as emotional attachment. For it is in its affectional dimension that love's sorrow and joy exhibit two qualities, empathy and equality, that make selling all and giving to the poor (i.e., that makes covenantal economics) a practical possibility. First, empathy is a moral quality that presupposes habits like Christian humility and vulnerability. Intersubjectivity, you will recall, is the capacity certain emotions possess that enable people who may otherwise differ greatly to share experiences in common. Max Scheler argues this point persuasively in his classic work *The Nature of Sympathy*. Love by its very nature includes not only a diversity of emotional experiences but also various forms of mutuality and sympathy. Two forms in particular are pertinent: First, "community of feeling," he says, is a kind of sympathy experienced only by those who are subject to the very same conditions that are giving rise to sorrow or joy. This "feeling in common" is an internal connection between two parents who experience the loss of a child, for example, or the poor of a community who suffer malnutrition. Those not experiencing these conditions, for example, the rich man, will not have access to this "feeling in common."[66] Scheler, however, speaks of a second form of sympathy, "fellow-feeling," which involves "*intentional reference* of the feeling of joy or sorrow to the other person's experience." Here, those (e.g., the rich man) who do not suffer or enjoy specific conditions of life (e.g., poverty) can nevertheless imagine such conditions and sympathize because of "its very capacity *as* a feeling."[67] This is the kind of loving empathy Jesus presupposes when he enjoins the man of wealth to "sell all and give to the poor": an intentional reference in which the sorrow of some invites the empathetic sorrow of others or joy's delight multiplies itself in others. A community enabled to feel for and empathize with the plight of another is inspired to undertake moral projects commensurate with that feeling. Jesus' command to the man of wealth presupposes that he feel in himself the same kind of sorrow the poor feel in their poverty. It is just such an empathetic feeling of sorrow that will enable him to care for the poor in a way that he would want to be cared for if he were poor. As the American bishops argue, Christian love implies just this sort of "mutual care" of one another, a "solidarity" and "social friendship" with the poor that inspires a community of faith not merely to feel with the poor but to participate with the poor in moral projects of economic justice.[68] This power of love to inspire empathy, accordingly, implies a heart disposed toward intimacy and vulnerability, a heart unafraid of the intimacy implicit in sharing with another, even with a stranger, feelings of sorrow and joy, a heart empowered to act with and for the poor.

Equality is a second quality that belongs to love's empathetic nature and that presupposes when practiced the presence of dispositions like humility and vulnerability. By feeling in himself the same kind of sorrow the poor man feels in his poverty, the man of wealth not only would empathize with his plight but simultaneously would show himself in his sorrow to be on common and equal ground with the poor. "One's neighbor," as Kierkegaard suggests, "[becomes] one's equal.... To love one's neighbor means equality.... He is your neighbor on the basis of equality with you before God; but this equality absolutely every man has, and he has it absolutely."[69] To "weep with those who weep," accordingly, not only consoles the sorrowful but challenges the caring one to relinquish categories of comparative worth and in evangelical humility acknowledge his or her vulnerability before God and with his or her poor neighbor. Perhaps this is partly why the rich man went away downhearted; for feeling sorrow with the poor would require him to share not only the intimacy of fellow-feeling with the poor but their vulnerability. Indeed, in feeling love's sorrow with them, the material and social boundaries whereby he protects himself and preserves his security and privilege over the poor fade. By empathizing and loving the poor as equal neighbor, one ultimately establishes a fellowship in which, as Kierkegaard puts it, "the contentious mine and yours have become a communal mine and yours. Therefore it is a fellowship, a perfect fellowship in mine and yours."[70]

The earliest Christian community, as a case in point, manifested both qualities (empathy and equality) of love's sorrow. Wealthy and poor together understood themselves as a humble, vulnerable, loving fellowship involving shared lives and possessions. Compassionate sorrow for widows and orphans inspired an outpouring of joyful generosity in which those who had plenty humbly shared with those who in need and in so doing shared in a kind of mutual vulnerability and security. Not only were needs cared for but love's command to sell all and give to the poor was satisfied. Had the man of wealth heeded Jesus' command to sell all and follow, he would not only feel love's sorrow in caring for the poor but at the same time would experience love's joy. Indeed, joy is a primary emotional force without which love's project of sorrowing with the poor, is unlikely to be accomplished. In sharing all he has with the poor the man of wealth would experience the joy of participating in God's project of liberating redemption, of transforming the world as it unfairly is into the world as God wills it to be. For the Christian community such redemptive projects are inspired by feelings of

compassionate sorrow for the poor and sustained by feelings of delight and gladness. The community's joy lies in the privilege of sharing with the poor the same
gracious kindness it receives from God, so that in the end both donor and recipient rejoice together. It is important to note that, as an empathetic feeling, covenantal joy arises from an attitude of sheer graciousness, so that love's project
remains a gift. For only as a gift can love be said to "seek not its own," as Paul
claims true love does (1 Corinthians 13:5). A feeling of joyfulness arises from the
fact that, as Kierkegaard puts it, love "gives in such a way that the gift appears
as if it were the receiver's possession" and not as if it were charity whereby the
"recipient gets to know that he is indebted."[71] Charitable giving risks degenerating
into judgments of comparative worth, into pride's condescension and to that
extent into self-love. Thus, the man of wealth who truly seeks not his own, insists
Kierkegaard, would give "precisely in such a way that it appears as if the gift were
the recipient's own possession. In so far as the lover is able, he seeks to help a
man to become himself, to become his own."[72] Both donor and recipient participate in a fellowship of rejoicing in which both experience the joy of liberation
from the destructive forces of poverty. Love's sorrow and joy, in other words, are
intricately interrelated, as the writer of John's gospel so vividly portrays in a
metaphor of childbearing. Although the experience of sorrow is undeniable and
unavoidable, "sorrow will turn into joy" just as when a woman experiences pain
and anguish when she is in labor. "But when she is delivered of the child, she no
longer remembers the anguish because of her joy that a child is born to her. So
you have sorrow now," comments John, "but I will see you again and your hearts
will rejoice, and no one will take your joy from you" (John 16:20–23). Sorrow
and joy are profoundly formative emotions for those whose lives are dedicated to
loving passionately as Jesus loves. Had the man of wealth understood love in this
way—had he felt sorrow and joy as analogous to giving birth to a child—perhaps
he would have been prepared for Jesus's challenge to sell all, give to the poor,
and "follow me."

We are now in a position to answer the question, What are the economic
implications of covenantal love, of weeping with those who weep and rejoicing
with those who rejoice? What significance does "Sell all, give to the poor, and
follow" Christ hold for developing a covenantal economics? The National Conference of Catholic Bishops' letter *Economic Justice for All* is a helpful guide in
understanding Jesus' teaching on wealth and poverty in general and his injunction
to sell all and give to the poor in particular. Ultimately, argue the bishops, "*The
dignity of the human person, realized in community with others, is the criterion
against which all aspects of economic life must be measured.*"[73] So what could Jesus
mean by "sell all and give to the poor"? First, Jesus is not establishing poverty as
a socioeconomic ideal. Involuntary poverty is not a condition the Christian community should tolerate or invite. Although poverty may be for some Christians a
valid call and vow, involuntary, oppressive poverty is not the way God wills the

world to be for those created in God's image. The bishops make this point. The practice of voluntary or "evangelical poverty in the church has always been a living witness. . . . [But Christianity] neither canonized material poverty nor accepted deprivation as an inevitable fact of life."[74] Rather the bishops go on to argue convincingly that it is precisely to alleviate poverty that Jesus enjoins the man of wealth to give his abundance to the poor and that the early Christians sold possessions. The conditions that prompt Jesus to challenge the man of wealth to give all to the poor are conditions that produce involuntary, oppressive poverty, a poverty that causes hunger and homelessness, suffering and sorrow, a poverty that savages human dignity and happiness.

Second, Jesus' command to the man of wealth to give to the poor does not mean that charity finally is the acceptable means for addressing conditions of poverty. Indeed, Jesus enjoins the man of wealth to so dispose of his wealth that he will no longer be in a position to give charitably; he will no longer possess an abundance to give. So, although personal, private acts of charity are surely acceptable, argue the bishops, such acts are in themselves woefully inadequate. "[A]lleviating poverty will require fundamental changes in social and economic structures that perpetuate glaring inequalities."[75] But if not poverty or charity, what could "Go, sell all, give to the poor, and follow me" possibly mean for Christians today? The nearest I can come to an interpretation that is faithful to both the character of Mark's story and to love's obediential dispositions and empathetic emotions is this. What is required is first of all a social and economic restructuring such that the economic privilege currently enjoyed by the wealthy is given up or "sold." Second, what is required are structures and policies that more equitably distribute economic goods in ways that no longer necessitate private, charitable giving. When private charity, to individuals or through social agencies, becomes the primary means by which Christians address poverty, then we can be sure that the Church, like the man of wealth, has sadly refused to heed Jesus's command and has capitulated to the fatalism of accepting poverty and deprivation as inevitable facts of life. Charity by its very nature presupposes social structures that generate unjust discrepancies in the distribution of goods. Charity by its very nature reifies class distinctions and structural inequalities that cause poverty and deprivation in the first place and the need for charitable giving in the second place. The need for charity is a symptom of the need for the radical renovation of economic structures, structures that mutilate the dignity of humans otherwise created in the image of God. For charity intensifies the distinction and distance between mine and yours, constantly placing and preserving the poor as in my debt. Kysar argues this point when he writes that charity "assumes a chasm between me and the needy other. It further assumes that chasm can be kept in place while I serve the other,"[76] assuring my excess and the poor's deficit. Because it does not require love's empathetic sorrow and joy, because it does not transform conditions of poverty into conditions of prosperity for the poor, charity is unable to establish the equality, fellowship, and communion between donor and recipient implied by covenantal love. Therefore, charity's indebtedness cannot be an occasion for the kind of sorrow and rejoicing characteristic of covenantal love. Charity no doubt suited the man of wealth just fine. We can easily imagine that it was his practice to give some of his excess to the poor in hopes that in doing so he could in a single stroke fulfill God's commands, secure eternal life, and maintain his economic privilege and advantage.

Third, covenantal love as empathetic affection enables a community to establish conditions of economic equality that logically emerge from love's fellowship, from feeling sorrow with those who are sorrowful. Establishing a fellowship of spiritual communion means at the same time establishing a fellowship of economic communion. The bishops argue that the "community of hope" that emerges from a community of faithful Christians implies inevitably and necessarily solidarity with and mutual care of the poor and disenfranchised.[77] Love's sorrow and joy, if genuinely and graciously felt, necessitate it. Failing to do so signals a failure of love. Indeed, Jesus and the early church presuppose the interdependence of spiritual and economic communion, so much so that absence of the one implies the absence of the other. Love's empathetic feeling of sorrow assumes "a sense of solidarity with the conditions of the other person," as Kysar puts it, "and [it]further assumes that service is rendered not from a distance but in relationship with the other." Covenantal love "seeks not the sharing of surplus on the part of a few with the many," as Kysar goes on to argue, "but the total redistribution of all the resources of society. It presupposes restructuring social systems rather than the maintenance of the status quo." Covenantal love inspires a community "to rebuild the total social system from the foundation up and not simply remodel [the] entry way [to wealth]."[78] Jesus' own Jewish tradition includes a rather intricate network of socioeconomic practices and institutions (gleaning, tithing, sabbatical and jubilee years, etc.) dedicated to distributing and redistributing property and wealth in a fair and caring way. Whether Israel uniformly implemented these practices is beside the central point that these social institutions and practices were intended as a system of economic distribution whereby the economic well-being of all members of the community, especially the poor, is addressed fairly.[79]

What socioeconomic theories and institutions might best accomplish this covenantal ideal today is difficult to say. What can be said, first, is that changing social and historical conditions require a change in economic systems and practices so that the new conditions are directly and successfully addressed. Second, it can be said that, given the widening economic discrepancy between rich and poor, the structures and policies currently in place not only lack the capacity to overcome this discrepancy but generally lack also the capacity to recognize and account for the fact that such discrepencies exist and are worsening. Sorrowing with the poor and disadvantaged around the world, the covenantal community will not want to be held hostage to capitalism's presumption of charity, which demeans the integrity of the recipient and validates economic inequality. Although charity may be temporarily necessary, the humility and vulnerability that invites love's empathetic sorrow will work toward gainful employment for all and equitable distribution of the economic goods over which God calls his community to be good stewards.

My assumption, defended in chapter 2, is that the universality of love's sorrow and joy is practically possible and justifiable through the particularity of a tradition's obediential habits. Love's joy and sorrow are empathetic emotions that can be and often are shared in common by people of faith. The question I have yet to address is, For the Christian community, on what basis is the experience of love's joy and sorrow, and the covenantal economics arising from it, justifiable and practical possibility? What reasons and incentives are able to justify and inspire the radical economic project implicit in covenantal love? The argument set forth in chapter 2 suggests that the justification and incentive for experiencing love's sorrow and joy reside not in the abstract metaethical heaven of universal laws and transcendent principles but instead in the concrete, local, and in the particular tribal tradition of a community. Those opting for the Christian tradition have only to look to the obediential dispositions of humility, intimacy, and vulnerability embodied in the life of Jesus in order to justify and inspire love's sorrow and joy and the covenantal economics inspired by them.

Love's covenantal version of economics would constitute, no doubt, a sour pill for Western Christian communities to swallow, one not likely to be digested unless compelling reasons and incentives particular to their own Christian experience could be marshaled. So it must be shown that the universal truths implicit in emotional judgments (such as "Poverty should not exist," "We should distribute socioeconomic goods fairly") are justifiable in terms of the particular, distinctive patterns of meaning implicit in the Christian community's narrative tradition. It must be shown how the obediential dispositions that shape the contours of that tradition justify and inspire convenantal economics.

The Apostle Paul's magnificent Christological discourse in Philippians 2 shows how Christ embodies in his own life the obediential dispositions of humility, vulnerability, and intimacy. Paul also indicates how these dispositions invite love's sorrow and joy in Christ's own life and empower him to undertake a redemptive project of serving even the lowliest of humankind. That covenantal economics is logically and practically compelling for the Christian is due to the truth of Christ's humility, vulnerability, and intimacy. Without these qualities of character there is no incarnation, no gospel story, no covenantal community. Paul himself makes these logical and practical connections between obediential dispositions and empathetic emotions. His pivotal injunction, "Have this mind among yourselves which is yours in Christ Jesus" (Philippians 2:5), is preceded by his desire for the Christian community to find some reason for "any incentive to love, any participation in the Spirit, any affection and sympathy" (2:1). The same injunction is succeeded by what he finds are compelling reasons for loving selflessly, namely, the incarnation, life, and death of Christ. Paul explains that the loving affection and sympathy that counts "others better than yourselves" and looks "not only to [one's] own interests but also to the interests of others" presupposes the kind of humility and vulnerability embodied by Christ. The same Jesus "who, though he was in the form of God, did not count equality with God a thing to be grasped . . . emptied himself, taking the form of a servant, being born in the likeness of men. And being found in human form he humbled himself and became obedient unto death, even death on a cross" (Philippians 2:6–8). Assuming this central fact of the gospel story, the Christian community is endowed both with justifiable reason and practical, spiritual power whereby it is inspired and enabled to devote itself to projects of covenantal economics. By becoming humbly incarnate, by taking on the form of a servant, Jesus embodies both qualities of love's affectional nature: empathy and equality. He shares in the risks and vulnerabilities of the disheartened, homeless, and poor. By becoming a humble servant Jesus makes himself equal with (not subservient to) humanity. He makes himself intimately vulnerable and "disposable," as Marcel puts it, to the human condition, thereby sharing the risks and dangers, weaknesses and temptations, joys and celebrations, sorrows and sufferings of being human, even to the point of despair and death on the cross.

Commensurate with his status as incarnate servant, Jesus is often reported to be in the company and service of tax collectors, prostitutes, the irreligious, the poor, and the disenfranchised. He befriends them, even eats with them, which, as Kysar points out, is "an expression of intimacy in which he opens himself to the influence of their character (e.g., Matthew 9:10–11)"[80] and they to his. Jesus even calls a tax collector one of his most intimate friends and disciples and praises one of them, Zacchaeus, for repenting and undertaking a radical project of personal economic reform. In fact, the story of Zacchaeus (Luke 19:1–10) portrays the way that love's obediential dispositions confer a power of practical justification on empathetic emotions. In humility Jesus accepts Zacchaeus's invitation to dinner and in so doing establishes with Zacchaeus a kind of intimacy and vulnerability for which he is criticized by the crowd: "He has gone in to be the guest of a man who is a sinner" (19:7). Luke's account suggests that there is a direct link between Jesus' act of humility and Zacchaeus's response of humble repentance. Jesus' own humility, intimacy and vulnerability provides a model for Zacchaeus to imitate, a model that in fact inspires in Zacchaeus humble repentance and intimate vulnerability. Moreover, Zacchaeus seems to understand immediately the practical economic implications of the salvation that has come to his house. His humble repentance invites the empathetic power of love's sorrow. Consequently, he is able to feel in himself the same sorrow felt by those he has defrauded and is able to undertake a radical project of personal and public economic reform in which "the half of my goods I give to the poor, and if I have defrauded any one of anything, I restore it fourfold" (19:8). Luke's account suggests that Zaccheus's repentance, salvation, and intimate fellowship with Jesus implies, justifies, and makes practically possible an economic communion, one in which economic exploitation and privilege is relinquished for the fellowship and equality of love's sorrow and joy. In short, Jesus' habit of humble, intimate vulnerability with the least of humanity is a habit of heart that the Christian community is to nurture and imitate. By inviting love's empathetic sorrow and joy, it calls forth emotions so profoundly powerful as to inspire and enable a community to place at the disposal of humanity not charity, not a temporary loan on its vast economic resources, but, like Jesus, all that it is and has. In loving, a community enters into a fellowship so intimately vulnerable that it finds itself delivering to humanity its very self, life, and being. By appealing to the tribal practices of a local Palestinian prophet, by imitating the humble and intimate vulnerability of Jesus' life and teaching, a community of faith is inspired and justified in undertaking projects commensurate with covnenantal economics. That Jesus humbly suffers with those who suffer and sorrows with those who sorrow is reason and incentive for the Christian community doing likewise. That Jesus invests himself personally and intimately in the lives of the poor and dispossessed, that he places himself and his resources at their disposal is reason and grace, justification, and inspiration enough for the Christian community doing so.

This approach reveals more clearly why the norm-centered approach to love, represented by the Kantian tradition's preference for rational law, is of itself inadequate. Commanded love by itself does not acknowledge and thus cannot solicit the emotional power and incentive required of any community committed to living lives of such radical obedience. Rational law by itself cannot and does not call a community to become emotionally, personally invested in the sorrow and joy of others so that it is willing to sell all and follow Jesus. What is required in addition to law is, as I have argued throughout, certain habits of heart (humility, intimacy, and vulnerability) that empower and inspire personal, emotional investment in the lives of those in need. To insist on the adequacy of commanded love by itself (as did the man of wealth) and disenfranchise the passionate, empathetic power of love's heart is to insist de facto that one ought to love yet must disown precisely those resources without which one cannot love as Christ loves. Our primary tendency as fallen creatures is to promote ourselves, to undertake projects that indulge our desires and guarantee our comfort. Although the man of wealth found it convenient and satisfying to obey all of God's commands, he found Jesus' demand that he care passionately for the poor disarming, disconcerting, and inconvenient. In contrast, whatever has the character of suffering love, of intimate vulnerability and compassionate sorrow with "the least of these," having escaped the fallen human preference for rational and personal distance, must have as its source the redeeming power embodied in God's gift of love.

Dutifully keeping all of God's commands by itself, as we learn from the man of wealth, requires neither that we learn habits of humility, vulnerability, and intimacy nor that we empathize passionately and personally with the plight of our poor neighbor.

Love's commandments are, however, integral to love's story. "Lawlike pronouncements have a prominent place in the Scriptures," as Hauerwas puts it, yet "they are certainly never treated as an end in themselves or as capable of independent justification."[81] Rather, they acquire their justification from the covenantal story of which they are an indispensable part and from which they should not properly be abstracted. Indeed, the Decalogue and the Sermon of the Mount seem quite unintelligible when treated as sets of rules independent of the plot of which they are originally a vital part. The exhortations that people should believe that "God is one," keep the Sabbath, not bear false witness, turn the other cheek, go the second mile, or love their enemies have little meaning or persuasive appeal independent of the historical narrative and moral character of the community out of which they arise. "The Decalogue is part of the covenant with Israel. Divorced from that covenant it makes no sense. God does indeed command obedience, but our God is the God who 'brought you out of the land of Egypt, out of the house of bondage' (Deuteronomy 5:6). Because of this action the demand 'You shall have no other God before me' can be made."[82] That commandments lose their meaning and indeed their practical possibility abstracted from love's obediential dispositions and empathetic emotions is as important to remember as to remember that the meaning of love's story cannot be told without recalling the moral pattern encapsulated in God's commandments.

To make the same point by analogy, God's commands and actions in history are to love's story as a melody line is to improvisational jazz. The musician who cultivates skills so as to be adept at playing improvisationally is one who both is clear about the melody line and remains creatively faithful to its basic pattern and demands. Indeed, improvisation is possible and makes musical sense only so long as its creative freedom remains clearly anchored to the original melody line. So too in Christian ethics. The story line, the plot of Christian ethics, is constituted by God's covenant with a chosen people; the basic elements of this covenant are God's mighty acts and commandments. These historical acts and commands give narrative shape to love's story, a story that could not be faithfully told, let alone faithfully experienced, apart from them. They give shape to the experience of Christian love and love's story, and it is on the basis of this shape that the church is called to creatively and constructively improvise in a morally chaotic world. Christian moral improvisation (casuistry) is possible and makes moral sense, in other words, only so long as it remain faithful to the original pattern of God's commandments and mighty acts. Abstracting those commands from a community's dispositions and emotional preferences makes no more sense than a musician abstracting and playing without feeling a few fragments of a piece instead of the composition as a whole. God's commandments are central and crucial to the practice of morality but only insofar as they remain embedded in the complex and intricate plot of love's covenantal history.[83] Furthermore, to extend the metaphor, the musician who is so skilled as to play improvisationally is one who has participated and continues to participate in a community that helped and helps her develop the elementary skills of playing jazz. Indeed, only by remaining faithful to that community, its traditions, and its elementary disciplines—only by imitation of its masters—is she able to achieve the creative freedom needed to play improvisationally at all.

The Kantian tradition's emphasis on the norm-centered, commanded love, therefore, must not be rejected; if it is, there will once more, as often in the past, be change but no progress. The Kantian understanding of love must be retained in the work of superseding it; obedience to God's commandments, as the writer of 1 John indicates, is crucial to love's story. When we love God with humble intimacy and passionate engagement, we obey his commandments (1 John 5:1–6), thereby conforming to the essential pattern of love's covenantal story. As such, to the man of wealth, as to the admirer and skeptic and downhearted, there is tendered in covenantal love the strongest and most reliable pledge: that in love's sorrow and joy God's promise of life eternal is assured.

The remainder of my discussion in part II, my analysis of peace and justice as Christian virtues, assumes the method I have been using to this point and the application I have made of it to love as a Christian virtue. The discussion of peace and justice, in other words, presupposes already the presence of covenantal love—presupposes a community whose character is shaped by humility, intimacy, and vulnerability and by the empathetic sorrow and joy these dispositions inspire. Although we do not yet know what conception of peace and justice this method will yield, we do know that it will require us to attend to the obediential dispositions and empathetic emotions that constitute the heart of Christian virtue.

4

Peace as a Christian Virtue

COMMOTION ON THE STREET attracted Jesus' attention. A woman, an adulteress, was in the custody of authorities, and they were bringing her to Jesus, a rabbi of recent and dubious reputation. Teacher, they said, this woman has been caught in the act of adultery. Now in the law Moses commanded us to stone such. What do you say? Jesus faced a dilemma. He knew the law well, and it was clear and unambiguous on this point. The woman legally and justly deserved death. Yet Jesus was rapidly gaining a reputation as a teacher for whom love and compassion, mercy and forgiveness constituted the true meaning of faith. What was Jesus to do? The woman heard Jesus say to her accusers, "Let him who is without sin among you be the first to throw a stone at her." She waited for what seemed like an eternity, but no stones fell. Again that voice, "Woman, where are they? Has no one condemned you?" "No one, Lord," she heard herself say. "Neither do I condemn you," said Jesus; "go and do not sin again" (John 8:3–11). Without undermining the law, Jesus grants the woman mercy, forgiveness, reconciliation, and peace. Today the Christian community faces a similar dilemma. When confronted with choices of punishment or mercy, violence or nonviolence, war or peace, what should it do? What is it equipped to do? Should it take national sides in international conflicts? If so, which ones and which sides? What is it that the church can bring to international conflicts that nations cannot provide for themselves?

Christian peace "does not begin so much as an ethical reply to the violence question (as it is often interpreted to do, especially by just war theorists)," says Cahill, "but as a practical embodiment of a religious conversion experience—as a way of life rather than a theory."[1] My aim in this chapter is to show that when peace is understood as a Christian virtue, the Christian community will dedicate itself to the practice of pacifism. More specifically I argue that in understanding itself as a pacifist community, the Christian community will understand itself as a kind of spiritual version of the Red Cross: its mission not to take national sides in times of conflict but to care for the afflicted regardless of national loyalties.

I follow here the method, set forth in chapter 2, for analyzing each Christian virtue. First, I examine the obediential dispositions (faithfulness, hopefulness, and lovingkindness) essential for obeying Christ's commandment to be peacemakers. Second, I examine certain empathetic emotions (mercy and generosity) elicited by these dispositions. Finally, I show how, together these two dimensions of virtue commit a covenantal community to the practice of pacifism. I assume throughout this chapter the fact that covenantal peace presupposes love as a Christian virtue– presupposes the obediential (humility, intimacy, vulnerability) and emotional (joy and sorrow) dimensions of love. Indeed, love is the seed without which the flower of covenantal peace cannot bloom.

Peace as Obediential Dispositions

Covenantal peace consists of certain obediential habits of heart that enable a community to conform to Christ's command to be peacemakers. Commands like "Swear no oaths," "Turn the other cheek," and "Love your enemies" are commands quite impossible to obey unless certain obediential dispositions of character are nurtured and internalized by the Christian community. Focusing on key passages in the Sermon on the Mount (Matthew 5:33–42), I examine three dispositions of character—faithfulness, hopefulness, and lovingkindness—that are essential to any community intent on obeying Jesus' command to live nonviolently as peacemakers. In doing so I find, with Walter Wink, that Jesus' teaching about peace is not simply a "pietistic exhortation" that emphasizes "the spiritual benefits to be gained by voluntarily undergoing humiliation"; nor is Jesus' message "one of non-resistance, as almost all commentators have argued." Rather, with Wink, I find that in exhorting his disciples to be peacemakers, Jesus is calling them to undertake risky projects of "active nonviolent resistance."[2] The vision of Jesus affirmed by Matthew in chapter 5 is a vision of a "countercultural polis," as Richard Hays puts it, a polis in which "the transcendence of violence through loving the enemy is the most salient feature."[3] Unless communities of faithful followers are willing to take the risk of living counterculturally, the hope that they will be "salt" and "light" in the world fades to nothing. From the fact that Jesus, according to Matthew's gospel, models such a countercultural style in all the various relationships of his life, not only in his personal but in his social and political relationships as well, one is compelled to draw the conclusion with Hays that what is sketched in the Sermon on the Mount is a comprehensive outline of the kind of countercultural relationships (personal, social, and political) that Christian communities ought to embody.

Faithfulness

Leading up to and logically preceding Jesus' core teachings on peace ("Turn the other cheek" and "Love your enemies") is the following passage: "Again you have heard it said to the men of old, 'You shall not swear falsely, but shall perform to the Lord what you have sworn.' But I say to you, 'Do not swear at all. . . . Let what you say be simply 'Yes' or 'No'; anything more than this comes from evil" (Matthew 5:33–34, 37). These comments regarding the second commandment lend themselves to a variety of interpretations.[4] My concern here is not so much with these interpretations but with the core meaning underlying Jesus' prohibition and its significance for understanding covenantal peace. The underlying meaning, I think, is clear: Jesus expects the speech, actions, and indeed the very life of his disciples to embody truthfulness so faithfully that swearing oaths is preempted and is irrelevant.[5] Loyalty to God and truth, in other words, should shine so brightly in one's life that swearing oaths, which imply the possibility of untruthfulness, is simply unnecessary, a need that does not arise. Indeed, the implication is that the covenantal community should be as faithful to God as God is to it, thus nullifying any occasion for swearing oaths. "The Bible is clear that such a life style of loyalty," as Katherine Sakenfeld puts it, "depends in every way upon God's faithfulness. Divine faithfulness provides a model of loyalty which takes commitment radically seriously. . . . The faithful God overcomes our failure of loyalty and with forgiveness sets our feet again and again on the right path."[6] Faithful discipleship, inspired by God's faithfulness, involves a life so committed to God's truth that swearing of oaths of loyalty to auxiliary authorities is an act of betrayal.

Jesus' expectation that his disciples will be single-mindedly faithful to God, of course, complicates somewhat the relation between peacemaking obligations of covenantal communities and Paul's injunction (in Romans 13) to the same communities to obey governing authority. How can the Christian community be both single-mindedly faithful to God and God's peaceable kingdom and at the same time obey governing authorities, who not infrequently require of citizens oaths of allegiance, military service, and warfare?

Many early Christian communities developed, as is well known, a pacifist stance in which faithfulness to Christ and Christ's peace excluded swearing oaths of allegiance to governing authority, military service, and warfare. In pre-Constantinian times, early Christians communities often considered it a betrayal of Jesus and transgression of his prohibition regarding oaths to enter military life and to engage in the wars of Rome. Faithful witness to Christ's peace very often involved refusing to swear oaths required for military service. Tertullian, for example, juxtaposes faithfulness and peace with swearing oaths and warfare. He asks "whether warfare is proper at all for Christians" and then adds, rhetorically, "Do we believe it lawful for a human oath to be superadded to one divine, for a man to come under promise to another master after Christ[?] . . . And shall the son of peace take part in the battle when it does not become him even to sue at law? . . . Shall he carry a flag, too, hostile to Christ?"[7] Roman military life entailed swearing allegiance to Caesar in a way that for Tertullian transgressed the second commandment and Jesus' prohibition of swearing oaths. Similarly, Marcellus, a Roman centurion and Christian, came to understand that faithfulness to Christ meant that he could not pledge allegiance to Caesar or engage in warfare. "I am a Christian, and I am unable to adhere to the military oath of allegiance, but rather serve Jesus Christ, the son of the almighty God the Father." Marcellus was put to death because he "abandoned his oath publicly," counting faithfulness to God more compelling that service to Caesar, counting the peace of Christ more compelling than allegiance to Rome and Roman warfare.[8]

Constantinian Christianity, which continues to dominate Western Christianity, supplanted this early pacifist tradition with a just war tradition derived largely from Roman sources. But pre-Constantinian pacifism did not disappear entirely, and during the Reformation it reasserted itself among some reformers. The Schleitheim Confession, for example, sets forth a pattern of thought that links magistrates, warfare, and swearing oaths. Christ's disciples should not serve as magistrates because magistrates, whose "citizenship is in this world," are required to use "the devilish weapons of force—such as sword, armour and the like" and because "the weapons of their conflict and war are carnal and against the flesh only." Moreover, because magistrates find themselves involved in conflict and fighting, they are required to swear oaths, for "the oath is a confirmation among those who are quarreling or making promises."[9] In short, the Schleitheim Confession presupposes a single-minded and exclusive faithfulness to Christ as an essential obediential disposition of heart without which Jesus' commands "Turn the other cheek" and "Love your enemies" make little practical sense. But what of biblical passages, like Romans 13 and 1 Peter 2, in which Christians are enjoined to subject themselves to those in authority, "whether it be to the emperor as supreme or to governors"? (1 Peter 2:13) How is single-minded faithfulness to Christ (swearing no oaths) possible for the Christian along with simultaneous obedience to temporal authorities who demand of citizens oaths of allegiance and military service? To pilot these turbulent waters safely, it would be well to keep in mind several landmarks.

First, nowhere do Jesus or the apostolic writers say or even suggest that being subject to authorities entails swearing oaths, serving in the military, or engaging in warfare. Victor Paul Furnish's analysis of Paul's Romans passage is compelling on this issue. He argues that requiring Christians to be "subject" to authorities is not the same as requiring them to "obey" every decree emanating from governmental authorities and that the opposite of being "subject" is not "disobeying" but "resisting" authorities. Like Peter and John, "One might . . . 'disobey' a law of the state and still 'be subject' to the political structure, namely, to the due processes and penalties administered in cases of [civil] disobedience."[10] One might, like Martin Luther King, Jr., commit acts of civil disobedience while remaining subject (i.e., without resisting), as he did, to structures of political authority and penalties. And one might very well disobey the call of governing authorities to swear allegiance to a state and take up arms in warfare while remaining subject to the structure and penalties of such governing authorities. Paul's injunctions in Romans 13, in other words, do not conflict either with Jesus' command forbidding the swearing of oaths or his commands to commit oneself to nonviolence and love of enemy—both of which seem to preclude participation in warfare. Moreover, the apostles, in their comments about subjection to authorities, nowhere indicate or imply (although Christians over the centuries certainly have inferred) that such subjection compels military service and warfare.[11]

Second, the state's function, as both Paul and Peter indicate, is to establish and preserve moral order in society. Paul says that rulers "are not a terror to good conduct but to bad" (Romans 13:3) and Peter similarly says that authorities are sent by God "to punish those who do wrong and to praise those who do right" (1 Peter 2:14). The state's proper function is to encourage those citizens who do good and punish wrongdoers. Paul employs the metaphor of the sword to indicate not just that the state wields "judicial authority" as Yoder suggests,[12] "but apparently that the state may also use force to maintain moral order." But whatever means the state employs to enforce order in society, the apostle Paul is unambiguous about the behavior of the covenantal community. If we take chapters 12 and 13 of Romans as a literary and theological unit, as I think we should,[13] then we must interpret his comments about Christians and governing authorities (chapter 13) in light of his comments about the character of Christian community (chapter 12). There Paul prefaces his comments about subjection to authorities with a series of moral injunctions that qualifies the nature and extent of that subjection. Paul commands Christians, for example, "Repay no one evil for evil"; "So far as depends on you, live peaceably with all"; "Never avenge yourselves"; and "Do not overcome evil by evil, but overcome evil with good" (Romans 12: 14–21). If governors are indeed appointed by God to do God's service, as Paul and Peter both insist, then the covenantal community, in obeying governing authorities, should not and must not, in doing so, falsify obedience to God by indiscriminate, naïve obedience to civil authorities. The community must not obey when civil authorities command repaying evil for evil, violence with violence, injustice with injustice. Furnish's analysis here again is illuminating. First, the authority of earthly rulers is derived not from themselves and not from the people but from God. Those rulers' reception of this moral authority is not to be construed as a sign of their inherent goodness and wisdom. Rather, it lays on them the responsibility to 'learn wisdom and not transgress,' and to long for divine instruction in the ways of holiness (Wisdom of Solomon 6:9–11). Paul uses the images of "servant" and "minister" to describe the role of authorities, not "king" or "master"; they are responsible, as stewards are responsible, "for governing wisely and justly"[14]—responsible for being servants and ministers and good stewards who distribute God's goodness throughout the realm. Paul's accent is as much on the government's obligation to rule righteously as on the citizens' obligation to be subject. Even if one allows that Paul is suggesting that the state may execute vengeance and wrath in service to moral order, one must still admit with Yoder, I think, that for the Apostle Paul this "function [vengeance, wrath] exercised by government is not the function to be exercised by Christians,"[15] who are forbidden by Jesus to avenge wrongdoers. Rather, they are commanded always to show mercy, a virtue with which the community of faith and not the state is endowed.

Finally, apostolic writers are keenly and personally aware that faithfulness to God and refusing to swear oaths of allegiance may lead to occasions in which civil disobedience is the only option if the faithful are to conform to God's moral order. Recall that Paul begins the discourse in which we find his comments on civil authorities by urging Christians "to offer themselves wholly and unreservedly to the spiritual worship of God"; as Furnish puts it, "[t]hey are not to be conformed to this present age, but are to live rather as transformed and renewed persons with in it, seeking out and doing God's holy will."[16] Governing authorities are properly servants and ministers of God's holy will in matters of civil order. When the rule of authorities is not in servitude to God's, then they are not longer ministers of that will, and Christians are no longer obligated to obey it, although all the while they remain subject to the institution of government that God has ordained. Although Christians are to be subject to governing authorities, they are not obligated to obey naïvely and without critical qualification, at the expense of faithfulness to God's peaceable kingdom. When Peter and other apostles suffer unjustly for the sake of the gospel, their response, "We must obey God rather than men" (Acts 5:29), justified for Christians acts of civil disobedience and shattered for all posterity the Constantinian view of Romans 13: namely, that, as Yoder puts it, the state's "mandate to wield the sword and the Christian's duty to obey the state combine to place upon the Christian a moral obligation to support and participate in the state's legal killing (death penalty, war)." Clearly, for the Christian community there are, insists Yoder, "contrary duties" to obeying the state, duties that "otherwise would seem to follow from Jesus' teaching or example."[17] The covenantal community is to obey governing authorities, but only to the extent that those authorities fulfill a divinely appointed role that does not conflict with God's call to peace. Yoder makes this very point—that although "whatever government exists is ordered by God . . . the text does not say whatever the government does or asks its citizens is good." He further insists that the participle usually translated "attending" (Romans 13:6) is better translated as "an adverbial modifier of the previous predication. We should then read 'they are ministers of God *to the extent* to which they busy themselves . . . to the assigned function.' "[18] Not only early Christians but many Christians throughout the centuries have assumed that the actions and policies of governing authorities are not self-justifying but are justified only to the extent that they are otherwise compatible with the life and teaching of Jesus. Jesus' own life and teaching, in fact, conflicted fairly often with the orders of governing authorities, as did the lives and teaching of those early Christians (e.g., Stephen) whom Saul persecuted. Indeed, very often their lives seem to reflect a "contrary duty," articulated by Martin Luther King, Jr., in his "Letter from a Birmingham Jail," that the Christian not only has a moral obligation to obey just laws but an equally compelling obligation to disobey unjust laws. Peter hints at the reality of contrary duties when, in speaking of the master–slave relationship, he acknowledges that, mindful of God, the Christian may, as a result of civil disobedience, endure "pain while suffering unjustly" (1 Peter 2:19) as Peter himself did. In short, the call to faithfulness underlying Jesus' prohibition of oaths implies that when God's moral agenda conflicts with the agenda of governing authorities, God's agenda takes precedence.

Since Constantinian Christianity has generally not kept these landmarks in sight, it is not surprising that it foundered on the shoals of what the writer of James calls "double-mindedness" (James 1). The Constantinian tendency is not exactly to prefer governing authority to God's authority but to divide one's loyalty between masters—between God and government, between church and state. James describes the character of those who attempt to parley divided loyalties; they will be like "a wave of the sea that is driven and tossed by the wind," "unstable," "unfaithful creatures" (James 1:6–7; 4:4). The great temptation for Constantinian Christianity has been a double-mindedness in which its loyalty is somehow divided between swearing oaths of allegiance to the state and faithfulness to God, between the false idols of the age and the truth of God's kingdom. In so dividing its loyalties, the church cannot be relied on, indeed, cannot rely on itself, to deliver to the world the one thing that it alone is empowered to administer: the healing grace of God's peace. Faithful obedience, as a habit of the Christian heart, dramatizes the gospel's decisive "Yes" and "No": "No" to double-mindedness and divided loyalties, "Yes" to faithfulness to God's kingdom and to what follows in the Sermon on the Mount, namely, "Turn the other cheek" and "Love your enemies."

Hopefulness

Jesus' prohibition of swearing oaths is immediately and logically followed, in the Sermon on the Mount, by a command that his disciples act nonviolently in their relations with others, especially with those who act violently or unjustly toward them. "You have heard it said, 'An eye for an eye and a tooth for a tooth.' But I say to you, Do not resist one who is evil. But if anyone strikes you on the right cheek, turn to him the other also; and if anyone would sue you and take your coat, let him have your cloak as well; and if anyone forces you to go one mile, go with him two miles" (Matthew 5:39–41). Two dimensions of Jesus' injunction are relevant to understanding covenantal peace: hopeful meekness and active non-violent resistance.

First, to conform to the conditions described here by Jesus requires a habit of heart that might properly be referred to as hopefulness or hopeful meekness.

Hopefulness, as a disposition of character, manifests itself as "meekness." Meekness, a word largely absent from modern moral discourse, refers to a habit of steadfast endurance in the face of opposition and suffering; one suffers in full and hopeful assurance that such enduring leads to liberation and redemption. Katie Canon calls this quality of character "unctuousness." For her, unctuousness is "the quality of steadfastness, akin to fortitude, in the face of formidable oppression. . . . [It is a] moral quality of life [set forth] not as an ideal to be fulfilled but as a balance of complexities so that suffering will not overwhelm and endurance is possible." The covenantal community learns unctuous meekness by imitating Jesus, of course, but also by imitating those in its community for whom that quality was and is most decisive for survival, namely, African-American women who are "twice stigmatized—once for race and once for gender."[19] A community that turns the other cheek is one that is characterized by unctuousness, patiently, meekly, hopefully enduring injustice and injury and at the same time "creatively straining," as Cannon puts it, "against the external restraints" that oppress and demean.[20] So by steadfast meekness I by no means want to imply a passive, subservient deferrence to forces of oppression. It is rather an irrepressible moral quality of character, an indomitable spirit that refuses to capitulate to despair in the face of seemingly insurmountable odds and actively seeks creative, even clever, ways of overcoming evil.

It follows that Jesus' command to turn the other cheek, second, requires of a covenantal community a commitment to act proactively and not simply passively. Wink rightly argues, I think, that the hopeful meekness implicit in Jesus' command is "not one of non-resistance" but one of "active nonviolent resistance."[21] By these commands to resist nonviolently, Jesus intends to condone neither harm and aggression nor passive quietism. Instead, in his three examples Jesus establishes, as Wink puts it, how "the oppressed can recover the initiative, how they can assert their dignity in a situation that for the time being cannot be changed."[22] Indeed, by commanding meekness of the covenantal community Jesus acknowledges that "suffering willingly endured is stronger than evil, it spells death to evil," as Bonhoeffer puts it, so that "[v]iolence stands condemned by its failure to evoke counterviolence."[23]

Jesus, of course, embodies most fully and forcefully both hopeful meekness and active, nonviolent resistance. Jonathan Edwards, in *Religious Affections*, makes this point with great clarity and passion. Meekness, or what he calls "fortitude,"

> is quite the opposite of brutal fierceness such as the boldness of beasts of prey. Rather, true Christian fortitude consists of a strength of mind, through grace . . . the steadfast maintenance of a holy calmness, meekness, sweetness, and a benevolence of mind that is sustained amidst all the storms, injuries, wrong behavior, and unexpected acts and events in this evil and unreasonable world. The Scripture seems to intimate that true

fortitude consists chiefly of this: "He that is slow to anger, is better than the mighty; and he that rules his spirit, than he that takes a city" (Proverbs 16:32).[24]

Imagine a community that imitates Jesus's fortitude and meekness. What will be its commitments regarding violence and nonviolence, war and peace? Since Jesus supremely exemplifies "the true nature of holy fortitude," says Edwards, "see how he has fought and won his glorious victories." At the time of his passion, for example, "when all His enemies on earth and hell made their most violent attack upon Him," Jesus responded "[n]ot in fiery passions, nor fierce and violent speeches, but simply in his silence. For he went 'as a lamb to the slaughter, and as a sheep before his shearers was dumb.' " Jesus also displayed the long-suffering patience characteristic of a meek person, says Edwards, "in praying that the Father would forgive His enemies." Nor did Jesus, like the Church so often after him, "shed other's blood, but with all conquering patience and love, He shed His own." Contrast this with tempestuous Peter, who represents Constantinian Christianity by manifesting a kind of worldly boldness, declaring that he would willingly die for the Messiah. He demonstrates that he intends to die not by following Jesus' path of nonviolent resistance but by doing violence. In the garden, says Edwards, Peter "began to swing about with a sword"; Jesus "meekly rebuked him and healed the wound he gave. Never was the patience, meekness, love, and forgiveness of Christ so gloriously seen as it was on this occasion."[25] Even when Jesus was betrayed and arrested, Peter and the other disciples had yet to learn what Jesus meant when he enjoined them to resist not one who is evil. They understood neither the nature of the battle to be fought nor the weapons with which it is to be fought. On the one hand, the battle to be fought was not, as Peter seemed to think, defensive, a battle to defend political allegiances or personal interests and reputation; instead, the battle was to be offensive, a holy war against the false idols of the age, whatever they may be. On the other hand, the weapons with which the battle is to be fought are not the weapons of those who do evil, not the fear and intimidation on which Peter and the church have so often depended. Jesus meant that the holy wars against false idols were to be fought not with the sword and shield of the zealots but with the truth and meekness of Zion. The Apostle Paul, in Ephesians 6:10–20, refers to the weapons with which the cov- ennantal community is to wage its spiritual battles as "the whole armor of God." They include: loins girded with truth, "the breastplate of righteousness," feet shod with "the equipment of the gospel of peace," "the shield of faith," "the helmet of salvation," and "the sword of the Spirit, which is the word of God." These spir- itual, moral weapons, not swords or other weapons of violence, are the means whereby the covenantal peace to which Jesus calls his disciples is secured. As is well known, there are several gospel passages that seem at first to run counter to Jesus' radical peacemaking model and Paul's preference for spiritual warfare. Two passages (Matthew 10:34 and Luke 22:36) use the word "sword" in a figurative sense, and a third passage (Mark 11:15–19) tells of the Temple incident in which Jesus dislodges, with a whip, money-changers from the Temple. I am in agreement with Hays's explanations and conclusion that, properly understood, these passages do not undermine the pacifist vision of the gospels.[26]

The question arises, then, Can the Christian community remain faithful to Jesus' command to act in hopeful, patient meekness toward an enemy, can it "turn the other cheek" and at the same time obey the state's demand that its citizens demonstrate loyalty by participating in or sanctioning its violent warfare? Apparently not! Acting violently or going to war seem to preempt the very possibility of turning the other cheek, of acting toward the enemy with hopeful meekness. Edwards seems to concur when he says that "the Christian must treat his enemy as a brother, and requite his hostility with love. His behavior must be determined not by the way others treat him, but by the treatment he receives from Jesus."[27] "Turn the other cheek" and "Go the second mile" are falsified to the extent that the Christian community advocates or participates in warfare.

Far from implying passivity and resignation, however, Jesus' injunction not to resist one who is evil means only that the faithful are to refrain from treating the evil one with the same violence with which the evil one treats others; or, as the Apostle Paul puts it, "[r]epay no evil for evil . . . but overcome evil with good" (Romans 12:17, 21). The church, as Outka points out, is to be proactive in its response to evil, striving "to convert rather than defeat opponents," to redeem rather than subjugate. "What is forbidden is complicity in the evil designs of the enemy";[28] what is forbidden is not resistance but resistance that employs the same evil and violence that makes the enemy evil in the first place. A covenantal community is to serve its enemies in all things not by avenging evil with evil but in hopeful meekness, by going the second mile, by doing good to those who hate, by "overcoming evil with good." In doing so, by resisting evil with kindness, Christians not only obey God's commands but, as Wink points out, retrieve their human dignity, reempower themselves in the face of humiliation, and recover from the evildoer the initiative[29] by heaping "burning coals upon his head" (Romans 12:19–21). Proactively resisting evil does not require the community to participate in violence, intimidation, and coercion. Indeed, the peace of Christ implied by Paul's injunction might be fairly contrasted with the dominant practice, the peace of Rome, in which a kind of uneasy, oppressive stability was coerced by means of intimidation, violence, and threat of violence. Jesus, Paul, and the early Christian community envisioned and embodied an alternative model of peace based on active nonviolent persuasion. This model presupposes a character shaped by hopeful meekness, a character that does not honor evil by resisting it in kind, a character that will not be lured into the fatal cycle of fighting fear and intimidation with fear and intimidation. By commanding that the church "turn the other cheek" and patiently endure aggression, Jesus is not enjoining the church to become "a doormat for Jesus,"[30] as Wink puts it. Instead, it is to be a community divinely empowered to offer the world what it cannot provide for itself, the grace to overcome evil with patient, hopeful, nonviolent resistance.

Lovingkindness

Jesus' injunction to "turn the other cheek" could easily be misinterpreted and misused "vindictively," as Wink points out; "that is why it must not be separated from the command to love enemies."[31] In the previous chapter I set forth the essential features of love as a Christian virtue and need not reiterate them here. Rather, for the purpose of understanding the nature of covenantal peace, I will focus on Christian love *in extremis* represented by the precept "Love your enemies." The saying is familiar: "You have heard that it was said, 'You shall love your neighbor and hate your enemy.' But I say to you, Love your enemies and pray for those who persecute you" (Matthew 5:43–44).

"Love of enemy" is a kind of litmus test for the church. Whether its love is extraordinary, divinely inspired love or not is measured in terms of the church's faithfulness in loving its enemies. Hebrew Scriptures never tell us to hate our enemies; indeed, they frequently tell us that we are to love them (see Genesis 45: 1–ff, Exodus 23:4–, 1 Samuel 24:7, 2 Kings 6:22, Proverbs 25:21–). Likewise, in Christian Scriptures, love is no more glorified, insists Bonhoeffer, than when it persists in the midst of enemy hostility. So "the more bitter our enemy's hatred, the greater his need of love. Be his enmity political or religious, he has nothing to expect from a follower of Jesus but unqualified love."[32] Lovingkindness *in extremis*, in other words, requires that one's righteousness exceed even the considerable righteousness of scribes and Pharisees (Matthew 5:20), for whom righteousness, at least in Matthew's interpretation of things, requires only that one love friends. Lovingkindness chides those righteous who love only friends, for in doing so they are in common moral company with society's morally despised, tax collectors and Gentiles (Matthew 5:46–47). The distinguishing features of a heart disposed toward peace, in contrast, includes lovingkindness toward one's enemies. Faithfulness to God's love draws us outside ourselves and makes us disposable not only to our neighbor but to our enemy. Nygren puts it succinctly: "just as God's love is a love for sinners, so the Christian's love is a love for enemies. God's love for sinners and Christian love for enemies are correlative."[33] "When Christian love is directed toward enemies, it shows itself to be real love, spontaneous and creative. It creates fellowship even where fellowship seemed impossible."[34]

If this is so, is advocating and participating in war, even just war, compatible with loving an enemy? Advocating warfare against an enemy by its very nature, it seems to me, forfeits the possibility of loving that enemy in a way that the enemy would recognize it as love. Jesus links them directly together: "Love your enemies and pray for those who persecute you, so that you may be sons of your

Father who is in heaven; for he makes his sun rise on the evil and on the good, and sends rain on the just and on the unjust" (Matthew 5:44–45). The two activities are exclusive; it is impossible to demonstrate to an enemy God's mercy and lovingkindness and at the same time inflict intentional harm and destruction on an enemy's life and welfare. Indeed, not only does "neighborly love include love for one's enemies,"[35] as Nygren puts it, but it transforms the enemy into neighbor. We must hear Jesus say not only "I was a stranger and you welcomed me" but also "I was an enemy and you made peace with me" (Matthew 25:35). It is true, of course, that the enemy's response to my love may be less than hospitable; my enemy may take offense at my love, even to the extent of taking my life, as many Christians throughout history have discovered. But very often, as in the story of the Samaritan woman and the parable of the good Samaritan, covenantal love transforms those who formerly were enemies into neighbors. I elaborate the full extent and implication of lovingkindness as love of enemy more fully in the context of my discussion of generosity as an empathetic emotion elicited by Jesus' command to love one's enemy.

Christians in general and biblical scholars in particular have often been perplexed by these passages depicting the countercultural polis at the end of Matthew's fifth chapter. The seemingly radical impossibility of taking these sayings literally has led many to search for ways of bracketing or defusing the literal, explosive force of these passages. Hays summarizes and persuasively dispels, in my estimation, six such conventional attempts to make Matthew 5 more palatable to the Constantinian mentality that currently dominates Western Christianity,[36] whereby "salt" loses its savor and "light" dims its beam. I have tried to show that these three habits of heart, faithful loyalty, hopeful meekness, and lovingkindness constitute the obediential dispositions shaping Matthew's story of Jesus' life. The same dispositions ought to shape the story of covenantal communities that are called to sustain the countercultural community exemplified by Jesus' life and teaching. But my analysis of the heart of such a community is not yet complete; these three dispositions of heart elicit certain empathetic emotions that empower the covenantal community, enabling it to practice in its own life Christ's call to peacemaking.

PEACE AS EMPATHETIC EMOTIONS

A covenantal community is obligated not only to obey Christ's command to live peacefully but also is obligated to nurture and sustain certain empathetic emotions that make obedience a practical possibility. Empathetic feelings, feelings of compassion for enemy as well as neighbor, are essential to actually practicing that peace to which Christ calls his people. I examine two such emotions: mercy and generosity, which are elicited by and inseparable from the obediential dispositions (faithfulness, hopefulness, and lovingkindness) just examined.

Mercy

As with all moral emotions, mercy is constituted by judgment, project, and energy. My aim in this chapter is to discuss mercy as a feeling without which the practice of covenantal peace is quite impossible; my aim in the next chapter is to show how mercy functions as an experience underlying the covenantal notion of justice.

Mercy consists of a family of tender feelings that dispose a community to feel caringly toward a neighbor or enemy who have done wrong, with the ultimate aim of forgiving the wrongdoers and reconciling with them. Feelings of mercy presuppose not only that a rather complex judgment has been made—that a wrong has been done, and the persons guilty of the wrongdoing deserve to be fairly punished for their wrongdoing—but also that, because God in Christ has been merciful toward it, the covenantal community should likewise deal gently and graciously with the guilty. The judgment, prompted by the belief that God has acted mercifully toward it, requires a community to act not only compassionately toward the one victimized by wrong but mercifully toward the one who has done wrong. As the author of Hebrews suggests, the wrongdoer, although guilty, should not receive his just due but rather in his unrighteousness should be shown merciful forgiveness (8:12).

Feeling mercy toward a wrongdoer, of course, is emotionally more difficult and demanding than feeling compassion for one victimized. But it is an emotion that distinguishes Jesus' disciples from those Gentiles who merely show kindness toward their own friends (Matthew 5:43–48). There are several reasons why mercy should distinquish the Christian community from other communities. First, mercy is at the heart of the gospel. God's mercy, embodied in the life, death, and resurrection of Christ, God, redeems humanity from sin and reconciles it with God (Luke 1:78). Indeed, without God's merciful sacrifice there is no remission of sins (Hebrews 9:22). Second, mercy is commanded of the faithful community throughout Scriptures. The prophet Micah, for instance, says, "What does the Lord require of you, but to do justice, and love mercy, and walk humbly with your God?"(6:8) Through the prophet Hosea the Lord says, "For I desired mercy and not sacrifice" (6:6), a text that especially impressed Jesus, who is recorded to have recited it twice (Matthew 9:13, 12:7). And along with the other Beatitudes, Jesus' declaration "Blessed are the merciful, for they shall obtain mercy" (Matthew 5:7), plays a normative role in the Kingdom of Heaven. More than its imperative status, however, showing mercy seems, third, to be a *condition sine qua non* for being forgiven. Jesus concludes his most famous prayer: "For if you forgive men their trespasses, your heavenly Father will also forgive you; but if you do not forgive men their trespasses, neither will your Father forgive your trespasses" (Matthew 6:14,15). If mercy consists of those tender feelings that make genuine forgiveness possible, then mercy is not optional for the Christian community in private and public life. Jesus is insisting that a kind of reciprocity exists between giving and receiving merciful forgiveness; one receives God's merciful forgiveness but only if one is willing to show mercy toward others. God's mercy, no doubt, is freely given, but it must also be freely received, which is to say practiced. This surely is the thrust of Jesus' parable of the unforgiving servant (Matthew 18:23–35), as well as the Epistle of James, whose author declares, "Judgment is mercy to one who has shown no mercy; yet mercy triumphs over mercy" (2:13; see also Job 22:1–11). In short, only those who show mercy show they have been willing to accept God's mercy.

Being merciful involves not just empathetic feelings of forgiveness, however, but specific projects of healing, reconciliation, and peace with God, self, and others. By showing mercy to the woman caught in adultery and forgiving her, Jesus demonstrates in a concrete way the kind of merciful forgiveness he expects his community of followers to show toward all humans. One of the Apostle Paul's crowning theological achievements is showing how mercy and forgiveness are indispensable for bringing about reconciliation and peace. In his classic study *Forgiveness and Reconciliation*[37] Vincent Taylor indicates that there are two dimensions to Paul's doctrine of reconciliation: first, human reconciliation with God and second, reconciliation of humans with each other. These two dimensions of reconciliation constitute the peace that Jesus says he came to offer to humankind. Paul's logic is that peace presupposes reconciliation and reconciliation presupposes mercy and forgiveness. Peace prersupposes mercy; mercy establishes the possibility of peace. How so?

"All this is from God," says Paul, "who through Christ reconciled us to himself and gave us the ministry of reconciliation." Mercy requires "not counting . . . trespasses against [people]." As a moral project, mercy is delivered first through Christ and then through the covenantal community to whose members God has "entrusted . . . the message of reconciliation" (2 Corinthians 5:18–21). As Taylor argues, reconciling peace "is accomplished by [mercy and] forgiveness and the proclamation of the Apostolic message."[38] Sometimes Paul emphasizes that in Christ humans are reconciled to God. In Romans, for example, he says that "while we were enemies we were reconciled to God through the death of his Son . . . through whom we have now received our reconciliation" (5:10–11). At other times Paul emphasizes the social implication of human reconciliation to God, that in Christ humans are reconciled with each other. In Ephesians Paul says, for example, that it is the peace of Christ that "has broken down the dividing wall of hostility" between races (Jews and Gentiles). Accordingly, Christ's mercy empowers a community to bring unity and oneness out hostility, "so making peace . . . [and] thereby bringing the hostility to an end" (Ephesians 2:11–16). What is noteworthy for my purposes are two points: one, that, as Taylor notes, there is a "close association between reconciliation and peace in the mind of St. Paul";[39] second, that reconciliation and peace together are rendered possible because God is "rich in mercy" and love (2:4–5).

Underlying and linking mercy's judgment and project is an affectional energy loaded with the power of a tender and gentle heart that seeks not to condemn or punish but to redeem and reconcile (Joel 2:12–14). Feeling merciful is itself a peacemaking project; by being merciful a community forgives the wrong done toward it or others and works for the reconciliation of the wrongdoer with God, neighbor, and self. As is evident in Christ's own passion and death, mercy requires a character consisting of the obediential habits examined earlier, namely, steadfast faithfulness to God, hopeful meekness in the face of suffering, and a lovingkindness toward those who are enemies of God. Mercy, in other words, is painstaking work, of which Christians themselves are incapable but for the grace of God. "Relinquishing vengefulness," as Mary Durham puts it, "means forfeiting pride or malice." But merciful forgiveness is quite another thing; it "is not an act that takes place when anger or hurt or revenge are spent. Rather it involves the introduction of a leavening agent . . . resulting in something new: a solution."[40] Not surprisingly, then, mercy and forgiveness constitute an ongoing spiritual process "which takes time, often protracted time, and which requires immense effort on the part of the forgiving one."[41] Indeed, it requires of a covenantal community the same grace whereby God in Christ forgives common humanity.

Generosity

A second empathetic emotion invited by habits of faith, hope, and lovingkindness is generosity, a feeling intimately related to and interdependent with mercy. Generosity is a general class of feelings of which mercy is a species. By generosity I refer to a family of empathetic emotions—gentleness, compassion, kindness, graciousness—that not only create conditions for peace but by their very nature are peaceful. Paul calls generosity or kindness a fruit of the Spirit (Galatians 5:22). He then enjoins Christians: "Let all bitterness and wrath and anger and clamor and slander be put away from you, with all malice, and be kind to one another, tenderhearted, forgiving one another, as God in Christ forgave you" (Ephesians 4:31–32; also Colossians 3:12–13). For the Christian, generosity involves more than the ordinary kindness one finds among friends and neighbors; it entails extending to enemies the same undeserved, gracious generosity that is extended to me by God in Christ. Hence, although I may feel vengeful toward those who do evil, vengeance belongs to God and not me.[42] What is my prerogative, indeed what is required, is that I extend toward the wrongdoer the same tenderheartedness and generosity that transformed me from an enemy into a friend of God. Consider, then, generosity's judgment, project, and energy.

Richard Stith identifies two ways in which generosity is extraordinary: first, as an emotional judgment it involves a duty without a right; second, as an emotional project it involves benefiting wrongdoers. Stith insists that insofar as it is constituted by an emotional judgment, generosity entails "a duty without a right."[43] Feelings of generosity, for example, are initiated by the judgment that I have a duty to act kindly and mercifully toward a wrongdoer even though the wrongdoer is not entitled to any rights that correlate with that duty. Ordinarily we think of "duty" and "right" as correlative: "that for every right there exists a correlative duty," as Stith puts it, "and that for every duty there exists a correlative right." But there are some duties that one should undertake in full knowledge that no benefits will be forthcoming in return. Stith insists that there are moral occasions when " 'duties with rights' can and ought to be rejected in favor of . . . 'duties of generosity.' "[44] Generosity is a kind of project, he insists, in which one makes the judgment that one has "a duty to benefit precisely and only those who do wrong."[45] How so? Stith employs a trivial example taken from etiquette: "Everyone has a duty to leave the last cookie on the table for someone else, and not to object if someone else takes the cookie." This duty to leave the cookie "cannot without contradiction be straightforwardly transformed into a statement of individual rights-claim."[46] The duty I have of leaving the last cookie for another transforms itself into an act of undeserved generosity when I dutifully and graciously allow another to wrongfully take the last cookie, a cookie to which that person also has no right. This notion of generosity as a duty without a right can help illuminate, I think, the extraordinary character of a kind of generosity that distinguishes covenantal from other kinds of love. God's acts of love toward humans are acts of gracious generosity, of undeserved kindness to which no rights are correlated. God expects of covenantal communities the same extraordinary generosity.

Hear, then, Jesus' appeal to his disciples to practice extraordinary generosity: "If anyone would sue you and take your coat, let him have your cloak as well; and if any one forces you to go one mile, go with him two miles." Can this injunction be translated into a correlative rights-claim? Apparently not, for it seems to presuppose a judgment that certain covenantal duties ("Let him have your cloak as well" and "Go with him two miles") will not correlate with any rights to which the one who compels the cloak and second mile is entitled. Because they are not correlated with any rights, these duties will sound dissonant in relation to the moral tonalities on which our rights-based culture has nurtured us. Indeed, the rule "Everyone has a right to more than they are allowed to sue for" is self-contradictory, if by "suit" we mean that to which another has a moral and legal right. By law, as one commentator has put it, a person did not have "to give as collateral an outer garment—more than what the law could require, which was merely an inner garment."[47] If one has a right *only* to X, then we cannot say that one also has a right to Y, without speaking at odds with ourselves.

The one who has a right only to X cannot also claim a right to Y without violating the rights of another, namely, the other's right to Y. However, there is no contradiction or confusion in Jesus' injunction. He means that his disciples are to give not only what is due another but also what is not due. Even to those who treat them unjustly, their generosity is to be of this extraordinary sort. Jesus' presumption is that even if one had a right (which one does not) to X (the initial strike, the first mile, the other's coat), one does not have a right to Y (the second strike, the second mile, the other's cloak). The generosity of the second mile is a duty the Christian should deliver even though the neighbor has no right to it.

What kind of moral project, then, is required of covenantal generosity? An extraordinary and extraordinarily difficult one, to say the least; one in which the wrongdoer undeservedly benefits from the intentional kindness of another. Such generosity, embodied by Christ and commanded of his disciples, is extraordinary because, as Stith says, it benefits "precisely and only those who do wrong." The context of Jesus' remarks about one's cloak and second mile is "Do not resist one who is evil. But if any one strikes you on the right cheek, turn to him the other also." In other words, the one who demands your cloak and a second mile is in Jesus' view a wrongdoer to begin with; he is already "one who is evil," one who "strikes you on the right cheek." Thus, to "let him have your cloak as well" and to "go with him two miles" will always be to the benefit of one who is evil. Perhaps Craig L. Blomberg is right to conclude that "[e]ach of these commands requires Jesus' followers to act more generously than what the letter of the law demanded. . . . Not only must disciples reject all behavior motivated only by a desire for retaliation, but they must also positively work for the good of those with whom they would otherwise be at odds."[48] Paul indicates similarly that we should not act wrongly toward the enemies of God who treat us wrongly ("Do not be overcome by evil") but that we should act kindly toward them ("overcome evil with good") (Romans 12:20–21). Clearly, unmerited generosity of this sort presupposes that Jesus' disciples possess a character of faith, hope, and love that predisposes them to mercy and forgiveness and not to vengeance and retribution; a character whose habits invite emotions, like gentleness and compassion, that inspire acts of kindness for which the aggressor can claim no right.

What is extraordinary about Christian generosity, then, is that no rights correlate to its acts and when this is the case such acts may very well benefit a wrongdoer. The generosity Jesus showed toward the woman caught in adultery was extraordinary because the grace of merciful forgiveness was directed toward one who was clearly a wrongdoer and deserving of punishment. Generosity so conceived does not quite cohere, of course, with the law of talion that is the basis for Western conceptions of justice and just war theory. Retaliation in some form comparable to the wrong done is essential, it is thought, to any society wishing to be civilized. But apparently, in Jesus' view, the way a covenantal community is to be civilized differ from the ways those communities that embrace the law of talion are civilized. Just vengeance is the prerogative of God alone and not the prerogative of the church or state, just as just retribution in a family is a prerogative properly assumed by parents and not by children. Instead of retaliation *in kind* to a wrong done, as demanded by the law of talion, the Christian is to respond with unmerited *generosity*. The reason for doing so, that "you will heap burning coals upon his head" (Romans 12:19), is fundamental: the merciful generosity with which God has redeemed the faithful is the same generosity with which the faithful are to redeem the world. Clearly generosity of this sort requires an extraordinarily potent emotional energy, one so great as to embolden the covenantal community to make judgments and inspire projects of generosity that few civil societies have the moral resources to replicate. By undertaking projects of extraordinary kindness toward especially the undeserving, a covenantal community bears into the world the same extraordinary grace whereby God in Christ redeems and reconciles the world and establishes a kingdom of peace.

Mercy and generosity, as emotional preferences of covenantal life, constitute the empathetic dimension of Christian pacifism. Together with the obediential dispositions I have identified, peace as a Christian virtue is established as a practical possibility. By nurturing habits of faith, hope, and lovingkindness, empathetic emotions, like mercy and generosity, manifest themselves in the daily life of a community and empower it to undertake extraordinary projects of peace. But before showing how these dispositions and emotions together generate and justify the practice of Christian pacifism, I must first discuss an emotion that in the experience of most humans is morally compelling and directly relevant to matters of peace and war.

Just Vengeance

Merciful forgiveness and generosity do not exhaust, for the Christian community, the range of moral emotions appropriate to issues of war and peace. Vengeance, as a species of anger, is another moral feeling about which the Bible has a great deal to say. I explore here the nature of vengeance and the extent to which it is relevant to covenantal attitudes toward peace and war. In chapter 5 I examine a gentler form of righteous anger and its relevance to covenantal justice.

Western conceptions of justice, as Solomon points out, are fundamentally derived from the ancient Hebrew tradition, a tradition in which justice is nurtured by a family of emotions that we ordinarily refer to when we speak of vengeance and revenge. The Bible assumes that feelings of vengeance are the fundamental source from which a sense of justice arises. Often in Hebrew Scriptures, as in Homer, notes Solomon, the term "justice" "refers to revenge" and related feelings of retribution and vengeance that are assumed to be appropriate. Indeed, the desire for " 'Getting even' " that constitutes feelings of vengeance "is just as much a part of the emotional basis for our current sense of justice as benign compassion."[49] The emotional landscape in which *lex talionis* thrives, in other words, presupposes a feeling of "just vengeance"; and certain kinds of wars, ones that arise from a godly sense of anger, are depicted in the Bible as morally appropriate, even holy. The Hebrew tradition, of course, does not sanction indiscriminate vengeance; restrictions are placed on it, such as "eye for eye, tooth for tooth" (see Exodus 21:24–25). In the context of such restrictions, the feeling of vengeance gives rise to a sense of justice, of just vengeance. Jesus' teaching regarding the law of retaliation and vengeance requires of a covenantal community even greater restraint: "Turn the other cheek," "Go the second mile," and so on. But Jesus and the early church never simply discard the ancient Hebrew notion of justice nor the feelings of vengeance and retribution that belong to it.

The several emotions belonging to vengeance properly arise when we make a judgment that the world as it should rightly be is not the world as it unjustly is. Indeed, vengeance is the emotional link between a sense of justice and injustice. "Vengeance means . . . putting the world back in balance. . . . Philosophers have been much too quick to attribute this sense of balance or retribution to reason, but . . . it is rather a function of emotion," argues Solomon. "Vengeance just is that sense of measure or balance that Kant (and so many other philosophers) attribute to reason alone."[50] Similarly, ethicists tend to attribute to reason alone the sense of justice presupposed, for example, in just war theory. But underwriting the criteria for making rational judgments about the justice of war are those emotions belonging to vengeance. This is as it should be; our feeling that something is amiss, that the world as it is is somehow unjust and should be otherwise, arises from a desire for just vengeance, a desire for social and moral balance, for rectification of a grievous wrong. Of course, compassion for those suffering injustice may very well inspire communities to undertake projects of justice; but such projects are also inspired by a desire to regain an equilibrium by avenging a wrong done, by punishing the wrongdoer. So Christians who appeal to the criteria of just war theory are at the same time quite rightly appealing to a biblical sense of vengeance as an emotional source of those criteria.[51]

One might fairly object that the biblical tradition is advocating two contradictory things—a dilemma on whose horns the Church, throughout its history, has managed to frequently impale itself. Indeed, the biblical writers are well aware of it. In response to injustice, act according to both just vengeance and merciful generosity. How can this be? First of all, it is clear that the biblical writers are not prepared to sacrifice the emotional, moral force of one horn of this dilemma (vengeance) for the sake of the other (mercy), and vice versa. What is clear is their unflappable affirmation of both just vengeance and merciful generosity. The biblical consensus is both that God is merciful and expects the church to show the same mercy toward others as God shows toward wrongdoers (Matthew 6:14–15, 18:23–35) and that God also renders just vengeance but with this qualification:

as an appropriate response to wrongdoing, the biblical consensus is that just vengeance is God's prerogative alone and not the church's or the state's on behalf of the church.

What moral project, then, is implied by a judgment for just vengeance? For the covenantal community, the answer to this question is not as simple and straightforward as one might want or think. For although feelings of vengeance are appropriately moral, the biblical tradition is quite consistent in calling the covenantal community to defer or transfer to God projects of vengeance, especially when it comes to war. In Hebrew Scriptures just anger as vengeance is sometimes forbidden: "You shall not take vengeance or bear any grudge against the sons of your own people, but you shall love your neighbor as yourself: I am the Lord" (Leviticus 19:18). At other times the Hebrew writers recognize the legitimacy of vengeance in interpersonal affairs, as suggested by the ordinances governing the domestic affairs of ancient Israel (Exodus 21; Leviticus 24). But when it comes to national and international conflict, Hebrew Scriptures recognize just vengeance as a legitimate, moral response, albeit one whose power and prerogative belong exclusively to God and not to humans. "The Lord is the one who takes vengeance" (Nahum 1:2). 'Vengeance is mine,' says the Lord, 'and recompense for the time when their foot shall slip" (Deuteronomy 32:35). The Psalmist instructs us not to take vengeance into our own hands but to wait on the Lord, for "He will bring back on them their iniquity and wipe them out for their wickedness" (Psalms 94:23). Christian Scriptures preserve this Hebrew teaching. The Apostle Paul and the writer of Hebrews reaffirm their Jewish heritage regarding vengeance; both retrieve the phrase " 'vengeance is mine, I will repay,' says the Lord" (Romans 12:19 and Hebrews 10:30) and extend it to covenantal life. Implicit in Jesus' "Turn the other cheek" and "Love your enemies" is the belief that just vengeance is not the prerogative of those who claim to be his disciples.

What of the many Hebrew wars of retribution that are recognized as "holy" and justifiable? There are those Christian thinkers who would answer this question by, as Yoder puts it, writing "off the holy wars of the Old Testament as due to the primitive culture of the time and therefore not relevant today."[52] Whether this view harbors Marcion sentiments in its dismissal I cannot say, but many Christians, as well as Jews, cannot so easily dismiss or "forget Joshua and David and Josiah."[53] For if Hebrew Scriptures are taken as seriously as Christian Scriptures, then another more serious and challenging tack must be attempted. A way of doing so is to suggest that those wars of the Hebrews that are recognized as "holy" and justifiable by the biblical writers are restricted to wars that are "covenantal."[54] By "covenantal" I mean wars that are justifiable on the basis of meeting two criteria: first, they are divinely ordained; second, they are eschatological. Reuven Firestone gathers together a great deal of scholarly research that shows how a biblical consensus forms to support these two criteria. First, as Firestone suggests, "[a]ccording to the broad outline of this [biblical] consensus, Israel's God, like the deities of other peoples in the ancient Near East, was seen as fighting on behalf of God's people."[55] This is to say that the Hebrew writers, in interpreting the history of Israel, understood that all wars profoundly affecting that history were "ordained or determined by God. This included wars destructive to Israel, such as the catastrophic destruction of the kingdom of Judah by the Babylonians. . . . Even such defeat [by a foreign power] was considered a divinely authorized event because God was understood as having ordained the outcome."[56] This is not to say that the Babylonians were conscious of playing a role in which they fulfilled some divine plan for Israel; only that the interpreters of Israel's history understood its God to ordain the outcome, in this case defeat, at the hands of the Babylonian military. "The Babylonian debacle was seen as an act of divine punishment realized through war, although punishment could also be administered through plague, drought, lack of fertility, or other 'acts of God.' "[57] The consensus of Hebrew Scriptures seems to be that any war that is justifiable is one that is ordained by God.

Second, a biblical consensus, according to Firestone, also revolves around the view that divinely sanctioned wars are eschatological wars, that is, wars "associated in the Bible with protection of the national unit or the acquisition and sanctification of its divinely ordained territorial inheritance."[58] God's faithfulness was and is to the covenant that Abraham would be the father of a great people in a specific geographical location. The texts of Deuteronomy establish "possession of the land of promise by God to Israel" as a justification "for divinely sanctified wars of Israel (1:6–8, 2:25–37, 3:1–22, 6:10–12, 7:1, 9:1–3, 11:23–25, 20:1–18; 29:6–8, 31:3–6)."[59] The first of these eschatological wars, whereby God reestablishes his territorial covenant with Israel, is the exodus, a war in which God delivers just vengeance to Israel's oppressors, in this instance without the use of military weapons. Records of other wars to establish and sustain covenantal integrity are found in the Pentateuch, in Joshua and Judges, and in the books of Samuel. Related to this eschatological criteria, according to Deuteronomy, are justified, divinely sanctioned conflicts whose aim is to ensure "that the national holding would remain free of idolatry, including those people practicing idolatry (7:1–5, 7:16–26, 12:1–3, 12:29–13:1, 13:2–19, 16:21–22, 17:2–7, 18:9–14)." Deuteronomy and the prophets call for just vengeance to be delivered by destroying both the idols and idolatrous people who live within the covenantal lands, even if the idolatrous people happen to be God's chosen people (7:1–4, 7:9–11, 8:19–20, 11:16–17, 11:26–28, 28:1–68, 29:15–27, 30:17–18).[60] Jesus' cleansing of the Temple might be interpreted as this sort of conflict, purging the Temple of the idolatry of greed and wealth.

For the people of God to justifiably engage in wars, the biblical consensus seems to be that those wars must be covenantal; they must be divinely ordained and eschatological, aimed at sustaining the territorial integrity of God's covenant with Israel. Wars not meeting these two criteria, at least in the biblical tradition of holy war, do not seem to qualify as justifiable. The wars, for example, of Saul and Absalom against David do not meet these eschatological criteria and are thereby illegitimate and unjustifiable. The Bible seems to restrict Israel, and other nations, to covenantal warfare: warfare ordained by God for the sake of Israel's territorial integrity. These covenantal criteria for justifiable war are drawn entirely from the biblical tradition and are properly seen as distinct and different from the criteria for justifiable war that constitute the just war tradition in Christianity. The criteria for the later tradition, as is well known, are derived originally from ancient Roman and Stoic traditions. In Constantinian Christianity the just war tradition is preserved and further developed by Christian thinkers such as Ambrose and Augustine. The conclusion to which my inquiry here leads is that the covenantal war tradition is biblically, theologically, and morally more compelling than the just war tradition. It acknowledges the powerful feelings underlying the desire for vengeance but acknowledges also, as I will show, that moral projects based on those feelings (i.e., warfare, violence) are entrusted to God and not his children, just as parents reserve for themselves and do not delegate to their children the duty and prerogative of punishment. The covenantal tradition develops criteria by which wars according to the biblical record are deemed justifiable, and these criteria are quite different, local, and particular compared to those of the just war tradition. I will show that these criteria are consistent with the life and teachings of Jesus and the apostles; they uniformly enjoin the Christian community to live peaceful lives, resisting evil and violence nonviolently while leaving the anger of just vengeance to the Lord.

Before sketching the profile of a community that actually practices covenantal peace, it might be well to place this discussion in the context of the classic 1932 exchange regarding peace and war between the brothers Niebuhr.[61] Much is remarkable about this exchange, both in regard to what is said and what is left unsaid. The church, for example, is a vital community in H. Richard's proposal, with an identity and loyalty quite apart from America and American interests. "Cells" of Christians, he says, "divorcing themselves from the program of nationalism and of capitalism, unite in a higher loyalty which transcends national and class lines of division and prepare for the future."[62] Accordingly, as H. Richard's essay's title "The Grace to Do Nothing" suggests, grace is central, since grace endows the church with the power to be different, to sustain loyalty to God's peaceable kingdom, and not simply succumb to the interests of the state. This view is certainly in keeping with the covenantal approach I develop here. In contrast, the church as a community with an identity and loyalties independent of American and American interests is noticeably absent from Reinhold's discussion. He apparently assumes that the American church's interests and loyalties are subsumed under the interests and policies of the state, at least when it comes to issues of peace and war. Reinhold neither mentions nor hints at the need for grace, and why should he? since he apparently assumes that the church's role is largely absorbed into the policies of states whose actions are entirely possible independent of God's grace.

Second, H. Richard proposes that the pacifist church in the midst of war must settle for the grace of inactivity. The church must do nothing; it must not take national sides in the conflict and must not try to find ways to justify the conflict. Of course, H. Richard does not mean Christians should literally do nothing; he does mean that since nothing "constructive" can be done immediately and directly about the certain conflicts, Christian activity must be mediate and indirect. He mentions two indirect activities, hope and repentance. In hope, although it can do nothing, Christianity lives eschatologically: it knows that God will do something, will eventually serve just vengeance—"it knows something is being done, something which is divine both in its threat and its promise."[63] In repentance, Christianity calls America to undertake a project of "self-analysis" through which it will come to understand its own self-interested motives in war and its own need of repentance. The covenantal view I set forth here both affirms and denies H. Richard's claims. It affirms, as I have just shown, that just vengeance is the Lord's and that the church, as God's children, should not assume that role for itself. But covenantal peace does not and should not, as I will show, resign itself, as H. Richard does, to an inactivity in which the church in the midst of war can do nothing directly, immediately, and constructively. Reinhold, in contrast, argues that realistically Christians are morally obligated in the midst of war to take direct and immediate and constructive action. With this I agree. But the action he insists Christians must take is in concert with nation-states who resort to coercion and violence in protecting, preserving, and promoting their moral, economic, and political interests in world affairs. With this I disagree. The activities and projects in which the church engages, as I show in the next section, must involve single-minded loyalty to God's Kingdom and must always involve acts of nonviolent peacemaking. How this is possible is a matter to which I now turn.

PRACTICING COVENANTAL PEACE

I may now combine the various dimensions of covenantal peace that thus far I have treated separately. Suppose a community's character is shaped by habits of faithfulness, hopefulness, and loveingkindness, and suppose these obediential habits inspire in it empathetic feelings of merciful generosity. What kind of peace and peacemaking is implied? Recall from chapter 2 the two ways these dimensions of virtue are interrelated. First, universals are accessible through particularity: universal judgments/projects of feeling merciful generosity are a function of specific obediential habits, in this case, faithfulness, hopeful meekness, and lovingkindness. Second, universals are justified in terms of the particular: practicing the empathetic emotions constituting peace is justified by the local particularity of the gospel story and the obediential habits shaping that story. I begin by examining the practice of peace and peacemaking implied by empathetic feelings of merciful generosity. I continue by examining how these peacemaking feelings are justified by those obediential-dispositions of heart (faithfulness, hopefulness, and lovingkindness) that shape the kind of peacemaking embodied and proclaimed by Christ.

For the Christian community, the practical consequence of feeling merciful generosity is pacifism. Always showing mercy and extraordinary kindness toward neighbor or enemy implies that a covenantal community should not act otherwise than in a peaceful, nonviolent way. Conversely, that community forfeits its identity as covenantal, as Christian, if in the midst of fear and violence it fails to practice the merciful generosity on which basis alone its identity as covenantal and Christian is justified. In devoting itself to mercy and generosity, then, a covenantal community must in times of conflict devote itself to what Ulrich Mauser refers to as the Red Cross model of peacemaking. This model envisions the church as a kind of spiritual version of the Red Cross. Mauser says, "As the Interantional Red Cross does not arm its members but participates in war only as a force upholding the power and hope of rescuing, healing, and reconciliation, so the Christian community should seek global recognition . . . as an organization dedicated to peace beyond national rivalries."[64] Or, as Clara Barton says, the mission of the Red Cross is to further the "progress of mercy" and provide "relief" in the midst of war.[65] H. R. Niebuhr tends toward this view when, in a lecture to the Berkeley Divinity School, he argues that insofar as the church genuinely manifests faith in Jesus Christ who reveals divine will, it transcends all forms of government. The church's loyalty and obligation is not to any particular government or form of government, whether monarchy or oligarchy or democracy, and not to the preservation of any particular government, but to the welfare of humans, regardless of what nation-state they happen to find themselves subject to[66] and regardless of what side of a war they may find themselves on in their suffering. In short, the mission of the Christian community in the midst of war is not to attempt to justify or not justify a particular war, nor is it to take national sides. Instead the mission of the church, modeled on that of the Red Cross, is to deliver to all those on all sides suffering the violence of war, both combatants and non-combatants alike, the healing grace of Christ's merciful generosity, which establishes conditions for and of peace.

We find recorded in Matthew's version of the Sermon on the Mount Jesus asking, "Or what man of you, if his son asks him for bread, will give him a stone? Or if he asks for a fish, will give him a serpent?" (7:9–10) Or what community, if nations desire peace, will offer them just war and violence? Or desiring mercy and reconciliation will give them retribution? Nations of the world, with few exceptions, desire peace but do not know how to give or get it. Is it not curious that the very community that has been inspired by God to bear into the world the healing grace and power of Christ's peace very often squanders, like the prodigal son, that inheritance by collaborating in the warfare of nation-states? Is it not tragic that the very community that God has empowered to deliver mercy and unmerited generosity in the world instead delivers to the world's nations little more that what nations without the aid of churches can very well deliver for themselves: retaliation, violence and war? Indeed, when a faith community feels compelled to decide whether or not to justify the wars of nations, it automatically forfeits and forsakes the very ministry of peace to which it has been called and for which it has been empowered. In so doing, it delivers to nations a stone instead of bread. In contrast, covenantal communities are called, like the Red Cross, to deliver to peoples on all sides of the conflict, aggressor and victim alike, the very mercy and generosity with which God in Christ redeemed and empowered those communities. Consequently, they need not scramble, as typically they do, to decide whether a particular war transgresses just war criteria or not. Their call, mission, and agenda is settled and clear a priori; they are to constantly and continually practice the peace of Christ, bearing into the midst of war the same merciful forgiveness and unmerited generosity whereby God in Christ redeems humanity. By deciding to favor national sides, covenantal communities betray the redeemer they are pretending to follow once more to the arrogance, violence, and insecurities of civil authorities. Indeed, preferring to take national sides in war to delivering mercy and generosity marks the difference between admiring Jesus and following. Appeals to just war criteria, accordingly, represent that Constantinian deception whereby admirers, at least on this particular moral issue, deceive themselves, believing that in so doing they are followers of Christ.

Take the Gulf War of 1991 as an example. Many individual Christians and most Christian communities felt compelled to decide whether the United States and its allies would be justified in going to war against Iraq. Applying the principles of just war theory, some Christian communities determined that such an engagement would be justified and made official statements to that effect, thereby sanctioning, according to just war principles, the warfare of nation-states against each other. In doing so, by taking national sides in this conflict, these communities undermined their own identity as covenantal and Christian. They instantaneously forfeited the possibility of fulfilling their own divine calling and mission, especially their mission to the enemies of the nations whose cause they sanction. For it is impossible for me to administer mercy and extraordinary generosity to those whom I myself have declared I am against and of whom I have made myself an enemy. Those Christian communities that, in the Gulf War, so declared and justified their allegiance to the allied cause at the same time forfeited their covenantal mission to deliver to aggressors and victims alike the healing that comes through God's merciful generosity. By taking national sides in wars of state, they abandoned their mission of merciful generosity. By sanctioning a nation's war, Christians cast the peoples of other nations in the role of enemy as well. In so doing, they invert Christ's project of turning enemies into neighbors to a project of turning neighbors into enemies. Yet no other community is so endowed with power to deliver God's healing grace of peace to the world. Jesus demonstrates the power of that grace when to the woman caught in adultery he delivers not law, judgment, condemnation, and retribution but the healing power only merciful forgiveness and extraordinary generosity can deliver. There is no doubt about Jesus' own judgments regarding the moral quality of the woman's adultery, but he understood his mission single-mindedly, as a mission of merciful generosity.[67]

Presupposing covenantal pacifism, how then can the covenantal community account for and assimilate just vengeance that, in the biblical tradition, is a legitimate moral feeling? First, we must remember that the wars of the Lord, as already shown, are not analogous to the just wars of church and state. The two criteria distinguishing covenantal wars (divinely ordained and eschatological) are nowhere included in the just war criteria. Any justifiable, covenantal war, accordingly, will involve in some significant way God's chosen people Israel and the integrity of the covenantal territory promised by God to ancient Israel. Mary Elsbernd makes this point. The wars of ancient Israel as "wars of conquest were understood as an expression of Yahweh's gracious intervention on behalf of the chosen people in times of national crisis."[68] The Christian community, of course, perceives itself as umbilically linked to God's chosen people Israel but perceives itself wrongly when it views itself, as sometimes it has, as a national, political entity. The church has no national, covenantal territory comparable to Israel that must be defended. Consequently, no national or territorial wars by the church, or by the state with the church's blessing, qualify as covenantal. Most, if not all, of the many "religious" wars littering the history of Western civilization, accordingly, are unjustifiable.

Are the criteria justifying covenantal wars relevant and operative for covenantal communities today? Is it possible to justify on covenantal grounds warfare on behalf of the current state of Israel? There are at least two ways of trying to answer these questions. First, the Christian community might make the assumption that the current state of Israel, with its national and territorial boundaries, is continuous in some general sense with ancient, covenantal Israel. Assuming this, it would follow that the criteria for justifying and engaging in covenantal warfare remain relevant throughout history. Since the Crusades certainly do not satisfy both covenantal criteria, they could not be justified as legitimate warfare. They do not appear to have been divinely ordered, and their manifest aim seems to have been Christian hegemony in the Holy Land, not the territorial integrity of the nation of Israel. Several wars during the Christian era in the West might appear to qualify as covenantal: the Second World War, for example, and the ensuing conflicts to reestablish Israel in its homeland. Insofar as the Jewish people interpret the Allied campaign against Hitler as a national crisis, insofar as it is perceived as divinely ordained, as a war in which God employs Gentile nations to deliver his people and reestablish the territorial integrity of Israel, then that war can perhaps properly be viewed as meeting the covenantal criteria and thereby, according to the biblical tradition, justifiable. Similarly, ongoing conflicts dedicated to preserving Israel's territorial integrity would on this basis appear to be justifiable, without thereby justifying military imperialism or terrorism by any nation involved in the conflict.

A second way of answering these questions would insist that such an assumption—that the current state of Israel is continuous with ancient Israel and its covenantal obligations—entails a leap far too great to reasonably take. On this view, the current state of Israel is discontinuous in significant ways with ancient, covenantal Israel and would not warrant a privileged status. Although the morally legitimate notion of just vengeance, retribution, and covenantal warfare is not to be abandoned, the covenantal community's mission of peacemaking in a violent and contentious world remains unchanged.

In either case (my preference tends toward the second) the faithful, covenantal community's aim must be prophetic, delivering to the world the same peace that God in Christ delivered to it, rejecting all wars, including those that meet the criteria established by the just war tradition. Assuming pacifism, the covenantal community would stand in constant tension with nation-states in a way reminiscent perhaps of the early Christian community's tension with the Roman Empire. Christians participating in the military conflicts of nation-states would be reckoned, as in the early church, traitors of the faith. If they refused to serve they would be reckoned, as in the early church, traitors of the state and suffer persecution. In a predominantly Christian nation, the impact of a covenantal community that remains faithful to pacifism could be rather significant and severe. Consider the prospects of a large peacemaking community that refuses to serve the military interests of the United States—refuses to take national sides in international conflicts. Not only might such a community's pacifism influence a state's decision to engage in a conflict in the first place, it might very well influence the outcome of international conflicts. It might very well earn a reputation and role as a peacemaking community on whom nation-states can depend for resolving and mediating international conflicts, such as those occurring in the former Yugoslavia.

So, in contrast to H. Richard Niebuhr's call to the grace of "inactivity" described earlier, there is a great deal a covenantal community can directly, immediately, and constructively do in the midst of local violence or global war. I mention here five kinds of activities or projects covenantal communities can undertake on a local, national, or international scale. All of them presuppose that the Christian's aim is to bring to war the healing grace of God's peace—a healing that is unavailable independent of that grace and a healing that nations cannot deliver for themselves. First, covenantal communities must cultivate within and without the context of war a reputation as peacemakers: as healers and not warmongers. This is a long-term process and activity that they must undertake if they are to practice Jesus' call to be peacemakers. Second, in the midst of local violence or global war, covenantal communities must minister to those on all sides who suffer the tragedies and devastations of war. At the end of his *Christian Century* article, H. Richard Niebuhr mentions that the inactivity he proposes "is not the inactivity of the merciless, for works of mercy must be performed though they are only palliatives to ease present pain while the process of healing depends on deeper, more actual and urgent forces."[69] Such acts of mercy toward those who suffer are immediate, direct, and constructive ways by which covenantal communities can make peace in the midst of local violence or global war. Third, covenantal communities, locally and globally, should appropriate the grace of speaking prophetically in the midst of a violent and warmongering world. Calling for peace and mercy is a voice with which God has gifted these communities. It is a voice that needs to be heard daily in sanctuaries, in media, and in homes. Fourth, covenantal communities should encourage and support all efforts and agencies seeking to secure a negotiated, mediated, and lasting peace. Ideally, local and global Christian communities should equip themselves with the necessary tools, skills, and reputation to be trustworthy peacemakers to which nations and factions can appeal. I need not belabor how vast is the distance Christianity must travel and how massive the renovations it must undertake to secure such a reputation and status. Fifth, covenantal communities must actively engage in "self-analysis" and repentance, as H. Richard Niebuhr refers to it, or what Martin Luther King, Jr., calls, in his "Letter from a Birmingham Jail," a process of self-purgation. Church institutions have their own economic and political and moral agendas, which very often so thoroughly corrupt covenantal communities that Christ's call to peacemaking is ignored, invalidated, or even entirely disowned. Covenantal communities should earnestly and repeatedly repent and purge themselves of such tendencies so that the healing grace of God's peace is available not only to them but through them to the world.

My assumption, defended in chapter 2, is that these feelings of merciful generosity that inspire the practice of covenantal peace are feelings that are universally accessible and justifiable through the narrative particularity of obediential dispositions like faithfulness, hopeful meekness, and lovingkindness. Implicit in this assumption is the related premise that the bases on which feelings of merciful generosity are justifiable and practicably possible are as diverse, particular, and local as the communities who value and experience them. The reasons and incentives why communities practice pacifism, in other words, are not lodged in some metaphysical heaven of universal, rational laws but in the local, tribal particularity of a community's narrative tradition—for the Christian, in the character, life, and teachings of Jesus. My task now is to show how the dispositions of character just set forth (faithfulness, hopefulness, and lovingkindness) give shape to Jesus' life and character, inspire empathetic emotions of merciful generosity, and shape the gospel story and the pacifism implied by it. These dispositions shape a community's character in such a way that pacifism is the logical and moral implication and application. A community need only appeal to the gospel story and those disposition of character that shape it in order to justify pacifism and inspire itself so to live. Indeed, that a community whose character is shaped by faithfulness, hopeful meekness, and lovingkindness can do nothing other than live pacifistically is a conviction advocated by the National Conference of Catholic Bishops, even though this conviction is ultimately abandoned for the sake of just war commitments. "Peacemaking is not an optional commitment," the bishops insist. "We are called to be peacemakers, not by some movement of the moment, but by our Lord Jesus. The content and context of our peacemaking is set not by some political agenda or ideological program, but by the teaching of his Church."[70] To the extent that the church does not honor that promise and commitment, to that extent it forsakes its role as a covenantal community embodying a gospel whose news is both unique and good.

Assuming that covenantal peace is a function of covenantal love, we might rephrase Jesus' saying as follows: "All humans will know that you are my disciples if you make peace with one another." This can not mean simply peace among those whom we count as neighbors, for even the most violent and oppressive live at peace with those whom they count as neighbors. One litmus test whereby a community demonstrates whether it is reliably Christian or not is in terms of its single-minded faithfulness to Christ, its hopeful steadfastness in the face of insult and violence, and its lovingkindness especially toward those whom it counts as its enemies or enemies of God, especially in times of war. Jesus himself teaches and demonstrates that the presence of these dispositions will inspire the kind of merciful generosity by which a community is enabled to devote itself to the practice of peace and peacemaking. A covenantal community will respond to evil and enemies not with the coercive power of vengeance, which is the Lord's prerogative, but with persuasive power of love; not with retaliatory violence but with proactive meekness. Indeed, a faithful Christian community distinguishes itself from other communities by showing unmerited generosity not just toward a neighbor, which is usually easy enough, but toward an enemy. Whether the enemy in question is a person, a people, or a nation, the litmus test of Christian morality is that extraordinary love be extended to it. Jesus identifies for us the radical lengths to which his followers are to go in loving enemies when he commands that the faithful community, although it is to resist evil, is to do so not violently but with steadfast meekness and lovingkindness. It is the particularity of these commands and the covenantal story in which they arise that supplies a covenantal community with the necessary and sufficient reason to live pacifistically. The traditional reasons for forsaking these commands and commitments, such as just war criteria, are simply irrelevant to the Red Cross model advocated here, although they may be relevant to nation-states interested in assuaging their consciences by waging wars. Attempts to defend the church's moral obligation to justify certain kinds of warmaking, such as those of Reinhold Niebuhr, Paul Ramsey, and the National Conference of Bishops, are impressive and compelling. But for communities who are passionately devoted to peacemaking, who have cultivated and internalized dispositions of peacemaking (faithfulness, hopefulness, and lovingkindness) as habits of covenantal life, the question of just warmaking simply does not arise. These communities, viewing themselves as continuous with the Bible's unique story of good news, feel no compulsion to swear allegiance to nation-states and their wars, feel no need to deliver to nation-states what they can very well deliver to the world themselves, feelings of just vengeance and the criteria for justifying wars that emerge from those feelings. No community of grace, no commitment to gospel, no faithful meekness, no habit of lovingkindness from which spring feelings of merciful generosity is required of those committed to preserving nation-states and sanctioning just wars. But to deliver healing, to act meekly and mercifully in the midst of war, to treat all people, perpetrator and victim, as creatures loved dearly by God and his people requires extraordinarily gracious dispositions of heart. Receiving these dispositions as a measure of God's redeeming grace is what justifies and inspires the empathetic feelings of merciful generosity that make possible the practice of covenantal peace in the midst of war.

That Jesus requires single-minded faithfulness, that he commands hopeful meekness and lovingkindness, that he requires followers who swear no oaths to auxiliary authorities and who turn the other cheek and love enemies means that Jesus requires followers who are are peacemakers, who practice the same merciful generosity toward others that God in Christ demonstrates toward humanity. That Jesus forbids covenantal communities the satisfaction of just vengeance in face of war is analogous, in the human family, to the conventional wisdom that just punishment is properly the prerogative of parents and not children. Caring parents generally do not allow children to assume the prerogative and power to punish each other, even for just cause. To do so would be irresponsible, dispatching moral power to those unqualified to wield it. Properly this power belongs to parents and analogously to God. Contemporary wars (even so-called just wars), accordingly, are analogous to children usurping their parents' (God's) authority, an authority with which they cannot be trusted. Any parent knows that children cannot be trusted to deliver retribution to their siblings fairly. Albanian refugees returning to their ravaged homes and lives in Kosovo demonstrate tragically what feelings of just vengeance and retaliation can mean. This is perhaps cynically to be expected of nation-states who opted to resolve the conflict in terms of violence in the first place. Hence it is urgent that the church leave matters of retaliation and retribution, including just wars, to the Lord. Commenting on Matthew's parable of the Last Judgment (Matthew 25:31–46), Eileen Egan says that "[i]n war, every work of mercy is reversed. Christ in the person of the enemy is blockaded and starved, is made to thirst for clean water, is made shelterless by bombing and uprooting, and is wounded and maimed."[71] The church must develop in itself the habits of faithful, hopeful, lovingkindness that prepare it to look into the eyes of the enemy and see the least of those with whom Jesus identifies and for whom he calls his followers to care. This does not mean that the righteous should not call upon the Lord to distribute justice and judgment into the world. As the Psalmist prays, "O Lord, thou God of vengeance, shine forth! Rise up, O judge of the earth; render to the proud their deserts!" (Psalm 94:1–2) Jeremiah prays for the Lord to "remember me and visit me, and take vengeance for me on my persecutors" (15:15) and to "take vengeance on her [Babylon], do to her as she has done" (50:15). Holy anger and just retribution are legitimate moral responses to injustice and injury, but just as just retribution in a household belongs to the parents and not to the children, so just vengeance among the nations is a response that belongs to God and not God's children.

Wink provides an example of how one covenantal disposition of heart, in this case, hopeful meekness, effectively and persuasively invites feelings of merciful generosity powerful enough to put into practice active, nonviolent resistance to violence. This example is based on his analysis of what he calls "the [three] examples of unarmed direct action" in Matthew 5:39–41.[72] Take the third example. Roman soldiers could impress labor on subject peoples by forcing them to function as beasts of burden for one mile but no more. "Such forced service was a constant feature of Palestine from Persian to late Roman times, and whoever was found on the street could be compelled into service." As we might imagine, this sort of forced labor was "a source of bitter resentment" toward Rome, as Wink notes, because, as some early sources indicate, soldiers would sometimes show " 'abuse and threats to private citizens,' " with the result that " 'the military [was] associated with arrogance and injustice.' "[73] In response to the humiliation, injury, and injustice of such coercion Jesus commands his disciples to "go the second mile" carrying the soldier's pack. Why so? Is not this aiding the enemy? One way of answering this question is, with Wink, to acknowledge that going the second mile "is how the oppressed can recover the initiative, how they can assert their human dignity in a situation that cannot for the time being be changed. The rules are Ceasar's, but how one responds to the rules is God's, and Ceasar has no power over that."[74] Another answer is that Jesus' own life and teaching demonstrate that love's persuasive power ultimately is more forceful than the coercive power of violence—that whereas coercive power destroys and subdues, love's persuasive power reconciles and renews. Although Jesus does not propose armed, coercive revolution against the oppressor, says Wink, "he does lay the foundation for a social revolution" based on love's nonviolent, persuasive power. Indeed, such a revolution "in fact did happen to the Roman Empire as the Christian church overcame it from below."[75]

In our own day the practice of merciful generosity and the force of nonviolent activism has proven itself more redemptive and reconciling than the coercive force of counterviolence. Based on his tradition of African-American Christianity, Martin Luther King, Jr.'s nonviolent movement proved itself more powerful than the forces of intimidation and violence (imprisonment, firehoses, attack dogs, lynchings, and bigotry) and generated a momentum toward justice that continues today. On the basis of the commitments of the tradition of his Hindu community, Mohandas Gandhi likewise harnessed the power of nonviolence and successfully forced one of the world's preeminent military powers to adhere to the basic tenets of justice. As Wink concludes, "[t]hose who have lived by Jesus' word—Leo Tolstoy, Mohandas K. Gandhi, Martin Luther King, Jr., Dorothy Day, Caesar Chavez, Adolpho Perez Esquivel—point us to a new way of confronting evil whose potential for personal and social transformation we are only beginning to grasp today."[76]

Why is it that most of the Christian and non-Christian world finds the biblical message of the redemptive power of peacemaking and loving one's enemies so hard to credit? Hays's answer is damning: because "the church is so massively faithless. On the question of violence, the church is deeply compromised and committed to nationalism, violence, and idolatry. (By comparison, our problems with sexual sin are tivial)."[77] If the Christian community is to be faithful, if an enduring and uninterrupted commitment to pacifism is to be possible and practical, the church must cultivate obediential habits of heart that invite the empathetic emotions of merciful generosity that make it possible to keep Jesus' command to be peacemakers. A heart of faithfulness to God's kingdom makes it possible for a community to obey the command to swear no oaths of allegiance to competing kingdoms; a heart of hopeful meekness makes it possible in the face of evil to turn the other cheek and go the second mile; and a heart of lovingkindness makes possible the extraordinary generosity required to love your enemies. Without these despositions of heart the Christian community's commitment to peace inevitably withers and dies.

This brings us to one more reason why the Christian community should neither sanction nor participate in warfare: it must be prophetic. The Christian must prophesy, as Collingwood says of the artist, "in the sense that he tells his audience at the risk of their displeasure, the secrets of their own hearts. . . . As spokesman of his community, the secrets he must utter are theirs. The reason why they need him is that no community altogether knows its own heart; and by failing in this knowledge a community deceives itself on the one subject concerning which ignorance means death."[78] The community to which Christians must prophesy is their own, and the secret of their own heart about which they must prophesy is Christ's message of peace. Failing this, the church forfeits Christ's eternal and peaceable kingdom and quickly withers with the demise of each nation-state. So if we presuppose love and peace as Christian virtues, we must conclude that a faithful Christian community will forsake the tradition of justifying war and taking national sides. The fact of human evil and violence jolts the world daily, challenging, even daring, the covenantal community to imitate Christ's life of nonviolent action. It cannot, of course, do so, if its loyalties are double-minded, divided between swearing allegiance to a particular nation-state and to God's kingdom. But it can do so by acknowledging that its mission is to deliver to the world, as Jesus delivered to the woman taken in adultery, the healing grace of God's peace and by acknowledging that it is uniquely empowered by God to do so. As Cahill concludes, "it inevitably is [God's] 'future' power in the 'present' that sustains compassion, forgiveness and even nonviolence as the edge of God's healing action amid the ambiguities, evils, and despair of history."[79] Jesus delivered to the adulterous woman as well as to those who killed him bread, not a stone; mercy and reconciliation, not punishment and condemnation. A church that faithfully, meekly, and prophetically commits itself to the gospel, a church marked by mercy and unmerited generosity, is one on which the world can depend for peace and reconciliation. As God's peace manifested in Jesus was a gift to the Christian community; so the church must be about the business of delivering God's peace to the world, and delivering it freely so that, as God intended, it remains a gift.

5

Justice as a Christian Virtue

Once a cluster of children approached the Hodja requesting that, in his wisdom, he settle a dispute that had arisen between them. One child said, "The four of us have gathered all the walnuts from under a tree; we have all shared equally in gathering them and would like to divide them equally among us. But when we do so, three walnuts still remain. It seems that one of us will be deprived of a walnut, but we do not know who it should be. How should we decide?" After some thought, the Hodja asked, "Do you wish God's justice in this matter, or man's?" The child replied, "I have seen man's justice, how vengeful and uncaring it can be; I vote for God's justice." The other children agreed; they preferred God's justice to man's. "You have chosen well," said the Hodja. So to one child he gave fifty walnuts, to the second child thirty walnuts, to another three walnuts, and to the fourth he gave none at all.[1] That God's justice is not the same as human justice is a point also made poignantly by Jesus in his parable of a householder who paid those who labored only one hour the same wage as those who labored all day. When those working longer hours complained that it was unfair that those working an hour should be paid the same wage, Jesus replied to the plaintiffs that since they had been fairly paid agreed-on wages they should not begrudge the householder his generosity toward the hourly workers (Matthew 20:1–16). God's sense of justice it would seem, sometimes differs from the sense of justice devised by humans. That justice may involve extraordinary generosity, as Jesus supposes, and not simply fairness runs counter to many conventional and popular notions of justice, including Christian ones.

The purpose of this chapter is to explore this apparent discrepancy between God's justice and human justice and to retrieve as far as possible a covenantal sense of justice that attempts to accommodate and account for the extraordinary sense of justice represented by the Hodja and Jesus. It is presumptuous, of course, to think that any human can begin to comprehend God's wisdom and justice. What I mean to explore is the difference between certain conventional conceptions of justice and an alternative interpretation of justice that presupposes covenantal love and peace.

Contemporary interpretations of justice tend to polarize into what Uma Narayan calls "rights discourse," or justice as fairness, and "care discourse," or justice as caring.[2] Rights discourse expresses a highly rationalistic version of justice as strict equity and finds its modern sources in Kant and his many contemporary interpreters, including Robert Nozick, John Rawls, and (in theology) Harlan Beckley. Care discourse expresses a relational, affectional version of justice that finds its modern sources in Carol Gilligan, Nel Noddings, and (in theology) Cahill. I develop here a discourse that articulates a sense of "covenantal justice," which is the kind of justice that should characterize communities that claim the biblical tradition. I show that although covenantal justice accomodates the concerns of justice as fairness and justice as caring, it cannot simply be reduced to one or the other. Although both fairness and caring should characterize any community that claims the biblical tradition, any notion of covenantal justice cannot be reduced simply to a balance between them, nor can its adequacy be measured simply in terms of their equilibrium.

My aim is to show that obediential dispositions and empathetic emotions are inseparable dimensions of covenantal justice. The term "obediential" refers to a dispositional dimension of covenantal justice that includes but is not reducible to many of the concerns and values belonging to justice as fairness. The term "empathetic" refers to the emotional dimension of justice and includes but is not reducible to those concerns and values belonging to justice as care. I show, on the one hand, that covenental justice, as constituted by obediential dispositions and empathetic emotions, is of sufficient moral and theological depth to embrace both the concerns of fairness and the concerns of care that are of primary concern in contemporary ethics. I show, on the other hand, that because it draws on a rich, biblical heritage, covenantal justice is not reducible to any other philosophical or theological tradition. I proceed by examining, first, the obediential habits that make up one thread of covenantal justice; second, I examine its emotional, empathetic thread; and third, I show how these two threads weave into the fabric of Christian community a unique sense and practice of justice. My aim in this chapter is not to show how covenantal justice is relevant to and operative in public life; I take up that task in chapter 6. Instead, my current aim is more particular and local: to develop a conception of covenantal justice as it emerges within the Christian community's tradition and commitments.

JUSTICE AS OBEDIENTIAL DISPOSITIONS

By "obediential," as already disccussed, I refer to certain dispositions or habits of character that are essential if a community is to put itself in a position to be able to dutifully obey God's commandments. Obediential, in other words, refers to a subjective dimension of justice whose corresponding objective dimension embraces rational principles, universal laws, rights, duties, and commands. The liberal, Kantian tradition in Western thought focuses on the objective dimension of justice, insisting that moral value is derived from duty to a rational pattern of universal laws that can be commanded. As argued in chapter 3, this tradition tends to reject or minimize the moral value of emotions and emotional attachments, arguing that since emotions are irrational at worst and nonrational at best, they cannot be commanded and therefore cannot be reliable guides to moral behavior. Kant is a modern source for contemporary philosophical (e.g., Rawls) and theological (e.g., Beckley) versions of this tradition.[3]

To be able to keep God's commandments, to make obedience a practical possibility, requires that a community cultivate specific dispositions of character. As Bondi says of love, so also we can say that justice can become a reality "only in so far as it is a disposition, a whole way of being, feeling, seeing, and understanding. . . . [It] is a deep attitude of heart or a . . . disposition."[4] My aim is to examine two obediential dispositions of heart remembrance and responsibility, by which any Christian story of justice is fundamentally shaped and reshaped.

Responsibility

Any covenantal version of justice begins with a profoundly spiritual sense of responsibility. By this I mean that justice first involves a person in a mutual and reciprocal relationship with God and with God's people. From this relationship emerges a habit of heart in which one willingly assumes the same kind of responsibility for others that God through a covenantal relationship assumes for humanity. Contemporary thinkers, such as Gilligan and Noddings, articulate a notion of just caring in terms of relationships and responsibilities. In her essay "Justice and Responsibility," for example, Gilligan locates the moral self in terms of its concrete social milieu and the interpersonal responsibilities belonging to that milieu.[5] Similarly, H. Richard Niebuhr, perhaps as forcefully as anyone in recent times, argues that the human self is an interdependent, social-historical creature whose moral life is and should be determined by a intricate pattern of relationships for which the self is responsible and to which it is accountable.[6] As Darlene Ehinger suggests, "[i]n order to account for the multiplicity of moral responses in this social-historical self, Niebuhr developed an ethic of responsibility that restored the contextual narrative to the moral question which he claimed could only be understood in social interaction, not separation."[7] "The contextual narrative" of an ethic of responsibility acknowledges, she insists, that "the moral self is not defined as a separated, autonomous individual reflecting on ethical ideals" but as a self that is "formed and responds to the community in which she lives."[8]

Niebuhr uses the words "fitting" and "fittedness" to identify the pattern of mutual relationships that constitute his ethic of responsibility. By "fittedness" he means something not so far different, I think, from the biblical notion of shalom. Whereas deontological ethics values most highly "the right" and teleological ethics values most highly "the good," an ethics of responsibility values most highly "the fitting." For Niebuhr "the fitting" is the most comprehensive moral category, so much so that it embraces both the good and the right. [F]or the ethics of responsibility the *fitting* action, the one that fits into a total interaction as response and as anticipation of further response, is alone conducive to the good and alone is right.[9] Any Christian conception of justice properly must be in terms of something like Niebuhr's notion of fittedness, a network of moral responsibilities. For a faithful community the practice of justice, accordingly, arises out of its devotion to the God whose covenant with a community inspires a spiritual and moral pattern of life. The good and the right to which this covenantal community commits itself are such that they *fit* into an intricate normative and narrative pattern—a fittedness presupposing that what connects people to each other (i.e., a covenantal relationship) is more fundamental and prior to what separates them (individual rights and freedoms). Fittedness involves, in other words, cultivating a disposition of responsibility constituted by a profoundly spiritual sense of interdependence and mutual commitment to every member of the community, to the community itself, and to its God. Possessing this disposition implies, on the one hand, that no member self can understand itself or be understood independent of the community to which she belongs and implies, on the other hand, that the community is responsible for the welfare of all of its members and that all members are accountable to the community for its welfare. In short, "fittedness" involves mutual responsibility for and accountability to the covenantal community.

Scarcely a line of Hebrew Scriptures can be properly understood independent of the idea of covenantal fittedness. Abraham's obedience to God's call, deliverance and exodus, revelation and law, land of promise and promised nationhood, exile and return, triumph and defeat, complaint and praise, apostasy and faithfulness all arise out of a keen sense of covenantal fittedness, of mutual responsibility and accountability. From deep in the rich soil of this "contextual narrative," as Niebuhr calls it, emerges the unique character of covenantal justice, a kind of justice whose fittedness retrieves and reenacts this covenantal relationship between God and his people. The Hebrew law of love is compelling, then, not because it is rational and can be commanded but because in gratitude to God a community is inspired to live fittingly—to live responsibly in accordance with the love that God has shown toward it. So the instructions "You shall love the Lord your God with all your heart, and with all your soul, and with all your might" (Deuteronomy 6:4); "You shall love your neighbor as yourself: I am the Lord" (Leviticus 19:18); and "Love the sojourner, for you were sojourners in Egypt" (Deuteronomy 10:19) are fitting ways in which a community assumes responsibility for its covenantal identity.

Jesus and the early church preserve this Jewish sense of justice as involving a feeling of mutual responsibility one for the other and as a function of this sense of communal responsibility. Partly it is this Jewish sense of righteous justice that Jesus claims to fulfill in his own ministry and not destroy. "The glory which thou hast given me I have given them," prays Jesus, "that they may be one even as we are one, I in them and thou in me, that they may become perfectly one, so that the world may know that thou hast sent me and hast loved them even as thou hast loved me" (John 17:22–23). This sense of oneness and covenantal solidarity was keenly and intimately felt by Jesus, so much so that in caring for "the least of these" Jesus said his disciples were in essence caring for him (Matthew 25:31–46). Two observations can be made, says Niebuhr, about Jesus as a paradigm of covenantal responsibility. First, he is one "who in all his response [to others] did what fitted into the divine action."[10] He exemplifies a character who is obedient not simply to universal imperatives but to a covenantal relationship such that his actions fit a pattern of what God has done and is doing in the world. Second, Jesus' actions do not fit conventionally into the pattern of spirituality discovered and devised by humans. The gospels portray those who witnessed Jesus' ministry as repeatedly astonished by what he did and said. Actions that fit Israel's covenantal paradigm are often in conflict with human paradigms, and this is often true, I will show, with regard to justice. Actions that fit into a divine pattern of convenantal justice, may very well conflict with provincial notions of justice devised by humans.

Niebuhr asks us to consider, for example, Jesus' interpretation of natural events. What is the covenantal pattern to which Jesus is responsible and how does his response to natural phenomena fit into that pattern? Jesus "sees as others do that the sun shines on criminals, delinquents, hypocrites, honest men, good Samaritans, and VIPs without discrimination, that rains come down in equal proportions on the fields of the diligent and the lazy." Those not attuned to Jesus' covenantal way of life interpret these natural phenomena fatalistically, as "signs of the operation of a universal order that is without justice. . . . But Jesus interprets the common phenomena in another way: here are the signs of cosmic generosity"; a generosity that, as I argued in chapter 4, benefits even the wrongdoer. Not only do the just benefit from sun and rain but the unjust as well; not because either merit sun and rain but because of God's grace. So it is also with the birds of the air and flowers of the field; birds are fed and flowers clothed not because of great deeds but because of God's grace.[11] So is the natural ordering of things indiscriminate and unjust or is it by God's grace indiscriminately just and gracious, favoring all? The point to which Niebuhr draws our attention is that for Jesus the righteous justice of God "is different in all its working from the provencial, even planetary righteousness that men have discovered or devised."[12] Covenantal justice, accordingly, is not simply "duty to universal law" but devotion to a covenantal way of life that requires a community to assume responsibility for the welfare of humanity in the same inclusive and gracious way that God in Christ assumes responsibility for the welfare of humanity.

Similarly, the Apostle Paul often uses the familiar metaphor of the body to articulate the interdependence and mutuality of responsibility that should characterize members of a covenant community. "For just as the body is one and has many members, and all the members of the body, though many, are one body, so it is with Christ. . . . But God has so composed the body, giving the greater honor to the inferior part, that there may be no discord in the body, but that the members may have the same care for one another. If one member suffers, all suffer together; if one member is honored, all rejoice together" (1 Corinthians 12: 12, 24–26). What is right and good in a covenantal community, in other words, is what is fitting, and what is fitting involves living in solidarity with God and the community of God. What is fitting may very well entail giving greater honor to those who are considered inferior or attending in a special and preferential way to the needs of the least of these. Or, as in Jesus' parable, fittedness may mean giving the same wages to those who have worked fewer hours. The proper Christian understanding of justice, in short, must take into account the necessity of fittedness, justice's place in a network of relationships that inspires the same sense of gracious responsibility for the welfare of humanity that God in Christ manifests.

That which is fitting, however, involves not simply the self's covenantal accountability to and solidarity with God and other selves. For the self's sense of fittedness, according to Niebuhr, involves also "the deep memories that are buried within us, of feelings and intuitions that are only partly under our immediate control."[13] Responsibility, in short, implies remembrance. A community characterized by an ethic of responsibility at the same time is characterized by remembrance, a sense of responsibility to its past.

Remembrance

"Remember" is one of the most fundamental and frequent commandments the people of Israel are called to obey. Memory is central both to its faith and to its sense of justice. Indeed, biblical versions of justice require of the faithful what Metz calls "dangerous memory"[14] and Russell Butkus, following Metz, defines as "the remembrance of suffering and freedom."[15]

What does it mean for a faithful community to nurture a disposition of remembrance and practice it? And what does such a disposition have to do with covenantal justice? And how is such a memory "dangerous?" The premise guiding any biblical notion of remembrance is that memory is not merely informative but formative and in this sense narrative. Memory is formative in the sense that the character of the one remembering, in this case the covenantal community, is shaped by spiritual and moral forces embodied in the act of remembrance. It is narrative in the sense that memory takes the form of stories, rituals, psalms, and dances that are imaginative interpretations of events in which patterns of meaning loaded with spiritual and moral power are constructed. The habit of remembrance that ancient Israel is commanded to cultivate is of this formative sort. Israel is not simply to recall a historical event but is to "possess it as something that is absolutely [its] own,"[16] something that shapes the memory and is reshaped by memory. Remembrance, then, involves imaginative reconstruction of the past by the one remembering. Moreover, the one remembering (e.g., Israel, church) imaginatively reconstructs past events on the basis of its practical concerns and needs. "To remember is not to duplicate," insists Brynolf Lyon. "The events or impressions that we recall from the past are not exact reproductions of the 'original event.' They are interpretations or reconstructions of the 'original event.'"[17] They are communal reconstructions of "past experiences and impressions in the service of [present] needs, fears, interests."[18] Put another way, remembrance is eschatological. In the act of remembering God's mighty acts, the covenantal community shapes and reshapes its present commitments and future prospects. Indeed, the possibility of the covenantal community's present faithfulness and future hope is established by remembrance, by retrieving what God has accomplished in the past. As Brevard Childs suggests, "[t]he role of memory here is not to relive the past, because much of what is remembered is painful, but to emphasize obedience in the future. Memory serves to link the present commandments as events with the covenant history of the past."[19] Remembering, then, not only says someting about "how our past was constituted," insists Lyon, "but also something about how we are presently constituting ourselves. We are retrieving and bringing to bear the influences of the past on our own present identity."[20] Remembrance is eschatological in that retrieving the past serves "the critical [moral and theological] function of orienting action for the future."[21] Remembrance establishes the possibility of prophetic vision, of repentance and redemption, of hope and liberation.

We are now in a position to see what rememberance has to do with covenantal justice. Childs, in his classic study *Memory and Tradition in Ancient Israel*, argues that the biblical act of rememberance involves two subjects, God and Israel, and the extent to which Israel acts fittingly, responsibly, and justly according to its covenantal relationships. Both God and Israel remember. "The essence of God's remembering," says Childs, "lies in his acting toward someone because of a previous commitment,"[22] in particular covenantal commitments. God remembers, of course, for many reasons,[23] but included in those reasons are occasions when the people of God suffer injustice and God hears their cry for help. In "complaint psalms," for example, God's people often plead to God for justice; they "remind Yahweh of the scorn of the heathen and the suffering of his people for the purpose of influencing and arousing his sympathy (Psalms 74:2, 89:51)."[24] Often Yahweh's response to such a complaint is to remember covenantal commitments and undertake acts of compassion and justice to redress injustices. "And the people of

Israel groaned under their bondage and cried out for help, and their cry under bondage came up to God. And God heard their groaning, and God remembered his covenant with Abraham, with Isaac, and with Jacob. And God saw the people of Israel, and God knew their condition" (Exodus 2:23–25 See also 6:5–7; Leviticus 26:40–42). God's compassion for suffering Israel is the occasion for remembering the covenant with Abraham. God's act of remembrance, in turn, reshapes the story and character of Israel. Not only does God call Moses to confront Pharaoh and demand justice and deliver Israel from oppression; God also requires that, since "I am the Lord your God, who brought you out of the land of Egypt, out of the house of bondage," Israel should live a life of extraordinary holiness (Exodus 20:1–17; See also Deutoronomy 5:6–21) and in so doing fulfill its covenant with God.[25] Remembrance, in short, is a disposition of God's heart that moves God to reaffirm covenantal commitments, including a commitment to resist forces of injustice and establish justice in the land.

That remembering the covenant disposes God toward justice characterizes not only the God of Israel but also the God of the Christian community. Early Christians inherited from their Jewish tradition the view in which God, now incarnate in Jesus, remembers the covenant and covenantal justice and in remembering reshapes the spiritual and moral life of the community. Matthew records in his gospel Jesus' claim that he does not abolish but retrieves and fulfills the law and prophets (5:17–18). And we find, in the succeeding section of Matthew's version of the Sermon on the Mount, that remembrance (i.e., remembering the covenant) is crucial to understanding how this is so. My concern here is not to determine how continuous or discontinuous with Jewish teaching the content of Jesus' remembrance is but to note how Jesus' remembrance of the covenant is central to a Christian understanding of justice. Jesus' interpretations of the laws of retaliation, of proactive nonviolence, and of neighborly love and loving your enemy are set forth in the context of remembering God's covenant with Israel (5:38–48). Indeed, the whole of Jesus' Sermon on the Mount, the center of his moral and religious teachings, cannot be properly understood except in terms of Jesus's remembrance of Israel's covenantal tradition.

Not only does God remember, but God's people are frequently commanded to remember: "And you shall remember all the way which the Lord your God has led you"(Dueteronomy 8:2). And one reason God wants his people to remember is for the sake of commiting themselves to covenantal justice. When Israel observes the Sabbath and Passover, for example, it is not only so that "all the days of your life you may remember the day when you came out of the land of Egypt" (16: 3), although observance includes that, but so that you might participate again in the Exodus event and retrieve that event and practice it in the days of your present life. Hence, as Childs suggests, for Israel "[m]emory functions as actualization . . . of the decisive event in her tradition." This is the thrust of commands such as "You shall not oppress a stranger; [remember] you know the heart of a stranger, for you were strangers in the land of Egypt" (Exodus 23:9; see also 22:21–24), and again, "When a stranger sojourns with youu in your land, you shall not do him wrong. The stranger who sojourns with you shall be to you as the native among you, and you shall love him as yourself; for you were strangers in the land of Egypt: I am the Lord your God" (Leviticus 19:33–34). Similarly, God's people are instructed to "Remember this day, in which you came out from Egypt, out of the house of bondage, for by strength of hand the Lord brought you out of this place; no leavened bread shall be eaten" (Exodus 13:3). For those who are intimidated, disheartened, suffering oppression, and in need of hope: "you shall not be afraid . . . but you shall remember what the Lord your God did to Pharaoh and to all Egypt, the great trials which your eyes saw, the signs, the wonders, the mighty hand, and the outstretched arm, by which the Lord your God brought you out; so will the Lord your God do to all the peoples of whom you are afraid" (Deuteronomy 7:17–19).

Likewise, in Christian Scriptures, remembrance is central to understanding and practicing covenantal justice. In the context of remembering the faith of the patrairchs, matriarchs, and prophets, for example, the author of the Epistle to the Hebrews says, "Recall the former days when, after you were enlightened, you endured a hard struggle with sufferings, sometimes being publicly exposed to abuse and affliction, and sometimes being partners with those so treated" (10:32–33). The writer encourages his readers, insisting that by remembering past sufferings God will give to them the faith, confidence, and courage needed to continue a life of compassionate justice. "For you had compassion on the prisoners, and you joyfully accepted the plundering of your property, since you knew that you yourselves had a better possession and an abiding one. Therefore, do not throw away your confidence, which has a great reward" (10:34–35). Indeed, remembering one's own suffering faith, the writer of Hebrew insists, retrieves a rich and diverse history of faith and suffering (chapter 11) that even today enable a community with the grace of courage to struggle against injustice. We are to recall the faith of Moses, who, when grown, refused, and refused to exploit, his inherited royalty but chose rather "to share ill-treatment with the people of God. He considered abuse for the Christ greater wealth than the treasures of Egypt" (11:23–28). And we are to remember women and men who "sufferd mocking and scouraging, and even chains and imprisonment" for the sake of remaining faithful to the covenant relationship to which they laid claim (11:36–38). In so doing, remembrance, then, mediates between history and practice, between God's faithfulness in the past and who we are and can be in the present and future. Remembering, then, is a disposition of heart whereby a faithful community is inspired to practice, among other things, the ancient art of covenantal justice.

The practice of this ancient art is precisely what is "dangerous" about biblical remembrance. Indeed, remembrance is dangerous in at least two interrelated ways. It is calculated not only to liberate those suffering injustice but also to undermine and subvert the attitudes and structures that perpetuate it. Remembrance not only retrieves narratives of painful suffering and oppression but demands liberation and justice. Biblical memory is dangerous, insists Butkus, "because of its capacity to subvert existing ideologies and unjust social structures and because it contains the possibility for promoting an emancipatory praxis for freedom and justice."[26] That members of the covenantal community recall that once they too were foreigners, for example, means at the same time that they must recall God's command not to mistreat or oppress foreigners but to treat them as Israelites, as neighbors. By retrieving this identity and commandment for themselves, Israel and the church retrieve a moral and spiritual power that begins to undermine prejudices against immigrants and threatens institutions and policies that would shun them as foreigners rather than summon them as neighbors. A community's habit of remembering is, as James Morgan points out, a "liberating force . . . [and] enables followers to be simultaneously rooted in their faith traditions so that they can live their heritage in a dynamic manner in the present and look forward in hope to a future."[27] Of course, in cultivating a disposition of remembrance a community risks false and corrupting memories, either by "succumbing to the disease of traditionalism or longing for a paradisiacal past" or by "envisioning a utopian or dystopian existence in the future that feeds upon people's fears instead of faith."[28] But the greatest risks are not forms of false memory but forgetfulness. Remembrance is dangerous and threatening because it casts doubt on the most profoundly held beliefs and values around which a community's identity and esteem revolves. As Lyon puts it, memories "appear to us as an unwelcome presence: an assault on our carefully hewn sense of self."[29] Hence it is not surprising that "we forget and so are able to sustain, however, precariously, these values around which the cohesiveness of our self is presently organized."[30] A disposition of remembrance is dangerous, in short, because it obligates biblical communities, such as Israel and the church, to commit themselves to a particularly risky form of covenantal justice that challenges conventional practices and provokes the practice of freedom and justice.

How then does the equation of remembrance and responsibility constitute an obediential orientation? Covenantal justice, as I have shown, requires of the community faithful obedience. This obedience serves not merely or most fundamentally a constellation of abstract laws and commandments, although commandments are crucial to covenantal justice, but a comprehensive, covenantal way of life for which remembrance and responsibility, continuity and solidarity, are essential habits of heart. Remembrance is a disposition of heart that retrieves for a community an ancient and ongoing story of justice; responsibility is a disposition that cares for the welfare of humanity in the same ancient way that God cares for human welfare. But although responsibility and remembrance are indispensable in shaping a community's character for practicing covenantal justice, certain empathetic emotions elicited by them are what empower a community to actually practice it.

JUSTICE AS EMPATHETIC EMOTIONS

The term "empathetic emotions," as already disussed, refers to certain emotional attachments that are crucial to the practice of Christian virtue, in this case, the practice of covenantal justice. Linking justice with empathetic emotions is nothing new, of course. Plato and Aristotle both find this relation vital to understanding and practicing justice. More recently, eighteenth-century thinkers, such as Reid, Hutcheson, Smith, and Hume, had a great deal to say about sympathy as a natural and irrepressible emotion that would guarantee justice in public (e.g., economic) life.[31] More recently, thinkers such as Gilligan, Noddings, Carroll Saussy, and William Werpehowski insist on the vital role of caring emotions in properly formulating any compelling conception of justice. My concern here is to show how certain empathetic emotions are presupposed by a covenantal notion of justice. The reluctance of some thinkers (e.g., Kant, Rawls, Beckley) to adequately account for this dimension of justice is due in part, I think, to inadequate conceptions of emotions, in part to inadequate attention to the biblical tradition's notion of justice, and in part to the privileging of reason and the dispossessing of emotions.

Solomon acknowledges justice's emotional dimension: "Without care and compassion," he insists, "there can be no justice."[32] For most people the notion that justice involves some measure of emotional investment is unsurprising and self-evident. They get angry at injustices or feel concern for those suffering unfairly. The biblical tradition's notion of covenantal justice likewise acknowledges this dimension. Empathy does not refer to any single emotion, of course, but to a diverse range of feelings, all of which I cannot hope to treat here. Accordingly, I have chosen to examine two emotions, anger and gratitude, that embrace between them a range of emotions that constitute the Christian practice of covenantal justice. Edwards acknowledges that "in gratitude and anger there is the exercise of some kind of moral sense. . . . [A]ll the moral sense that is essential to those affections, is a sense of *Desert*; which is to be referred to that sense of justice before spoken of."[33] Although, he goes on to argue, "it is not absolutely necessary to the being of these passions of gratitude and anger, that there should be any notion of justice in them," when justice as a true virtue "consists in public benelovence," he says, the affections of gratitude and anger are necessarily implied in it. Accordingly, gratitude and anger as affections "imply some delight in public good, and an aversion of the mind to public evil." Thus, "every time a man feels anger for opposition or gratitude for any favour, there must be at least a supposition of a tendency to public injury in that opposition, and a tendency to public benefit in the favour that excites his gratitutde."[34] I will show, first, that insofar as anger is an emotional preference of Christian life, its normative value for justice is as an effective gauge for detecting injustice. Second, I will show that insofar as gratitude is a fundamental emotional preference of Christian life, its normative value for justice is as an effective gauge for distributing what I shall refer to as equal mercy.

Anger

In chapter 4 I concluded that a particular form of anger, just vengeance, is morally relevant to peace as a Christian virtue. I extend that discussion here in an effort to show that anger is also an emotion crucial to the practice of justice as a Christian virtue. Righteous anger or indignation is, ironically, an empathetic, caring emotion that belongs fundamentally to God in relation to fallen creatures and God's desire to redeem them. God's plan of salvation, culminating for the Christian in the death and resurrection of Jesus, exemplifies at a profound depth the spiritual and emotional sources of anger as just caring. To show this, I shall first examine anger as a powerful emotion that is constituted, like other emotions I have considered, of three essential dimensions: judgment, project, and energy.

The key to understanding anger, insists Solomon, is to see it as a "judgment": an "indictment," an "accusation,"[35] that generates a response of frustration, indignation, outrage, or offense. It is a common experience; we encounter an event that we feel is unfair, and this judgment, "offering an interpretation" of the event, as Saussy puts it, "energizes a response of anger."[36] Anger, in other words, involves a judgment that the world as it is for some is not what it could and fairly should be. The basis on which this judgment is made is, for the covenantal community, its constellations of beliefs and values. Consider again the story in which Nathan tells David of the rich man who, not wanting to slaughter one of his many lambs, pirates the only lamb of a poor man in order to entertain a sojourner. David's emotional response is predictably and properly anger, a righteous indignation toward the rich man who for further economic advantage unfairly exploits the poor man. David's empathy with the plight of the poor man is triggered by a judgment he makes, that the world as it is (the rich man's treatment of the poor man) is not what it should be according to the values of the covenantal community to which he belongs. If we remove from David's mind the particular valuation he makes regarding the rich man's behavior, or alter it significantly, then David's anger disappears or alters with it. Or consider how the profiteers in the Temple elicited Jesus' anger (Mark 11:11–14). The Temple was the center of Jewish worship and symbolic of God's holy presence among the people of Israel. Certain practices occurring in this holy place were, in the judgment of Jesus, unacceptable. Those who had made it into "a den of thieves" were selling animals needed for sacrifice for "their own large profit," as William Temple puts it. "The place which should be ordered with the reverence appropriate to the dwelling-place of God is cluttered up with worldly ambitions, anxieties about our possessions, designs to get the better of our neighbors."[37] The judgment Jesus makes, that the unfair profiteering of vendors has made the Temple into a den of thieves, generates in him a passionate response of righteous outrage.

As a moral emotion anger is constituted, second, by a project arising from and continuous with its judgment. Certain moral projects are implied by and morally appropriate to anger's judgment. Anger's project sets out to right a wrong, to make the world as it unfairly is into the world as it fairly ought to be, thereby actualizing the purposeful intention implicit in its judgment. The project initiated by David's judgment is already stipulated by the community to which he belongs. Accordingly, David knew immediately the nature of the project to be undertaken. Injustice must be redressed with justice. The rich man must "restore the lamb fourfold" and "deserves to die" (2 Samuel 12:5–6). Not only has David's community cultivated in him the appropriate emotional response to injustice, but it has nurtured in him the kind of emotional project appropriate to that judgment. Similarly, Jesus' judgment that God's house has been made into a den of thieves implies an appropriate and intentional project, an action that will make the world as it unfairly is into the world as it ought to be, a temple, a place of worship. If anger toward injustice does not compel a community to actively work to overturn it and to reprove and redeem the offenders, then either the emotion is not genuinely felt or it is not of the righteous sort.

Finally, anger is constituted by an emotional energy that functions as a dialectical link between anger's judgment and project. Anger involves affectional forces of such potency as to actualize or propel into existence the project triggered by anger's judgment, thereby transforming the world as it unfairly is into the world as it ought to be. Anger possesses an energy that drives a person to take action, to undertake a project commensurate with anger's judgment. David's initial anger toward the rich man is transformed into guilt and anger toward himself when he recognizes himself as the rich man in Nathan's story. His anger's force inspires him to undertake a project appropriate to feelings of guilt and repentance. Along with feelings of guilt and remorse, anger as emotional spring sets in motion a project appropriate to the judgment triggering it. Similarly, Jesus' indignation toward the Temple profiteers is loaded with affectional forces of such potency that the action he undertakes seems almost beyond his capacity to command. As Temple puts it, "[i]t is a tremendous scene. The Lord dominates the multitude by the righteousness of his energy and the energy of his righteousness."[38] Jesus' judgment (the Temple has become a den of thieves) and correspondent project (drive the profiteers out) is mediated and actualized by his anger's affectional force, which aims to transform the Temple into the holy place it properly should be.

What then does anger have to do with justice as a Christian virtue? We can first speak of the kind of anger that is unrelated to justice, is unholy and unhealthy, and in fact very often leads to acts of injustice. Such anger, which Saussy calls the anger of despair, possesses two destructive qualities—retribution and despair—that are interrelated. Despairing anger, she explains, involves, on the one hand, a defensive, self-indulgent posture in which one feels personally offended, condemns the offender, and seeks to retaliate against the perceived cause of anger. Such anger involves, on the other hand, a desperate feeling of hopelessness in which the possibilities of reproving and redeeming evaporate and nothing short of destroying the object of anger is sufficient to assuage the desire for justice. As such, a person's anger is expressed defensively as vengeful hostility that seeks retribution and that aims "to punish and injure persons or institutions; it tears at the fabric of society by destroying relationships."[39] Cain, for example, embodies this anger of despair. His "downfall was not his anger that God did not accept his offering," says Saussy; rather, his failure was that "he did not accept God's invitation to talk about his anger." He was warned not to let the sin of despairing anger "couching at the door" master him. Instead he was to master his anger, finding healthy ways of expressing it and constructive projects for practicing it. Cain "made a fatal choice." Instead of talking to and contending with God, as did Job, about the hurt and resentment he felt in being treated (as he perceived it) unfairly, he "expressed the anger of despair, destroying the brother whose gift was favored by God."[40] Feeling anger was not Cain's problem so much as the (perhaps understandable) despair implicit in his anger. His feelings of hostility and vengefulness, his desire for retribution, feed off his sense of desperation that his condition is irredeemable. Ultimately his feeling of angry despair destroyed not only his brother but himself. Jonathan Edwards, as Werpehowski points out, makes a similar point in discussing when anger is and is not appropriate for the Christian community. Anger can be inappropriate in at least two ways. First, it is inappropriate when it is inspired by pride, "when its occasion is moral evil conceived exclusively as an offense against the self." Second, it is inappropriate "when it malevolently desires that an offender suffer. The passion for revenge is excluded from the range of covenantal emotions, though this is distinguished from 'Christian reproof' that redresses evil through an attempt to correct the wrongdoer."[41] Cain's anger (and the anger of Job's wife), as a response to his feeling of being treated unjustly, is despairing in both of these ways. He took God's rejection of his offering, on the one hand, as a personal affront instead of as God's desire for him to do well. And instead of mastering his anger, on the other, he allowed it to master him and malevolently redirected the anger he felt toward God toward a scapegoat, his brother.

The kind of anger that constitutes feelings of justice, the "anger of hope" as Saussy calls it, is a holy, righteous, constructive, albeit dangerous anger and is characterized by two qualities, gentleness and hope. A Christian community must assume a particular moral and theological posture, according to Werpehowski, when feeling angry. This posture is based on the belief that the wrong done, the injustice suffered, is first of all an offense against God and God's sense of justice and only derivatively an offense against others.[42] Taking this posture is important for two reasons. First, as an offense against God, every instance of injustice invites God's empathetic suffering with humanity, all of which suffering (past, present, and future) is recapitulated in the incarnation and atonement. Recognition that God suffers along with humanity provides hope and added incentive for feeling that the conditions producing injustice are, with God's presence and help among us, redeeemable. Second, seeing injustice as an offense against God and not merely humanity inspires not only hopeful possibilities for redemption but a family of feelings that Edwards refers to as anger's "gentleness" and that lead to "reproof" and "chastisement" and not revenge and retribution. Without hope and gentleness, in other words, anger degenerates into wrathful vengeance and condemnation.

What is the significance of saying that anger should involve hope and a gentle, temperate spirit? Edwards notes that the Apostle Paul includes gentleness among those fruits of the Spirit characterizing a redeemed community. He goes on to distinguish "Christian reproof" from retaliatory punishment, arguing that Christian reproof requires a spirit that is "gentle," "calm," "equable," or "mild," "never getting angry," as Werpekowski puts it in speaking of Edwards's view, "except on justifiable grounds and for a reasonable length of time."[43] Furthermore, the anger of hope is not an exclusively Christian feeling. Aristotle, in speaking of anger, similarly argues that "the gentle person is not given to retribution . . . but is rather inclined to sympathetic understanding."[44] Seneca, in his work *On Anger,* goes even further, as Nussbaum points out. He argues against the moral viability of retributive anger and in favor of anger that is characterized not simply by gentleness but by a particular form of gentleness, namely, clemency or mercy.[45] Anger's gentleness of spirit implies that in response to injustice a gentle person or community will seek not retribution, which is inspired by feelings of desperation and retaliation, but reproof, which is inspired by a desire for redemption and reconciliation. Reproof and chastisement assumes that there is hope that the offender might be redeemed, reconciled, rehabilitated. The writer of John recognizes this distinction when he writes that Jesus has not come into the world to condemn it but to redeem it (3:17). The hopeful anger that belongs to covnenantal justice, then, necessarily includes gentle feelings of anger that inspire care and compassion for the victim of injustice in order to alleviate her suffering and reproof for the unjust offender in hope of redeeming him. Covenantal anger is indeed outraged and offended by the injustice suffered by victims, by "the experience of being ignored, injured, trivialized, or rejected."[46] But it is likewise a gentle, measured "empathetic response to witnessing of someone else being ignored, injured, trivialized, or rejected," as Saussy puts it, an appropriate "response to the awareness of social evil such as prejudice, oppression, and violence."[47] Or, as Werpehowski puts it, anger is an appropriate response "to being wronged in one's rightful domain"[48] or the rightful domain of another with whom one empathizes. But toward the unjust offender a community's anger, if it is righteous, must also be a gentle, measured response, intended to deliver reproof that seeks transformation and redemption and not retaliation and vengeful punishment, which are God's prerogative alone.

Both biblical events—David and Nathan, Jesus and the Temple profiteers—exemplify the anger of hope and its qualities of reproof with gentleness. The sense of justice presupposed in both instances (the exploitation of the poor man by the rich, the unfair profiteering of the Temple merchants) are perceived as offenses against the spiritual and moral order of God's creation. And both inspire feelings of anger from which arise projects of gentle, hopeful reproof in which proper moral and spiritual order is restored. The reproof David suffers is just in that his family suffers death and other calamities for his sin; but it is gentle insofar as he does not suffer the punishment he justly deserves, for his own life is spared and kingly rule restored. Jesus' reproof of the profiteers is just in that it cleanses the Temple of corruption but gentle in that the profiteers, though they are dramatically driven out of the Temple, apparently are not prohibited from properly worshipping in the Temple. In short, holy anger seeks a delicate balance between indignation and gentleness, compensating the injured for the injustice suffered, reproving and redeeming wrongdoers instead of condemning them. Wherever and whenever injustice exists, then, holy anger is the gauge that detects injustice and provides an emotional impetus by which the covenantal community is enabled to undertake projects that transform conditions of injustice into justice and that provide hope for the weary and downtrodden.

The roots of hopeful anger are deep in the soil of the Christian story. God's anger toward sin in the world inspired God to undertake a project of righteous justice, of making the world as it wrongfully and unjustly is into the world as it should justly be. This project of salvation was so inspired by truly righteous anger toward injustice that sentimentality on the one hand and hostility on the other are feelings that are precluded. Righteous anger inspires the Christian community to care for victims of injustice and deliver gentle reproof to the unjust offender in full assurance that God's grace is sufficient to redeem. For the Christian community this feeling of righteous anger properly arises out of an experience of gratitude, to which I now turn.

Gratitude

A case could be made, I think, for the view that gratitude is an emotional experience in and through which Christian faith and practice, theology and ethics, most profoundly coincide and interact. This can perhaps most readily be seen in the fact that a feeling of thankfulness is at the heart of the eucharistic experience. Fletcher notes its centrality when he says that "[t]he Christian ethic is peculiar because it is a eucharistic ethic, an ethic of thanksgiving. It comes from the compulsion to behave according to the belief of the Christian faith, Christian

behaving according to Christian believing."[49] Indeed, in that it is eucharistic, covenantal justice contrasts most dramatically with other versions of justice, including Christianized versions of liberal and communitarian justice.

What, then, is the nature of gratitude as an empathic emotion and how is it
related to justice as a Christian virtue? I will show that the notion of justice
implied by gratitude requires of the covenantal community a profoundly spiritual
sense and practice of what I call "equal mercy," distinguishing it from the more
familiar Rawlsian notion of "equal fairness." The feeling and sense of equal mercy
is encapsulated as normative in the injunction "Do do unto others as God in
Christ has done to you." Eucharistic gratitude calls the Christian community to
deliver to others the same kind of mercy that God in Christ delivers to it. Just as
Christians feel grateful for God acting mercifully toward them, so also they should
act mercifully toward others, so that the recipients of equal mercy will feel toward
the Christian community the same gratitude the donor community properly feels
toward God. My premise, then, is that covenantal justice centrally includes the
complex experience of equal mercy and that any faithful eucharistic community
obligates itself to this notion of justice. Eucharistic gratitutde, in other words, is
an experience, a familiar feeling, in which the recipient of an unmerited gift is
genuinely thankful to a donor for graciously making the world of the recipient
qualitatively better than it otherwise would be. So grateful is the recipient community that now as donor it is inspired and empowered to act similarly, to graciously give unmerited gifts to others in like manner as it received. How so?

First, the feeling of gratitude involves a judgment made by a recipient that she
is the beneficiary of an unearned and unmerited gift. A recipient makes a judgment—that her world is significantly better because of a donor's gift. This judgment invites certain feelings of thankfulness and appreciation that properly empower and inspire the recipient to undertake projects of gratitude in which she
is now the gracious donor who acts toward others (recipients) in ways that invite
in them similar feelings of thankfulness and appreciation. As Paul Camenisch
says in his careful analysis of gratitude,[50] the recipient believes that a gift or "an
unearned benefit has been received from a donor."[51] The gift is "not a windfall
. . . [but] something of value given to one unearned and undeserved by another
agent at some cost to that agent and for the benefit of the recipient." Similarly,
Christians believe (make the judgment) that God freely and graciously delivered
to the world an unmerited gift in Jesus Christ, a gift of mercy and forgiveness to
fallen humnanity. Whoever acknowledges and believes that Jesus is God's unmerited gift properly feels thankful to God for the gift, a thankfulness that is expressed individually and communally and repeatedly in the eucharistic event. Participation in eucharistic gratitude makes sense only for a community of believers
that judges itself to be the beneficiary of an unmerited gift, Jesus as redeemer
and lord.[52] As judgment, gratitude entails what Camenisch calls certain kinds of
"obligations"[53] or moral expectations. Consider Jesus's parable of the unforgiving

debtor (Matthew 18:23–35). Although the text does not explicitly say so, we assume that the servant who pleaded for and received mercy from his master judged himself to be the beneficiary of an unmerited gift. We also assume, as Jesus does, that the recipient's appropriate response to such a gift should be a feeling of thankfulness. Moreover, although the gift, insofar as it is and remains a gift, can require nothing in return, nothing reciprocal from the recipient that would disqualify the graciousness of the gift, there are clearly, Camenisch insists, certain moral expectations the donor has of the recipient. The master's moral expectation for the servant, for example, is summed up in the notion of equal mercy. The master expects that just as he, the donor, has shown mercy, so likewise the recipient will show mercy toward others. Gratitude, in other words, involves a normative, emotional attachment that establishes between donor and recipient a moral relationship. It is the moral character of this relationship that justifies the donor's expectation that the recipient, if he truly judges himself to be the recipient of a gift and is genuinely grateful, will act in certain appropriate ways. When, in the parable, the recipient does not meet the expectations of the donor, the donor is portrayed as justified in punishing the recipient for his failure to conform to the moral expectation of a relationship based on the judgment that a gift was freely given and freely received.

Implied in gratitude's judgment, as already suggested, is a moral project that the thankful recipient is expected to undertake. In feeling gratitude, the recipient of an unearned gift establishes a normative, emotional attachment to the donor, what Camenisch refers to as "a relationship of moral community."[54] It is this relationship that requires the recipient to undertake, when appropriate occasions arise, projects of equal mercy. What project is implied in feeling gratitude? Camenisch points out that, although freely given and freely received, a gift "is given for some reason(s). And in accepting the gift, the recipient cannot strip it of its connection to the donor's will and intention, with the donor's reason(s) for giving it. To accept the gift is on some level to consent to that total complex reality and to consent to become a part of it."[55] An essential part of this total complex is that the recipient of a gift is in some sense called or expected to participate in a moral project commensurate with the feeling of gratitude, a moral project that encapsulates the principle of equal mercy. One might object that a gift graciously and freely given cannot be delivered with the strings of obligation attached. But, as Camenisch points out, "[m]oral relations between mature agents will most often be reciprocal relations."[56] Reciprocal, in this case, not in the sense that the donor must be compensated somehow for the gift, which not only would discredit the gift but presumably exceed the servant's means, but reciprocal in the sense that the recipient is rightfully expected by the donor to act similarly. Upon feeling thankful for mercy received, a recipient is expected to act mercifully toward others, including toward the previous donor if occasion arises. The expectation of the master, in Jesus' parable, that the servant act toward his fellow servant with the same unmerited mercy from which he had personally benefited establishes a pattern of moral activity that if neglected, Jesus makes clear, invites rather severe consequences.

Gratitude is constituted, finally, not only by judgment and project but by emotional energy, by a powerful feeling of thankfulness that serves as a potent dialectical link between the judgment (that I have been the recipient of a gift) and its actualization in moral projects. A community's eucharistic experience of believing that it is the recipient of an eternal and unmerited gift in Jesus Christ, accordingly, transforms and empowers it with such grace as it needs to go and do likewise. Gratitude's transformative power enables the Christian community to imitate Christ in its moral life in a distinct and distinguishable way; for gratitude empowers it to practice a life of just and equal mercy in a world that defines its public and private life largely in terms of just deserts or fairness. But in and through the eucharist, a covenantal community is endowed with the power of holy affections that enables it to hear God's call to go and do likewise and to do it.

As the emotional experience that is central to an eucharistic ethic, gratitude arises from the very *heart* of what is distinctive about Christian life and thought. When Christians confess (make the judgment) that in Jesus God freely and graciously delivered to fallen humanity an unmerited gift of compassion, mercy, and forgiveness, it properly feels and expresses its gratitude individually, communally, and repeatedly in the eucharist. But expressing thankfulness eucharistically does not exhaust the feeling of gratitude. Every genuinely felt emotion, especially a moral emotion like gratitude, generates a project commensurate with the experience, a project of equal mercy, a project in which the thankful community receiving God's unmerited gift is empowered to act mercifully toward others, just as God in Christ has acted mercifully toward oneself. The feeling of gratitude is inauthentic and disingenuous if the recipients of God's gift does not in turn employ the power present and available to them in that gift and gratitude to become equally donors of God's unmerited grace and mercy to others. Consider again the parable of the unforgiving servant (Matthew 18:23–35) in which we find contrasted Jesus's covenantal version of justice and a liberal version of justice, a contrast between treating others as God has treated me and treating others according to what they deserve. The servant to whom mercy and forgiveness are shown by his master, we know, is not genuinely and fully grateful; for when opportunity arises he refuses, as donor, to graciously bestow on his fellow servant the same mercy and forgiveness his master bestowed on him. What was graciously done to him, he refused to graciously do to another. The forgiven but unforgiving debtor does behave according to a conventional, liberal notion of justice when he adamantly refuses to show mercy and requires his fellow servant to pay his debts. He is demanding nothing more than what just fairness requires, what is owed. Indeed, he is behaving, as Archibald Hunter says, "as we do ourselves every day. Making his case on the basis of a contractual notion of justice, he sought to recover his debt in accordance with the law,"[57] in accordance with just deserts. The touchstone for covenantal justice as a Christian virtue, as suggested by this parable, is not equal fairness or just deserts but equal mercy. Accordingly, the Christian community, insofar as it is covenantal, is obligated to treat others as God in Christ has treated it, with undeserved, unmerited mercy and forgiveness.

This covenantal conception of justice as equal mercy, as I have already shown, is in keeping with the teachings and practice of Jesus. In concluding a prayer, Jesus says, for example, "For if you forgive men their trespasses, your heavenly Father also will forgive you; but if you do not forgive men their trespasses, neither will your Father forgive your trespasses" (Matthew, 6:14–15). Elsewhere Jesus enjoins his disciples to "Be merciful even as your Father is merciful" (Luke 6:36). For Jesus, " 'the quality of mercy,' so far from being something to be granted on single and exceptional occasions, had the nature of an ordinance, that is, something providentially written into the moral constitution of things,"[58] a quality of heart that constitutes an essential component of covenantal justice. In short, eucharistic gratitude, as an empathetic emotion of covenantal justice, compels the Christian community to undertake projects of equal mercy and not merely projects of minimal impartiality. Herein, then, lies the fundamental empathetic dimension of justice as a Christian virtue: the gift that God graciously and undeservedly delivers to the covenantal community ought to be graciously and gratefully delivered by it to others in turn. This is the force of the biblical injunction "Freely you have received, freely give" or, as Gustafson paraphrases it, "you have freely received, therefore you ought to freely give."[59] The feeling of gratitude becomes, as Camenisch puts it, "the salient characteristic, the dominant mood or theme of a total way of life,"[60] a joyful life of responsibility and remembrance, a fittedness whereby the community retrieves and reenacts the same gift of mercy with which it is enriched by God. As Georg Simmel suggests, "Gratitude . . . is the moral memory of mankind. . . . If every grateful action, which lingers on from good turns received in the past, were suddenly eliminated, society (at least as we know it) would break apart."[61] Conversely, if the Christian community would faithfully remember and in remembering hear God's call to deliver to the world the same covenantal justice, the same gracious and equal mercy, that God bestows on it, then society would be elevated to a qualitatively higher level of moral practice.

PRACTICING COVENANTAL JUSTICE

If we gather together these various strands of justice, what results? My way of answering this question is by now familiar. First, I show that universals are accessible through particulars: the universal judgments and projects of righteous anger and grateful mercy are manifested through the particular obediential dispositions (responsibility and remembrance) that shape the gospel story. Second, universals are justified in terms of the particular: practicing justice's empathetic anger and gratitude is justified by the local particularity of the gospel narratives and the obediential dispositions shaping them.

In all communities for whom holy anger and grateful mercy are desirable and normative, something like a covenantal practice of justice is implied. On the basis of my argument in chapter 2, I can claim with assurance that these empathetic emotions are intersubjectively available and accessible to all humans, that persons of diverse traditions experience them in common in their nature as emotions. The covenantal practice of justice suggested here, in other words, has universal appeal as a persuasive way of embodying justice. But what practice of justice emerges from the covenantal community's experience of holy anger and grateful mercy? In answering this question, I distinguish two dimensions of justice: *broad justice*, which emerges from feelings of holy, hopeful anger, and *deep justice*, which is rooted in feelings of grateful mercy.

Righteous anger is broad in two senses: first, it is a universal and universally appropriate human response to injustice, and, second, it arises naturally as a desire for treating all humans fairly, equally. This broad sense is the basis for liberal versions of justice such as Rawls's and involves feelings of anger that function in at least two ways: first, diagnostically and descriptively, as an emotional gauge that detects and registers for and in the heart of the community the presence of injustice; second, prognostically and prescriptively, as an emotional compass that indicates the direction a community's moral project ought to take if it is to rectify conditions of injustice. Implicit in this feeling of broad justice is an assumption that all humans ought to be treated impartially, as indeed the Epistle of James (2:1–13) insists. For a covenantal community that possesses well-developed habits of responsibility and remembrance, the judgment that the world as it unfairly is is not what it fairly should be naturally triggers feelings of holy anger. Isaiah, for example, speaks of how "the anger of the Lord was kindled against his people" because of injustice, because they would "acquit the guilty for a bribe, and deprive the innocent of his right" (5:22–25). Similarly, because David's community cultivated in him a keen sense of responsibility and remembrance, he immediately and rightfully feels anger when Nathan tells him of the rich man's unjust treatment of the poor man. And Jesus' anger at the Temple merchants is triggered by their unfair, exploitative practices. The covenantal community's feeling of anger, in other words, is occasioned by the judgment that injustice has occurred and that justice must be served. But what does it mean for a covenantal community to serve justice? Does broad justice, the covenantal community's feeling of righteous anger, embrace entirely within itself the range of feelings on the basis of which justice and just deserts are served? For the covenantal community, the answer, it seems, must be yes and no; Yes in that implicit in the feeling of anger is a principle of fairness that is central to any compelling conception of justice. Indeed, broad justice, in so far as it is an expression of hopeful anger, entails both a law of equal fairness (treat all impartially) and a law of retribution (an eye for an eye). The offended victim ought to be treated fairly and the unjust offender should be punished. The answer must be no, however, in that vengeance, retaliation, and retribution are for a covenantal community mercifully superceded and, as argued in chapter 4, are the prerogative and privilege of God alone and not of God's children—no, in that anger's desire for fair and equal treatment, although preserved, is nevertheless transformed in and by the eucharistic experience of grateful mercy from which emerges the notion of deep justice.

Whereas feelings of anger appropriately diagnose and register conditions of injustice, they are not the primary emotions that should be the basis of the covenantal community's treatment of the unjust offender or victim of injustice. The biblical tradition, culminating for the Christian community in the life of Jesus, points the way to a deeper, more profound sense of justice that is rooted in feelings of grateful mercy powerful enough to transform retributive feelings into an increasingly compassionate and merciful practice of justice. Anger's desire for equal fairness is internalized in the experience of grateful mercy. Feelings of grateful mercy in turn transform just anger in such a way that it is not inappropriate to speak, as Edwards does, of gentle anger, a desire to reprove and not retaliate, to redeem and not condemn, to reconcile and not repay.

What, then, is deep justice? How do feelings of grateful mercy preserve yet transform anger's desire for fairness and impartiality? How are they able to supercede anger's intense feelings of vengeance and retaliation? By "deep" I mean a dimension of justice that emerges in a covenantal community when it lives primarily in relationship to God and derivatively in relationship to humans. It refers to that profound feeling of grateful mercy triggered by a community's relationship with transcendence—its habits of remembrance of and responsibility to God.[62] This feeling of gratitude for God's mercy distinguishes deep from broad justice by endowing with spiritual depth the covenantal community's desire to embody in its practice precisely that merciful compassion it receives from God in Christ. By taking this spiritual dimension seriously, a community distinguishes its own practice of justice from other versions. For the Christian community, spiritual depth is conferred on justice by and in the eucharistic experience of gratitude, by and in that feeling whereby the covenantal community thankfully appropriates God's loving mercy as its own, as the way in which it is now enabled to live. Accordingly, with a keen sense of justice, a grateful community desires to do unto others as God in Christ has done unto it, to imitate and practice that action of Christ in its relations with all humans. By participating in the eucharist a community receives God's mercy and thereby commits itself to deep justice, to delivering equally to all that same grateful mercy. For the Christian community, absent this spiritual dimension of justice as primarily a network of covenantal relationships, justice devolves to something like a liberal version in which equal fairness instead of equal mercy is primary.

David's encounter with Nathan's parable of the rich man's unjust treatment of the poor man is especially instructive. David's "anger was greatly kindled against the man. And David said to Nathan, 'As the Lord lives, the man who has done this deserves to die; and he shall restore the lamb fourfold, because he did this thing, and because he had no pity' " (2 Samuel 12:5–6). Not only does David's feeling of anger rightly gauge the presence of injustice, but implicit in that anger is a moral project that includes fair retribution for the unjust offender, namely, death. The feeling of grateful mercy is, at this point, absent from David's experience. But note how God through Nathan deals mercifully with David when David acknowledges that he is the unjust offender and repents of his offense. David's initial feeling of anger leads him to condemn the rich man to death; David's anger at this point is an anger of despair, seeking vengeance and retribution instead of reproof and reconciliation. When David discovers that he is the offender, his anger turns to hope as he repents and seeks God's mercy and forgiveness. Although anger properly registers the presence of injustice, it is not the feeling that inspires God to deal reprovingly rather than retributively with David. Anger's desire for fairness is tempered by David's hope that God will deal mercifully with him, reproving him certainly, even severely, but not retaliating, redeeming but not condemning. In reproving David, God acted graciously and mercifully and not vengefully (i.e., death). Yet God's expectation is that a grateful David will in turn deal mercifully with unjust offenders, as indeed he tried to do with his son Absalom. Covenantal communities, insofar as they remain covenantal, should do the same. If they do not, the consequences are severe. Recipients of God's merciful forgiveness who fail to deliver to others the same mercy delivered to them condemn themselves, as Jesus' parable of the unforgiving servant makes clear. In so doing they abandon themselves to the wrath of God's retributive justice.

What contrasting implications, then, do liberal versions and covenantal versions of justice bear for policies such as affirmative action? Popular, conventional versions of liberal justice tend to hold that, since at bottom justice is fairness, all people should be treated symmetrically with strict and equal impartially. This is to say that all should be treated rigorously and strictly alike without appeal to distinguishing features. Indeed, fair impartiality generally rejects and veils as irrelevant to justice those features of a person's biography that distinguish that person from others, features that may otherwise be used to endorse asymmetrical treatment.[63] This popular version of justice as fairness is understandably suspicious of claims that policies of affirmative action are fair. Indeed, it claims that since affirmative action policies treat humans asymmetrically on the basis of distinguishing features, they are guilty of preferential treatment, even of unfair reverse discrimination. Fairness dictates that, all things being otherwise equal, the hourly workers, in Jesus' parable, should properly receive wages less than those of the day workers, commensurate with the number of hours labored. This, in fact, is the complaint of the day laborers. They assume that justice requires that each worker receive exactly the same compensation for each hour worked. Measured against this popular version of equal fairness, affirmative action falls under suspicion as a policy in which something unmerited is given to the undeserving. This "something" (e.g., contracts, hiring, promotion, admissions, quotas) is undeserved because such policies do not confer benefits on the basis of equal fairness or impartial application of universal law but on the basis of and with sensitivity to unique, local features of a person's biography, features that distinguish one person from others. Not surprisingly from the perspective of equal fairness, affirmative action infringes the rights and freedoms (e.g., equal opportunity for all) of those not included in the particular tradition on which favorable treatment is conferred.

Suppose that, in contrast to the day laborers, the hourly workers, in Jesus' parable, were known to be of an immigrant group who for decades were unfairly disenfranchised from society, suffering discrimination, living in abject poverty. Would this be a difference relevant to rendering wages as Jesus did? Not if we conceive justice as strictly a matter of fair and impartial treatment, as popular versions of liberal justice have it. Although the immigrant laborers may very well deserve reenfranchisement and equal opportunity, there is no justifiable basis for paying them wages higher than those of other workers. To do so would be to treat the hourly immigrant workers preferentially and the day workers unfairly. For fairness requires that all workers be treated symmetrically, simply as human beings, no different from or better or worse than one another. Any deviation from equal fairness, any principle that accounts for and distributes goods on the basis of difference, tends toward deep justice and feelings of grateful mercy. Admittedly, this view of justice as equal fairness possesses a certain power. Not only does its simplicity and clarity properly endow it with popular appeal, but certain philosophical and theological versions of it are sufficiently sophisticated and modulated to endow it with great conceptual power and intellectual appeal.[64] But whatever its appeal to those nurtured on liberal notions of justice, justice as fairness must be viewed as, by itself, somewhat attenuated for those committed to covenantal justice, justice as a Christian virtue.

When considering justice issues (such as capital punishment, distribution of goods, affirmative action) from a covenantal perspective, we can infer at least two characteristics that distinguish it from other versions of justice. First, covenantal justice may legitimately concern itself with those features of a person's biography distinguishing the person from others. Feeling grateful mercy may very well require a community to consider features unique to a person's experience to be relevant. As Nussbaum says of the views of some Greek and Roman thinkers, that "the decision to concern oneself with the particulars [of a person's situation] is connected with taking a gentle and lenient cast of mind toward human wrong-doing,"[65] so we can say of covenantal justice. This suggests, second, that by considering a person's distinctive biographical features, the practice of eucharistic mercy may require, as it did for the Hodja and Jesus, a kind of asymmetrical distribution of justice, a distribution that nevertheless does not infringe the requirement of minimum fairness for others. On the basis of unique biographical features, in other words, social goods might be distributed mercifully and not simply impartially. So just as love of neighbor is a minimum but insufficient practice of covenantal love, so broad justice's concern for minimum fairness, although essential, is for the covenantal community by itself insufficient. Just as covenantal love requires love of enemies and not just friends, so also covenantal justice requires grateful and equal mercy and not just fairness.

Affirmative action as a social policy coheres nicely with the purpose and promise of covenantal justice. First, for the victim of injustice, affirmative action embodies both hopeful anger and grateful mercy. The hopeful anger of broad justice compensates the victim (e.g., African-American women) for injustices, not only by guaranteeing fair, impartial treatment but by going the second mile, by transforming unjust structures into just ones. Similarly, the grateful mercy of deep justice graciously delivers to the victim a benefit that when measured against the principle of minimum fairness is preferential and unmerited. So the householder gives to the hourly workers (who, we might imagine, have greater financial needs) more generously than to the day workers who nevertheless are fairly paid and whose needs, presumably, are adequately met. Second, for unjust offenders, affirmative action avoids the retaliatory vengeance of just anger and advocates the equal mercy of hopeful, reproving, and gentle anger. The gentle mercifulness of anger's reproof is implicit in the fact that the offenders (e.g., white Euro-American males)[66] must now live in the context of policies whereby they may suffer the same sting of victimization suffered by those whom affirmative action benefits. Yet affirmative action, rooted in feelings of grateful mercy, does not attempt to deliver to the unjust offender "an eye for an eye"; it does not require nor even desire retaliatory retribution equal in severity to the centuries of oppression against women and non-Europeans. Moreover, relatively few European males will directly and personally feel the sting of affirmative action at all. Indeed, such a policy is liberally merciful, given the centuries of patriarchal oppression and given that affirmative action is a morally compelling option only so long as it is needed, only until the social conditions that produce and perpetuate injustice are dismantled and supplanted by just ones. By advocating affirmative action, then, the covenantal community extends to society the same measure of equal mercy that God in Christ extends to it. On the one hand, it delivers anger's fair compensation to victims of discrimination while at the same time mercifully delivering, in affirmative action, a benefit that strict impartiality itself cannot deliver. On the other hand, affirmative action distributes reproof (not retribution) and mercy to unjust offenders without infringing justice's requirement of fair treatment. Indeed, the confluence of these two emotional streams, hopeful anger and grateful, equal mercy, gathers to such a greatness, it can be fairly be said that the practices of it will "let justice roll down like waters, and righteousness like an everflowing stream (Amos 5:24).

My assumption, retrieved from my argument in chapter 2, is that the feelings of hopeful anger and grateful mercy constituting covenantal justice are universal and are universally accessible through the particularity of a wide variety of sacred and secular traditions. The only requirement for any person or community experiencing these emotions is that they value them and cultivate within their own local tradition dispositons of heart suited to eliciting such emotions. The question remains: On what basis can practicing just anger and equal mercy be justified as a practical possibility for the Christian community? What reasons and incentives are sufficiently compelling to inspire in Christian communities the empathetic emotions that empower them to actually put into practice projects of covenantal justice? What justification is there for acting with hopeful instead of despairing anger, with equal mercy instead of merely equal fairness? My answer here parallels a refrain familiar by now. The justification and motivation for practicing hopeful anger and grateful mercy lie not in some metaethical heaven of universal law but in concrete, local obediential habits of heart that shape the Christian story. Yet Christianity is not the only tradition on the basis of which covenantal justice can be justified. Nussbaum, in her essay "Equity and Mercy," for example, argues that ancient Stoic philosophers recommend a version of justice similar to the covenantal one set forth here.[67] But for the Christian community, participation in the eucharist, and thereby in the historical event it retrieves, inspires and empowers it with holy affections necessary and sufficient for practicing a covenantal version of justice. How so?

The feelings of hopeful anger and grateful mercy, without which the practice of covenantal justice is inconceivable, are elicited by obediential habits that are embedded in and give shape to the gospel story. The gospel story, shaped by obediential habits of responsibility and remembrance, in other words, invites the feelings of anger and mercy that inspire a community to practice covenantal justice. The reason for this is that habits of remembrance and responsibility provide two ingredients, identity and moral orientation, essential for practicing covenantal justice. The message of the Hebrew prophets in general and of Amos in particular is that Israel has become morally disoriented. It irresponsibly tolerates and promotes injustice in its land; it has become morally disoriented because it has forgotten its original identity as a *covenantal* community; it has forgotten who and whose it is. It has forgotten Abraham and Moses and Mount Sinai and Jerusalem; it has forgotten Yahweh; it has forgotten the ancient stories that preserve its origins and shape its identity as a community. Without remembering this tradition and identity, Israel becomes morally disoriented. Without remembering who it is in the past, it loses its sense of responsibility in the present and future. Without recalling and retelling the stories of God's deliverance and care, Israel loses a clear sense of its identity as a community and becomes confused about its covenantal fittedness and moral orientation. Similarly, the obediential habit of remembered fittedness is pivotal for Jesus' own sense of identity and mission. As already noted, the power that enables him to fulfill his mission is derived from his keen sense of acting in continuity and solidarity with Israel's ancient covenant. Jesus declares, "Think not that I have come to abolish the law and the prophets; I have come not to abolish them but to fulfill them" (Matthew 5:17). Remembrance endows Jesus' life and ministry with a powerful identity, one that gives them an unambiguous moral direction. In the remainder of this discourse Jesus speaks of how exceedingly dangerous remembrance can be when a community retrieves and reenacts all the law and the prophets, swearing no oaths, turning the other cheek, loving even its enemies. The specific historical identity that memory retrieves for him fittingly places him within the context of a covenantal community to which he is accountable and for which he is morally responsible. Similarly, when Jesus stands in the synagogue and reads the lesson from Isaiah, it is an act both of remembrance and responsibility, an act of identity and moral commitment. He derives inspiration and justification for his ministry by claiming for himself an identity continuous with Israel's ancient covenantal tradition, in which God and his people stand in solidarity not only with the poor, captive, blind, and oppressed but also with foreigners like Zarephath from Sidon and Naaman the Syrian. Luke tells us just how threatening such remembrance is for guardians of conventional wisdom. Those that heard Jesus rose up and put him out of the city, and led him to the brow of the hill . . . that they might throw him down headlong (4:28–29).

What happens when a community loses the dispositions of remembrance and responsibility that are crucial for establishing a community's identity and moral orientation, for inspiring hopeful anger and grateful mercy, is analogous to the fate of a person suffering from Korsakoff's psychosis, a neurological disorder involving the loss of memory. Oliver Sacks writes movingly of a patient, Mr. Thompson, who suffers from Korsakoff's psychosis: "he remembered nothing for more than a few seconds. He was continually disoriented. Abysses of amnesia continually opened beneath him, but he would bridge them nimbly, by fluent confabulations and fictions of all kinds."[68] Because of his failed memory, Mr. Thompson suffers a loss of identity, of the awareness of who he was, is, and can be. What Sacks says about Mr. Thompson, it seems to me, accents the significance of habits of remembrance and responsibility for eliciting those empathetic emotions necessary for practicing covenantal justice. Memory functions as a source and basis for both self-identity and moral orientation. If we want to know a person, a community, "we ask," says Sacks, " 'what is his story—his real, inmost story?'—for each of us is a biography, a story. . . . Biologically, physiologically, we are not so different from each other; historically, as narratives—we are each of us unique." Memory reminds a community of its story, its history, its identity, without which it becomes morally disoriented. A community "needs such a narrative, a continuous inner narrative, to maintain [its] identity, [its] self."[69] Remembrance of its narrative history shapes a community's identity, orients its moral life, and endows its life with meaning, its raison d'être. The antidote for a community wrestling with forgetfulness and disorientation is cultivating habits of remembrance and responsibility. If it is to know who it is and what it is to be, it must possess and repossess its life story, re-collect the gospel narrative without which it loses both its identity and its sense of moral orientation. By combining habits of remembrance and responsibility, moreover, a community renders itself dangerous, as Sharon Welch argues in *A Feminist Ethic of Risk*. Together these habits subvert attitudes and structures of injustice in all its subtle forms, while at the same time liberating the oppressed. That is why the eucharist is such a dangerous event in the life of the community and why Fletcher rightfully calls Christianity's ethic a eucharistic one. In and through the eucharist a community not only recalls who it is and what it is fitted to do but is empowered to practice a radical pattern of covenantal justice justified by the gospel story. Failing to practice covenantal justice, accordingly, indicates a failure of remembrance and therein a failure of identity so profound that instead of delivering redemption the community of faith finds itself in need of redemption.

What consequences await the community whose memory fails, that suffers a spiritual version of Korsakoff's psychosis? Like Mr. Thompson, the forgetful community does not stop telling stories, for deep in the human soul there is what Sacks calls a "narrative need." This need coupled with forgetfulness leads to a kind of "desperate tale-telling," a "verbosity." "Deprived of continuity, of quiet, continuous, inner narrative," the forgetful community is "driven to a sort of narrational frenzy—hence [its] ceaseless tales, [its] confabulations, [its] mythomania." Unable or unwilling to recall its genuine narrative tradition, the forgetful community is "driven to the proliferation of pseudo-narratives, in a pseudo-continuity, pseudo-worlds peopled by pseudo-people, phantasms."[70] Forgetfulness drives Christians to invent or co-opt alien stories of justice that for a genuinely covenantal community are disingenuous pseudonarratives discontinuous with its own gospel story. No community survives without story. In spite of its loss of memory, a community will attempt to improvise on the spot, continually inventing or co-opting new and different stories of justice; inventing, as Sacks puts it, "bridges of meaning over abysses of meaninglessness,"[71] inventing and reinventing its identity, its world, its orientation in order to keep it from vanishing entirely. For the Christian community, the antidote for loss of memory, for being co-opted by alien stories, and for vanishing entirely is, again, the eucharist. For in this event most profoundly the community is summoned to remember who it is and what its responsibilities are. In this event most profoundly it remembers God's merciful justice toward humanity. In this event most profoundly it participates in the covenant of redemption. In this event most profoundly it expresses its gratitude and is empowered to deliver to the world the same depth of covenantal justice that it receives from Christ.

What follows for a Christian community that remembers who it is and what it is to do? First it acknowledges that liberal versions of justice as fairness are in themselves of insufficient depth to embrace and sustain justice as a Christian virtue. It acknowledges that anger's desire for fairness must be transformed by eucharistic feelings of grateful mercy, according to which justice is primarily a manifestation of a spiritual relationship and not merely of a human relationship, of a relationship with God and not merely with humans. That empathetic feelings of equal mercy are common and universally accessible to humans does not diminish but rather intensifies the need for them to be urged upon Christian communities that are uniquely situated to practice them. Second, it follows that, for the Christian community, the incentive and justification for practicing deep, covenantal justice cannot simply be an appeal of universal, rational laws that can be commanded. Rather, justification and incentive for feeling hopeful anger and grateful mercy require particularity. The universal, empathetic feelings that empower a community to practice covenantal justice are elicited and inspired by the local, tribal particularity of the gospel reenacted in the eucharist. It is this story, shaped by those obediential habits of remembrance and responsibility, that invites precisely those empathetic emotions necessary and sufficient for a faithful community to practice covenantal justice.

Although I think this view of convenantal justice (as well as covenantal love and peace) is compelling, questions linger. Is not this covenantal version of Christian virtues, set forth in part II, an entirely sectarian one, one so local, tribal, and confessional that it cannot withstand the scrutiny of critical reason? Is it not so tribal and confessional that it renders itself irrelevant to communities different from itself and incomprehensible to society as a whole? Is it not a terribly private, Christian ethic and not a public one at all? These are provocative and legitimate questions, all of which are addressed in part III. In particular, I try to show how covenantal love, peace, and justice converge in the experience of compassion in such a way as to render the covenantal ethic of Christian virtue entirely relevant and comprehensible to society as a whole and resilient when scrutinized by critical reason.

Another a question, posed in chapter 1, for attention at this juncture: What is the difference between the Pharisee and the disreputable woman, between admiring Jesus and following him? The answer to this question, fidelity of heart, is now clearer. Following requires, in a way admiring does not, that a community faithfully cultivate and nurture certain virtues of the heart, especially covenantal virtues of love, peace, and justice. Following Christ requires that it develop all the obediential dispositions I have set forth. These dispositions elicit certain empathetic emotions whose collective power is sufficient to inspire it to devote itself personally and passionately to Christ, lavishing on him, as did the disreputable woman, its self, its heart, and its life.

PART III

The Heart in Public Life

The grace that is the health of creatures
Can only be held in common.

Wendell Berry, "Healing"

6

Compassion as Public Covenant

WHAT BOTHERED THE LAWYER MOST, as he listened to Jesus' story about the Samaritan, was not that religious leaders were disparagingly depicted nor that as a Jew he should be required to show compassion even toward his enemies. What bothered him was a gradual realization that, according to this rabbi at least, his duty to show compassion places him on equal moral footing with people of other, even hostile, traditions. What bothered him was that fact that in remaining faithful to his own religious commitment and community he would be obligated to share common moral ground with Samaritans and Romans.

The aim of this chapter is to answer the question, How is a public covenant possible? How is it that people of diverse and sometimes hostile traditions can possibly find ways to cooperate on matters public and political? The resources currently available for constructing a "public covenant"[1] tend to polarize into two camps, liberal and communitarian. "On the one side are those who champion the priority of the right, or justice, for determining ethical norms." Defending this turf are neo-Kantians such as Rawls, William Galston, and Beckley. "On the other side," says William Rehg, "stand those for whom more substantive notions of good [or virtue] or community are ethically prior,"[2] the likes of MacIntyre, Michael Sandel, and Hauerwas. The ensuing battle is often formulated in terms of justice versus virtue, individual versus community, command versus character. My purpose is to show that, although on the surface these two traditions tend to polarize, justice and virtue are in fact morally and logically connected by the common experience of compassion.

Quite a number of efforts, dedicated to mediating this liberal–communitarian conflict, assume that by adjusting one claim or another a compromise can be struck.[3] In my estimation, these endeavors for the most part are unsuccessful because they fail to recognize that compassion is an experience common to both traditions. My thesis is that love, peace, and justice as Christian virtues converge in the experience of compassion and this experience underwrites the moral worth of both justice and virtue and forms the basis on which a covenant in public life is possible. I begin by contrasting the concerns of liberal justice with the concerns of communitarian virtue. Second, after analyzing the nature of compassion, I show that it is an experience of sufficient moral depth to embrace the concerns of both liberal justice and communitarian virtue; indeed, that compassion is the basis on which justice and virtue are morally justified. Third, I show how compassion functions as a guiding principle of public policy. Finally, I argue that if compassion is normative for public life, it must be a central feature of public education.

Liberal Justice and Communitarian Virtue

One way that liberal justice and communitarian virtue differ is this: whereas liberal values presuppose that public life should be determined by what I shall call contractual attachments, communitarian values presuppose that it should be determined by constitutive attachments. For the purposes of this chapter, let "liberal justice" stand for contractual attachments in public life—for individual rights and freedom; let "communitanian virtue" stand for constitutive attachments—for community and for mutual, social responsibilities. My immediate aim is not to provide a comprehensive analysis of liberalism and communitanianism—I believe both contribute important moral values to public life—but distinguish them in order ultimately to show how each is rooted in the common soil of compassion. In doing so, I let the work of Rawls, Galston, and Beckley stand for the concerns of liberal justice and the work of Sandel and Hauerwas for communitarian virtue.

It is well known that liberal versions of public life have traditionally employed the term "social contract" to refer to the kind of attachments that should obtain among citizens, hence the phrase "contractual attachments." John Cobb suggests that in the liberal tradition what separates individuals from each other is prior to what connects them. The question of how an individual relates to others is still a relevant question, "but since these relations will have no fundamental effect on the relata, this will remain a secondary question. Primary will be what each thing is in itself.[4] Not surprisingly, then, liberalism develops a view "in which social allegiance is generated only to the extent to which persons' rational self-interest is served"[5] (Hobbes) or private property is protected (Locke). In either case, *Homo economicus* remains "self-existent and only incidentally bound up with families and communities, . . . a self-enclosed individual who calculates self-interest rationally."[6]

Social allegiances based on rational self-interest and private property imply a liberal, Rawlsian conception of justice that Beckley suggests is congenial with the basic convictions of Christian faith. Beckley argues that Christian love, as equal regard, "affirms each of the beliefs that underlie Rawls's original position, even though Christian love requires more than justice." Christians should promote human rationality, freedom, and equality as those Rawlsian values around which a conception of public life should revolve.[7] Moreover, these liberal values "carry weight," Beckley insists, "without being derived from prior duties or obligations owed to society or assigned to their particular social role."[8] Instead, liberal values are derived from something like Rawls's "veil of ignorance." Beckley observes that Rawls's veil of ignorance entails that our principles of justice must be "general (include no references to individuals), universal (hold for everyone), [and] final (they are the ultimate court of appeal for disputes about justice), must order conflicting claims, and must be public (both the principles and the grounds of the justification must be known to all).... The veil of ignorance... brackets knowledge of... particular conceptions of the good and actual interests."[9] Indeed, since liberal justice requires that attachments in public life remain contractual (i.e., abstract, objective, and impersonal), it follows that they will bear only accidentally and incidentally on the self's identity. Accordingly, as Cobb observes, the contractual attachments of liberal justice can be subtracted without altering the identity of the self. So if any attachment of liberal justice (e.g., religious freedom) is subtracted from the public experience of a Mennonite, Marxist, or Buddhist, their identities and values as Mennonite and Marxist and Buddhist will remain fundamentally unaltered. Whether a person is guaranteed freedom of religion or ideology, of course, is important, but because the attachments liberal justice establishes are general, abstract, and impersonal they are attachments that a person can stand apart from without altering self-identity. One's identity as a Buddhist (e.g., the Dalia Lama in Tibet) or Christian (Solzhenitsyn in Soviet Russia) remains unchanged whether freedom of religion is guaranteed or not. This is not to say, of course, that in a liberal society communitarian values and ends cannot be pursued, only that, as Rawls and Beckley point out, they cannot be pursued publicly as a matter of public policy. Indeed, communitanian virtue and ends, as Rawls insists, "cannot be upheld by the coercive apparatus of the state."[10]

In contrast, advocates of communitanian virtue insist that public attachments among citizens should be primarily constitutive. In some important sense, what connects persons to each other (mutual responsibilities) is in public life prior to what separates them (rights and freedoms), so that the identity of a person essentially, and not merely incidentally, involves relations with others. Public life is so constituted that the identity of any self necessarily involves reference to certain communal attachments and responsibilities from which that identity is inseparable. As Cobb puts it, in society there are "no units [i.e., selves] that can accurately be understood apart from the communities that they constitute with one another." The interests of individuals cannot be separated from the interests of the total community, for "the well-being of any one entity is largely dependent on the well-being [of the public whole]."[11]

Sandel advocates a conception of public life based on communitarian attachments. "We cannot regard ourselves as independent in this [liberal] way without great cost to those loyalties and convictions whose moral force consists partly in the fact that living by them is inseparable from . . . [who we are] as members of this family or community or nation or people." Communitarian allegiances demand more than "justice requires or even permits, not by reason of agreements I have made but instead in virtue of those more or less enduring attachments and commitments which taken together partly define the person I am."[12] The meaning Sandel gives the phrase "constitutive attachments" corresponds quite precisely to what communitarians mean by public virtue: a self whose identity is integrally shaped by allegiances to others, to a community. Accordingly, "a person incapable of constitutive attachments . . . is not," Sandel insists, "an ideally free and rational agent, but . . . a person wholly without character, without moral depth."[13] Constitutive attachments presuppose and preserve the integrity of personal relations and mutual responsibilities that persons ought not be required to separate themselves from in public life.

In theology, the writings of Hauerwas tend toward a communitarian approach to public life. "The church," he insists, "doesn't have a social strategy, the church is a social strategy. Consequently, "the church need not worry about whether to be in the world. The church's only concern is how to be in the world, in what form, for what purpose."[14] Drawing on the work of Yoder,[15] Hauerwas opts for a model of the church as confessional community. This model "finds its main political task to lie, not in the personal transformation of individual hearts [conversionist model] or the modification of society [activist model], but rather in the congregations determination to worship Christ in all things."[16] Indeed, no community exists for whom constitutive attachments are more important than a worshiping community, a community for and to whom each member is essentially interrelated much as are the parts of a body. Members of a confessing community maintain with each other commitments and loves that they cannot imagine standing apart from without being radically changed. That is why Hauerwas argues that in public life "*faithfulness* rather than effectiveness is the goal of a confessing church," for a community's faithfulness to God and to itself results in truthful witness in and to society.[17] Society, accordingly, needs the church to be faithful "because, without the church, the world does not know who it is" and how it can be redeemed.[18]

Hauerwas is not terribly clear about the shape a society's public life might take if a society is persuaded by the church's faithful witness. Presumably it would look something like the Christian community itself, a society somehow incrementally absorbed into the Christian way of life. Indeed, that seems to be what Hauerwas advocates when he approvingly quotes Lindbeck's hope that theology would now undertake "the ancient practice of absorbing the universe into the biblical world."[19] The point to which I want to draw attention here is not the details of Hauerwas's picture of what public life might look like but the communitarian values that would underwrite it. For him, a society's public life will be one in which relations among citizens are somehow constitutive, one in which, as Robin Lovin suggests, "the members are bound together by choice, by mutual commitment; one in which the members see their moral obligations as growing out of this commitment. Above all, the covenant creates . . . mutual accountability not only to one another, but before God."[20]

PUBLIC COVENANT AS COMPASSION

Given the differing priorities of liberal justice and communitarian virtue in public life, how is it possible for the Christian to construct a public covenant? Any answer to this question worth serious consideration must somehow account for both liberalism's concern for justice in public life and communitarianism's concern for virtue. My premise is that compassion is an experience of sufficient moral depth to embrace in public life both the values of liberal justice and communitarian virtue. In the common experience of compassion, these values are woven together into a fabric strong enough to bear the weight of a public covenant. Furthermore, compassion, as I will show, involves no single emotion but families of emotions correlated to the occasion that warrants a caring response. For the Christian community, the many obediential dispositions and empathetic emotions of heart belonging to covenantal love, peace, and justice contribute to the community's experience of compassion. Occasions for compassion call forth and upon the Christian community's experience of virtue in such a way as to thrust it into the heart of the public square.

Beginning in the seventeenth century, but especially in the eighteenth century, as Norman Fiering puts it, "the idea of irresistible compassion became a psychological dogma, and more than ever a touchstone not only of true civility but of human status itself."[21] Thinkers such as Malebranche, Hutcheson, Hume, and Smith argued that compassion is a natural and irrepressible passion by which public life, and even reason, should be guided. Although many of the attributes these philosophers ascribed to compassion would today be considered doubtful,[22] the spirit and force of their arguments are commensurable with what I am proposing here. More recently, Scheler's perceptive phenomenological work *The Nature of Sympathy* gratefully critiques the nineteenth centurys naturalistic theory of sympathy and places it on its proper moral footing. Regrettably, twentieth-century philosophers and theologians, as Prior argues, in large part abandoned "the sentiment of compassion" and as a result "produce a distorted picture of our moral lives."[23] Hauerwas is a case in point. In a chapter titled "Killing Compassion" in *Dispatches from the Front: Theological Engagements with the Secular,* he argues that compassion is the quintessential "liberal virtue" that sometimes leads liberals to engage in violence (e.g., capital punishment, war) that kills. He quotes approvingly from Oliver O'Donovan, who likewise identifies compassion as "the appropriate virtue for a liberal revolution, which requires no independent

thinking about the object of morality, only a very strong motivation to its practice."[24] Hauerwas finally comes to reject compassion as a genuinely Christian
virtue because it is rooted in an ethos of liberalism that he insists is destroying
us. Hauerwas's dismissal of compassion on the pretext that it is, apparently exclusively, a liberal value smacks of political posturing instead of keen analysis of
an otherwise compelling and common moral experience. Regardless of his motives for disowning compassion, however, the reasons he gives for doing so con-
ceal certain assumptions characteristic of the Enlightenment tradition he otherwise is eager to critique. First, his portrayal of compassion as basically a liberal
virtue ironically habors an ahistorical habit of mind. He assumes that a local and
narrowly parochial "liberal" version of compassion, rooted in eighteenth-century
England, somehow constitutes what compassion has been, is, and can only be.
He assumes reductively that a fairly recent and restricted liberal version of compassion embodies and exhausts the moral nature and practice of compassion.
Second, Hauerwas's view of compassion too much favors Enlightenment sentiments insofar as he seems to accept O'Donovan's view that those emotions constituting compassion are somehow irrational, noncognitive experiences that "require no independent thinking about the object of morality."[25] The time has long
since passed, I think, in which emotions, such as compassion, can be simply and
carelessly discarded by treating them as if they were simple, noncognitive, amoral
natural states, as Hauerwas, at least at this point, seems to. Emotions are cognitive
experiences and by their very nature make comprehensible judgments about objects of morality and the moral projects implied by those judgments. Hauerwas
seems to represent at this point a general tendency of narrative theologians to
ignore or diminish the significance of emotions in moral thought and practice,
even though, as I argued in chapter 2, narrative and emotions are interdepen-
dently and inexorably related to one another. Compassion, of course, is a normative moral experience deeply rooted in biblical tradition and properly practiced
by Christian communities over the centuries quite independently of any knowledge or interest in the recent, parochial political agenda of liberalism. I suspect
that compassion is partly an incorrigible moral category for Hauerwas because
he has not undertaken a clear and careful analysis of the nature of human emotions, of their affinity with narrative frameworks, and of the critical role they play
in the character and life of moral communities. Given the narrative inclination
of his theology and the fact that narrative is the means whereby we naturally and
logically access and educate moral emotions, it is not surprising that his writings
do include discussions of emotions such as love, anger, patience, forgiveness,
mercy, peace, and honor. Yet his inclusion of emotional experiences is largely
incidental to his chief concern, the narrative dimension of moral communities.

This contemporary neglect of compassion contrasts with the biblical portrait
of Jesus' public life, which is sketched largely in terms of compassion. Jesus'
passion, death, and resurrection, of course, cannot be properly understood in-

dependent of the experience of compassion. Nussbaum notes this fact when she comments that "the universal compassion for human suffering which one associates with Christianity at its best is difficult to imagine apart from the paradigm of human suffering and sacrifice exemplified in Christ."[26] For Christians, God's compassion for humanity is a paradigmatic moral category for relationships among humans and human communities. Indeed, compassion is central to the gospel story and the character of Christian community in at least two ways. First, of the many ways the biblical writers understand and interpret the incarnation, one of the most common and compelling is the way they envisage God entering human life by sharing emotionally in its joys and sorrows. The love that bridges the abyss between divine and human means little if not that, as Irenaeus long ago suggested, God in Christ recapitulates human experience in his own life, somehow sharing the emotional life of those whom Christ seeks to redeem. The writer of Hebrews especially insists on this point when he says that because Jesus participates in human suffering, temptations, and weaknesses, he is able to redeem humanity (Hebrews 2:17–18, 4:14–16). Similarly, Nussbaum grants that "in order to imagine a god who is truly superior, truly worthy of worship, truly and fully just, we must imagine a god who has actually lived out the nontranscendent life and understands it in the only way it can be understood, by suffering and death."[27] Compassion is the supreme moral experience through which God truly enters human experience in order to redeem it; and it is the common moral experience whereby humans share that redemption among themselves.

A second way that compassion constitutes the meaning of Jesus's life is suggested by the Apostle Paul, who enjoins us to have in ourselves the same love, joy, affection, sympathy, and humility of mind as does Christ Jesus (see Philippians 2). Compassion ought to be a primary way in which Christians relate to others. It is the balm that heals and redeems wounded lives. The poignancy of the parable of the good Samaritan dramatizes the healing powers of compassion. Estranged by ancient habits of racial, religious, and cultural animosities, the Samaritan is nevertheless persuaded of the redemptive quality of compassion. Similarly, a primary way in which the Christian community appropriates and projects into the public square the life and death of Jesus is by internalizing compassion and making it a habit of its public life. In short, compassion is a normative moral experience that for the covenantal Christian community ought to determine the shape of public life. Before showing how this should happen, I will examine the nature of compassion,[28] an examination I undertake here in terms of the other, the self, and the relationship of self and other.

The Other

Who is "the other," or the proper object, of compassion? Lawrence Blum's answer restricts the other of compassion to "a person in a negative condition, suffering some harm, difficulty, danger."[29] Virtually all who treat the subject of compassion

agree with Blum, including Solomon, who insists that "the most obvious speci-
fying feature of compassion ('suffering with') is that the object of one's concern
is somehow 'in pain.' "[30] But of course humans experience many negative conditions that are perhaps occasions for personal but are not properly occasions for
public compassion, for example, what is endured by the parents whose child dies
of a congenital disease. Certain criteria are needed, therefore, whereby we can
judge when the distress of others is a legitimate object of public compassion and
policy. I note three: that suffering be relatively central, involuntary, and social.

First, Blum suggests that compassion is appropriate when the condition of
one's suffering is "relatively central to a person's life and well-being, describable
as pain, misery, hardship, suffering, affliction, and the like." This does not mean
that a person's "overall condition [must] be difficult or miserable," only that she
is experiencing some significant suffering.[31] A wealthy person who loses a plane
and yacht in a hurricane no doubt suffers, but her suffering is not such as to be
considered central to her well-being and survival. On the other hand, the suffering
of a laborer who loses his job because a factory closes involves a suffering central
to his well-being.

Second, the suffering must be involuntary: the result of conditions for which
one is not directly responsible and from which one possesses neither power nor
the means to extract oneself. The single mother who lives in poverty and is unable
to find employment suffers involuntarily and is properly an object of public compassion. The requirement that suffering be involuntary allows for the fact that it
is not uncommon for people, for whatever religious or ideological reasons, to
willingly place themselves in conditions that cause them suffering. This sort of
voluntary, sacrificial suffering is crucial to a Christian conception of compassion
and vital for embodying love in public life. Such cases, insofar as they are voluntary and sacrificial, are not properly objects of public compassion.

Third, limiting the object of public compassion to "social" suffering recognizes
that not all involuntary suffering is properly the concern of public policy. Suffering must result from negative social, rather than personal, conditions. In suffering involuntarily the illness and death of a child, parents are indeed in need
of compassion. But since the source of that suffering is the result of personal and
not social conditions, their suffering is not an occasion for public compassion
but is properly an occasion for compassion from those with whom one is related
personally. If the illness and death are due to social conditions, then they become
a matter of public health and hence of public compassion.

The Samaritan's compassion for the injured man satisfies these three criteria.
Certainly the injured man suffered greatly; he was half dead. His suffering was
involuntary, at the hand of robbers; he found himself in conditions out of which
he was unable to extricate himself. Finally, his suffering was the result of conditions produced by a social phenomenon (i.e., violence), not personal.

The Self

What, then, does it take for a person to be compassionate? What does it take for a community to cultivate in its members habits of compassionate concern? By all accounts, the experience of compassion consists of two qualities; empathetic emotion and narrative imagination. Although when we think of compassion we think of feelings, "compassion is not a simple feeling-state," Blum insists. Rather, it is "a complex emotional attitude toward another, characteristically involving imaginative dwelling on the condition of the other person, an active regard for his good, a view of him as a fellow human being, and emotional responses of a certain degree of intensity."[32] But what sort of emotional experience does compassion entail? Must the compassionate person "feel with" the other, feel the same thing the other feels? Or must one only "feel for" the suffering other? Adrian Piper at times seems to suggest the former. He argues that compassion involves empathy, the capacity "to comprehend viscerally the inner state that motivates the other's overt behavior by experiencing concurrently with that behavior a correspondingly similar 'inner' state oneself, as a direct and immediate quality of one's own condition. . . . I empathetically experience subliminal sensations of pain in interpreting your wincing, grimacing, and putting your hand to your forehead."[33]

However, if compassion requires that I experience empathetically inner states similar to those of others, it would seem that many occasions appropriate for compassion would be inaccessible to me. In Toni Morrison's novel *Beloved*, for example, Paul D can't understand why Sethe has taken into her home Beloved, a stranger and apparent vagabond woman who wandered onto Sethe's stoop one day and about whom she knows precious little. Paul D wants Beloved out; Sethe replies: "Feel how it feels to be a colored woman roaming the roads with anything God made liable to jump on you. Feel that."[34] But Paul D seems unable to empathize, and not surprisingly: the pain, hurt, and humiliation a colored woman experiences when threatened with sexual assault are no doubt inaccessible to Paul D as a man; he cannot empathetically experience a "similar inner state"—he cannot share with her the character and intensity of her pain. But although he may not be able to "feel with" Beloved, he can, as Blum and Solomon suggest, "feel for" her. This distinction between "feel with" and "feel for" is a distinction Scheler similarly makes when speaking of various forms of sympathy. What he calls "feeling-in-common" parallels "feel with" and is in intensity and degree accessible only to those actually experiencing the event and the "keenness of emotion internal to the event." Abused women, for example, have feeling-in-common with one another. What Scheler calls "fellow-feeling" parallels "feel for" and is a feeling accessible even to those who are not experiencing the event itself but who can, with "intentional reference to that event, imagine what it might feel like, even though the intensity of that feeling will not be as keen."[35] Hence a man might have fellow-feeling for the experience of women who have been abused, though not having had the experience himself. Although Paul D cannot feel-in-common with Beloved, he can experience fellow-feeling with her in her pain.

A person can "feel compassionately for an other," accordingly, by attempting what Blum calls some degree of "imaginative reconstruction."[36] The capacity to imagine the conditions suffered by an other establishes the possibility of feeling for that other. Compassion, as imaginative reconstruction, does not require that the self "experience the sort of suffering that occasions it." However, Blum notes, the imagination does permit us to "commiserate with someone who has lost a child in a fire, even if we do not have a child or have never lost someone we love."[37] Certainly I should attempt to imagine the conditions, attitudes, values, and sensations the other must be experiencing. Yet I may not be able to feel exactly what the other is feeling but only able to begin to "feel for" the other. The weight my imagination must bear, then, is not that of generating some similarity of "inner states" but that of dwelling on another's plight such that I feel for her in her suffering, even if the full intensity and depth of her pain is inaccessible to me.

But is imaginative reconstruction a sufficient condition for all occasions warranting compassion? Nancy Snow thinks not. For her, although she accepts the imagination as sufficient for compassionate identification in many cases, it is not sufficient in all. Sometimes, she says, "imagination is impotent in portraying the experiences of others in distress." Yet she goes on to argue that we still "are able to identify with them in a way that allows for a compassionate response."[38] How so? Snow's answer is in terms of beliefs. Although the details of Snow's theory lie beyond the scope of this analysis, the gist of it is relevant, namely, that even if we are not able to imaginatively feel for suffering others, we can still "identify with their distress because we believe that we, too, or those close to us, can suffer misfortune, as they have."[39] Even though Paul D cannot imaginatively identify with the plight of a colored woman and her vulnerability to assault by "anything God made," still, as a colored man in post-Reconstruction America, he is vulnerable to indiscriminate assault by any white man and through his vulnerability he can identify somewhat with Beloved's plight and understand Sethe's feeling for her. Hence, failing imaginative reconstruction, belief in "our own vulnerability and that of others is sufficient for the rationality of compassion."[40] Of course many people fail on both counts at times. Belief in one's invulnerability or in the security of employment or simple conceit may prevent us from feeling compassion when occasions call for it. Nevertheless, Blum's "imaginative reconstruction" along with Snow's "belief in one's own vulnerability" together form the two foci on the basis of which the self is able to identify with and feel for suffering others.

Relation of Self and Other

How then can we characterize the compassionate relationship between self and other? Two elements are pertinent to answering this question: emotional intersubjectivity and beneficent action.

Of the many ways in which humans relate to one another, one of the most profound involves experiences of emotional intersubjectivity; these are common experiences, both positive and negative, wherein humans share the intimacy of their emotional lives. As Solomon suggests, in emotion "we 'open ourselves' to others, allow ourselves to share their experiences and opinions, their world views, and, ultimately, their other emotions."[41] Similarly, Blum argues that "compassion involves . . . a sense of shared humanity, of regarding the other as a fellow human being. This means that the other person's suffering is seen as the kind of thing that could happen to anyone, including oneself insofar as one is a human being."[42] What compassionate intersubjectivity calls for, then, is a self "engrossed"[43] in the experience of the suffering other. Engrossment, as Jean Grimshaw explains, involves the self in a process of "apprehending the reality of the other . . . a putting aside of self and an entering into the experience of another as far as possible."[44] Engrossment is the sacrificial suffering which Jesus embodies in his ministry and to which he calls his disciples. What is important to note here is the significance compassionate engrossment has for social and political life. By requiring me to share in the emotional life of another, by requiring the experience of another to become mine, compassion equalizes our identities, at least in terms of suffering. Perhaps this is why compassion in public life is so readily neglected: it presupposes a fundamental equality among humans. As Blum observes, the practice of compassion promotes "the experience of equality, even when accompanied by an acknowledgement of actual social inequality. Compassion forbids regarding social inequality as establishing human inequality. This is part of the moral force of compassion: by transcending . . . social inequality, it promotes the sensed experience of common humanity."[45] The parable of the good Samaritan suggests that the social distance dramatized by the indifference of priest and Levite is overcome by the Samaritan's act of compassionate care.

That compassion presupposes a fundamental social equality introduces a second feature of the self's relation to the other: beneficent action. It may seem obvious that beneficent action is a constituent of compassion, but compassion is often confused with related feelings like sympathy or pity that do not necessarily entail such action. As Snow suggests, sympathetic feelings are generally both less intense and less altruistic, though still desirable; compassion requires a greater investment of the self in the other. A "concern for the other's good . . . expressed in benevolent other-regarding . . . actions" partly distinguishes compassion from related experiences like sympathy.[46] "It is not enough," insists Blum, "that we imaginatively reconstruct someone's suffering: for, like belief, such imagining is compatible with malice and mere intellectual curiosity." Hence, the self and object are related not only emotionally but altruistically, not only by feeling for an other but also by undertaking projects on behalf of the other. Compassion is not therefore "a momentary feeling of concern, it is rather to act consistently and reliably 'in such a way calculated to relieve the other's distress.' "[47] Jesus' identification with human suffering and weakness was not simply sympathetic feeling, as the writer Hebrews makes clear, but practical, so that he might help those who are in need (see Hebrews 2:17–18; 4:14–16).

All this is again provocatively portrayed in the parable of the good Samaritan, where compassion involves more than imagining and feeling what the injured man must be suffering. For all we know, the priest and Levite might well have imagined this and still passed by. As altruistic, compassion ultimately includes other-regarding projects and compels us to think of ways whereby we might alleviate the other's suffering. Indeed, "compassionate acts often involve acting very much contrary to one's moods and inclinations. Compassion is fundamentally other-regarding; [and] its affective status in no way detracts from this."[48]

JUSTICE AND VIRTUE AS COMPASSION

This analysis of compassion—as care for those whose suffering is central, involuntary, and social—allows me to show more concretely how liberal justice and communitarian virtue are justified and reconciled by the experience of compassionate care.

Liberal notions of injustice are most often construed as violations of rights and freedoms. If I were to ask a person committed to liberal justice why discrimination according to race is wrong, most likely the answer would be "Because it violates a persons right of fair treatment." This kind of discourse, what Mary Ann Glendon refers to as our "rights dialect," is generally familiar and persuasive to Americans.[49] Yet, although we are able to articulate legal justifications for public policies, we often are at a loss in public discourse to articulate the relevant moral justifications. Justice, equal opportunity, discrimination, and so on are not merely matters of rights and freedoms, although they are that. For Christians, rights and freedoms sprout from seeds of moral conviction regarding the dignity of humans created in God's image. Compassion is the normative moral experience that connects this basic human dignity with political rights; it is an experience that endows justice with moral justification and emotional depth. How so? In that injustice causes involuntary social suffering, and any moral society should care for those whose suffering is social and involuntary and protect its citizens as far as possible from such suffering. A society is obligated therefore to act compassionately toward those suffering injustice.

Consider Galston's treatment of justice.[50] It revolves around three principles: individual choice, equal distribution according to individual need, and equality of opportunity. His discussion focuses on equality of opportunity and, persuasive as it is, is almost entirely lacking in moral depth. He speaks of equality of opportunity in terms of "gifts and talents," "social and natural differences," "need and desert," "fair competition," "personal development," and so on. This contractarian discourse, like Rawls's (and Beckley's) "veil of ignorance" and "principle of difference," is clearly articulated and essential to any society aspiring to embrace justice. Yet it is a "rights dialect," for the most part a one-dimensional, political dialect, and Galston's discourse is largely confined to it. It lacks the depth and power it might possess if it were to explicitly articulate the common experience of compassion that underwrites it. For Galston to say, for example, that "many opportunities . . . are to be allocated to individuals through a desert-based competition in which all have a fair chance to participate" (equality of opportunity)[51] presupposes but fails to articulate the substantive moral good (i.e., compassion) anchoring his views. Any infringement of equality of opportunity, and a *fortiori* of any rights or freedoms, produces the involuntary kind of negative social conditions that are legitimate occasions for compassion. As Nussbaum insists, "compassion [is] an essential ingredient of any human justice."[52] Grounding liberal justice in the normative experience of compassion, then, is to uncover its moral fiber and ultimately to recognize, as I will here, its connection to virtue.

My quarrel with advocates of liberal justice, like Rawls, Beckley, and Galston, then, is not so much that they fail to acknowledge compassion as a source of justice; certainly they do. My quarrel is that they neglect to articulate this moral source and justification of compassion as fully and explicitly as they do its rational source and justification. As Sandel suggests, the view of the moral self implicit in Rawls's theory of justice and in most theories that restrict public life to justice concerns remains underdeveloped. Why? Whereas "for Hume, we need justice because we do not love each other well enough, for Rawls we need justice because we cannot know each other well enough for even love to serve alone."[53] Rawls may very well have a way to respond to this objection, but he would be compelled to include in his response, it seems to me, a fuller analysis and articulation of the self as agent of the moral quality, compassion, that constitutes the moral source of and justification for justice in public life. Furthermore, by undertaking such an analysis of compassion, Rawls would ultimately discover that compassion is not only the moral source and justification of justice but equally the justification for enfranchising the values of communitarian virtue in public life. To the extent that advocates of liberalism neglect to accent compassion as justice's moral source, accordingly, to that extent they unwittingly dramatize the priest (in Jesus' parable) whose public indifference to the man in need, absent the call of compassion, appears as an act of "self-absorption."

By "self-absorption"[54] I mean that liberal justice tends to invest the energy called for by public compassion only when the self perceives its own rights and freedoms as directly or indirectly threatened in the experience of an other. When self-absorbed, one's sense of public compassion tends to restrict itself to those occasions when one feels one's own self (i.e., rights) threatened by and in the plight of another. Why this is so results from a certain mixture of beliefs and attitudes about justice in public life that excludes a public sense of mutual accountability and responsibility when the suffering of others does not directly or indirectly place one's own rights in jeopardy. So the liberal tradition properly encourages public compassion when any individual's rights and freedoms are infringed because telescoped within that individual's plight is potentially the plight of every self, but it does not encourage public compassion when values of communitarian virtue are at stake. Rawls insists on this: "We need not suppose that persons never make substantial sacrifices for one another, since moved by affection and ties of sentiment they often do. But such actions are not demanded as a matter of justice by the basic structure of society."[55] By so arguing Rawls fails to recognize that the moral source and justification underwriting justice in public life, namely, compassion, is common to and interdependent with the moral source and justification for virtue in public life. This failure is why he, along with Beckley, can argue that only concerns of liberal justice, and not concerns of communitarian virtue, can be "publicly recognized . . . and upheld by the coercive apparatus of the state."[56] So the self-absorbed priest, not perceiving his own welfare threatened by the injured man, passes on by. But if, because of the man's injuries, governing authorities had decided to disallow solitary travelers on that stretch of road, the self-absorbed would feel their rights and freedoms threatened and lobby in opposition to such illiberal policies. Restricting "the coercive apparatus of the state" to concerns of liberal justice inadvertently requires that we be willing to abdicate, in public life at least, the welfare of others to the hinterlands of self-reliance, except when the ideal of self-independence itself is threatened. Rawls's insistence that the "substantial sacrifices" people typically make for one another possess moral value but "are not demanded as a matter of justice by the basic structure of society"[57] surely manifests his keen awareness of compassion's moral value. But by excluding from public life occasions that require "substantial sacrifices," Rawls both fails to recognize the full extent to which justice in public life involves citizens in "substantial sacrifices" for one another and obscures the fact that the "substantial sacrifices" that constitute liberal justice originate in the same logical and moral species (i.e., compassion) as the substantial sacrifices that constitute communitarian virtue. If it insists, as Rawls does, that matters of virtue are not demanded by the basic structure of society, a society is likely to develop a culture of self-absorption and breed habits of insensitivity, indifference, and social neglect.

In contrast, communitarian notions of vice are generally construed as neglect of constitutive attachments. Since for communitarians the identity of a person is conceived fundamentally in terms of the community to which she belongs, public life must concern itself with attitudes, practices, and policies that treat citizens as independent selves only incidentally related to each other. Public life must concern itself with a community's character and with the attachments from which a person's identity cannot be separated. "To imagine a person incapable of constitutive attachments," Sandel insists, "is not to conceive an ideally free and rational agent, but to imagine a person wholly without character, without moral depth."[58] Humans inevitably cultivate self-identity in terms of the communities to which they belong, and these communal attachments should not be neglected or ignored in public life.

If I were to ask a communitarian why a society should take care of its poor, the answer would be in terms of charity, as Hauerwas suggests;[59] this because charity is a virtue of character reflecting attachments essential to community life. But charity and other virtues are not in themselves self-evident categories of public life. Their moral connection to public life is justified in terms of compassion for suffering others who are created in God's image. As with justice, so also public occasions for virtue are morally justified on the basis of compassion as normative in public life. How so? Vice (the neglect of virtue) causes involuntary, social suffering; any moral society should care for those whose suffering is involuntary and social and protect its citizens from such suffering.

Yet often communitarians unwittingly dramatize the Levite in public life by minimizing concerns for liberal justice. Hauerwas, for example, insists that "the current emphasis on justice and rights as the primary norms guiding the social witness of the Christian is in fact a mistake."[60] Although Hauerwas is not suggesting that justice be swept away entirely, he is suggesting that liberal notions of individual rights and freedoms be swept away. He does not, however, make clear what conception of justice should replace the liberal notion, except to appeal to Aristotle's and MacIntyre's treatment of justice as one of the virtues. But the difficulty with liberal justice is not, as Hauerwas seems to suggest, that it endows individuals with liberal rights and freedoms but that it excludes from public life communitarian virtues that, along with justice, are rooted in the moral soil of compassion. Hauerwas's tendency is to sacrifice rights and freedoms to the community, to claim that, first of all, the church must "hold before any society . . . not justice but God."[61] But by separating the two (God and justice) he is in danger of establishing conditions that in the past have threatened the foundations of civilized life. This propensity of communitarians to minimize liberal justice produces a disposition I call "vicarious possession."[62]

The self is vicariously possessed by a community through its constitutive attachments, and individual rights and freedoms tend to get subordinated to those attachments. "As the independent self finds its limits in those aims and attachments from which it cannot stand apart," observes Sandel, "so justice finds its limits in those forms of community that engage the identity as well as the interests of the participants."[63] Sandel's stance here seems measured and accommodating, but there is a danger. Historically the tendency of societies to subordinate individual rights and freedoms to the will of the whole has produced a tragic legacy represented *in extremis* by Fascist Italy, Nazi Germany, and Soviet Russia. I am not suggesting that communitarians like Sandel and Hauerwas are advocating anything like ideological fanaticism. What I am suggesting is that communitarian virtue, unqualified by compassionate justice, exposes itself, perhaps even lends itself, to the possibility of a not so benign sectarian fanaticism in which the self is vicariously possessed and often oppressed by the community. Without the clear and compelling call of justice, persons and parties are susceptible to being absorbed into the identity of the community and exploited for its will and pleasure.

The Puritan sources of communitarian virtue in colonial America, unmixed with liberal concerns for natural rights and freedoms, tended toward a kind of benign totalitarianism. By law, in the colony of Virginia, for example, citizens might place their lives in jeopardy if they should "speak unpiously or maliciously against the holy and blessed Trinity . . . blaspheme God's holy name . . . use any traitorous words against his majesty's person."[64] Or consider Americans who wish to make fallen America Christian again by assimilating everyone to the identity of their own community. Unqualified by liberal justice, communitarian virtue threatens important values any society must possess if it is to aspire to the civilizing ideal of compassionate care. So although communitarians, like Sandel and Hauerwas, do not neglect compassion entirely, they do neglect to recognize that the moral source (i.e., compassion) of virtue in public life is identical to the moral source for justice in public life. Vigilance is required against the drift toward fanaticism; a liberal sense of compassionate justice is just the force with which to resist this drift.

Neither liberalism's "veil of ignorance" nor communitarianism's "virtue of character," therefore, but compassion's "vale of tears" should take priority in public life and policy. Compassion's pattern of shared emotions provides the moral depth whereby the concerns of both liberal justice and communitarian virtue can be accommodated. Adversities occasioned by social neglect are as relevant to compassionate public policy as are infringements of justice. Homelessness or poverty or unemployment or urban blight or public health are as properly occasions for public policy as are all forms of discrimination, bigotry, and oppression. In both cases, compassion supplies a moral justification for public projects aimed at redressing involuntary, social suffering. To justify the one (justice concerns), as did the great liberal founders of America's social contract tradition, is to implicitly justify the other (virtue concerns), as did the great covenantal theologians of colonial America. For although differing, as do convex and concave, justice and virtue share a concrete, moral ground in compassion.

COMPASSION IN PUBLIC POLICY

Space does not allow an extensive application of compassion to specific public policy issues here. I can suggest, though, what such an application might look like. Two levels can be identified on which compassion is relevant to public policymaking—preventative and curative. On the one hand, policies should prevent conditions that give rise to involuntary, social suffering. For example, a comprehensive health policy should be enacted that prevents the kind of suffering that requires using hospital emergency rooms as primary care units by those without adequate health insurance. On the other hand, curative policies should be developed that address the needs of those who already suffer and eliminate the conditions that produce suffering. For example, policies should address in a serious and substantial way conditions that have produced a cycle of poverty and social decomposition in many urban communities. But what of those not infrequent instances when suffering cannot be entirely avoided or when the suffering of persons conflict? In cases where it cannot be entirely eliminated or avoided, suffering should be, as far as possible, minimized. This *principle of minimum suffering* requires that public policy not only not cause needless suffering and not only protect against it but also reduce as much as possible whatever involuntary, social suffering is unavoidable.[65]

For example, public policy regarding abortion must take into account potential involuntary, social suffering: the ill health of the unborn and its potential for a healthy life; the desire of mother and father for a child and their capacity to care for that child, and the burden society potentially must bear for the medical, financinal, and social well-being of parents and child. If compassion functions as normative guide, it seems to me that abortion is allowable until the point at which science determines that the unborn's brain and nervous system matures and the unborn begins to feel pain. Beyond that point, and presupposing the principle of minimum suffering, the suffering of the unborn takes precedence over the mother's. Why? Because suffering abortion is more central[66] to the unborn's well-being than the suffering a mother experiences in waiving her right to make decisions regarding her body. Since they are intimately related to and mutually responsible for unborn sentient life, the mother, father, and society must find just and virtuous ways of minimizing the mother's pain while protecting the unborn from avoidable suffering. The mother's suffering, for example, might be reduced by reassuring her that her unwanted baby will be adopted and cared for. But compassionate care for protecting a sentient being from suffering pain and death, a suffering central to her well-being, takes priority over the pain parents suffer from an unwanted pregnancy and the mother's right, now superseded, to abortion. Of course, abortion may also be allowed in special cases, for example, rape and incest, since these factors intensify the involuntary, social nature of the mother's suffering. No doubt both those whose moral convictions disallows abortion entirely and those whose convictions allow it routinely will find this policy unsatisfactory. But to elevate one's personal, moral convictions to the status of public policy in a way that precludes compassion's holistic care is to arbitrarily privilege simple justice or simple virtue. Personal convictions need and should not be relinquished, only absorbed in public life into the moral depth of compassion to which both must ultimately appeal. In this way compassion, as a moral experience undergirding both sets of values, provides a common, covenantal basis for concord in public life.

Implicit in this brief application of compassion to abortion are certain assumptions about the relationship between the citizen and the state. First, it assumes that compassion in public life is a moral commitment that a society, a state, can rightly expect of its citizens. The state can expect citizens to carry out certain social responsibilities as much as it can expect them to recognize the rights and freedoms of others. Citizens may well be expected to care for the hungry by serving in a soup kitchen as properly as they may be expected to serve fairness in hiring practices. They may be expected to assume responsibility for urban blight and violence as fairly as they can be expected to allow freedom of speech and religion. Second, compassion in public life is a moral commitment that citizens can rightly expect of public policy. Citizens can expect the state to act on their behalf when they suffer illness or homelessness as readily as they can expect the state to act on their behalf when freedom of speech or religion is infringed. Public policy guided by compassion should not only protect equal freedom of employment, production, and exchange for its citizens but promote and protect a fair distribution of social goods. By enfranchising compassion in public life in this way, a covenant between citizen and government is not only conceivable but a practical possibility.

COMPASSION AND PUBLIC EDUCATION

If we assume what I have been arguing, namely, that compassion should be a normative moral guide in public life, then it follows that nurturing this virtue in citizens ought to be a central responsibility and focus of public life. Indeed, if compassion is to be successfully practiced as public policy, then it is a habit that must be taught and learned not only in the home but in the schools, both public and private.[67]

One might fairly object that teaching compassion in public schools exceeds First Amendment restrictions on church–state relations. Given America's constitutional tradition and the pluralistic character of American society, how is it possible to justify teaching principles of morality, like compassion, in public schools? My treatment of compassion in this study has been distinctively Christian, and my own commitments to compassion in public life are rooted in that tradition. How can I presume to impose on citizens of diverse religious and secular traditions a moral experience rooted in the particularity of one religious community? I do not presume to do so. Compassion is not the exclusive possession of any single tradition, religious or secular. Compassion is an experience that is both common to all humans and rooted in the particularity of local narrative communities. Accordingly, compassion is an experience that can be taught and learned by drawing on the stories, rituals, values, and beliefs of any and all traditions. As a common human experience, compassion traverses, rather than transcends, the distinctive stories, values, and beliefs of all traditions; all traditions possess stories and beliefs that value compassion. It is thus an experience that people of diverse, local communities can, should, and in fact do share with each other; it provides a common instead of a sectarian basis for a covenant in public life.

As an experience common to and traversing all traditions, moreover, compassion lends itself to a special kind of justification whose logic I set forth in detail in chapter 2, I will summarize it here. Insofar as compassion consists of emotional experiences, it is not justified in terms of objectivist strategies, not in terms of other abstract, foundational beliefs whose rationality is somehow independently grounded. Rather, the appropriateness of compassion in any given instance is justifiable in terms of the local stories, values, and beliefs of the persons confronted with occasions for compassion. Thus, a single instance of compassion will have as many justifications as there are narrative traditions for which compassion on that occasion is deemed appropriate. Confronted with an instance in which several people of diverse traditions make a judgment that the poor ought not be exploited by the rich, for example, the ensuing project of compassion will be justified in as many different ways as are represented by those undertaking the project. The Jew might justify a project of compassion in terms of Yahweh's deliverance of Israel from Egypt, the Christian in terms of Jesus bringing good news to the poor, the Marxist in terms of class struggle, the Muslim in terms of emulating Allah, The Compassionate, and so on. One's narrative community, in other words, endows one's compassionate projects with a justification and intelligibility unique to that community's tradition, but this does not rule out other legitimate ways of justifying compassionate projects in public life. Accordingly, public school, as an institution dedicated to the education of citizens, is a forum in which compassion may and properly should be taught and learned. The diversity of religious and secular traditions represented in public schools enriches rather than impoverishes the pedagogical process, enhances rather than constricts religious freedom. Indeed, by drawing on the contributions of a variety of narrative communities, the student not only learns *about* compassion but *participates in* it, by imagining and entering into experiences of compassionate suffering present in the stories and histories of traditions other than his own.

Does teaching stories drawn from religious as well as secular traditions violate the establishment clause? Not at all. Teaching compassion in the schools is in relevant ways analogous to teaching American history, the aim of which is to nurture in students a sense of identity, a sense of what it means to be American. An American history teacher properly draws on sources from a wide variety of secular and religious traditions—Native American, European, African, Asian, and Latin American as well as Puritan, Anglican, Mormon, Presbyterian, Anabaptist, Catholic, Jewish, deist, atheist, and other traditions. The history teacher's aim, of course, is not religious or the establishment of any religion; her aim is identity, and it is quite impossible to teach students what it means to be American without drawing on a diversity of source traditions, including religious traditions. The student will identify more nearly with one or more of these traditions but will fail to understand what it means for him to be American unless a knowledge and appreciation is gained of other founding traditions. Similarly, the aim of teaching compassion in public schools is not religious or the establishment of religion or any particular religion; the aim is compassion in public life. To learn that a wide variety of narrative communities, both religious and secular, value compassion as a desirable moral habit can only enhance a student's education.

But what of the First Amendment? Stephen Carter is probably right in arguing that "the metaphorical separation of church and state originated in an effort to protect religion from the state, not the state from religion."[68] It turns out that the First Amendment also has been found useful by the courts for protecting the state from religion and undue religious influences. This use accounts for the origin and appeal of the Lemon test, which generally is thought to presuppose a rather broad, liberal reading of the First Amendment. Yet even if we assume Lemon's three criteria, teaching compassion in public schools remains within the bounds of the amendment.

A policy's "legislative purpose," asserts Lemon,[69] must first of all be "secular." Cultivating in public life policies that advance compassion aims at an entirely secular purpose, namely, to prepare students for public life; it does not aim to indoctrinate them in any tradition, religious or secular. The second criterion is that a policy's "principal or primary effect . . . neither advances nor inhibits religion." The effect of teaching compassion will be the practice of compassion in public life; that teaching the stories and values of a wide variety of religious and secular traditions may contribute to nurturing habits of compassion does not in its primary effect advance or inhibit religion. Finally, a policy must not foster "an excessive government entanglement with religion." The ethicist, like the historian, draws on a variety of historical and narrative materials in order to accomplish a secular purpose. The government need entangle itself with the teaching of compassion no more than with the teaching of history. Of course history is not compassion. History is largely a descriptive-interpretive enterprise, whereas compassion is largely a normative, moral enterprise. But both are essential to the health of a society.

By proposing compassion as a compass for public policy, I have been concerned not with abstract realities lodged in some metaphysical heaven but with the facts of our own place and time. The fact of human suffering forces itself upon us and calls us to undertake in public life policies of compassionate care. For the Christian, this reality is especially compelling; incarnation and atonement have no practical meaning at all if not compassion in face of human suffering. But compassion is not exclusively a religious experience, nor is it the private privilege of a single tradition. Even the parable of the good Samaritan, as Prior points out, "is not exclusively or even primarily a religious story: the representatives of organized religion are not cast in a favorable light, the hero is a member of a nation of religious outcasts, and he does not justify his actions by appeal to religious principles." Compassion is a common moral experience "shared by civilized people of many religious and cultural backgrounds, including those who profess no religious faith at all."[70]

If we want to supersede the stalemate of liberalism and communitarianism, and if we want to construct something better, we must begin by understanding them. Accordingly, I have examined the differences between these two traditions as well as how deeply they both are rooted in the soil of compassion. As a normative measure for constructing public life, compassion advances the best of America's political and moral resources while fortifying against their defects. Compassion may not be the whole of public life, but it should be one of its touchstones.

7

Educating the Heart for Compassion

As jesus walks by the Sea of Galilee he sees the fishermen brothers Simon and Andrew and says to them, "Follow me, and I will make you fishers of men." Immediately they drop their nets and follow. Further on he sees two other brothers and calls them to follow, and immediately they leave what they are doing and follow. What does "following" Jesus entail? Among other things and most immediately it involves practical, on-site training for his disciples, a kind of apprenticeship. They travel with Jesus throughout the region of Galilee, observing, serving, and emulating him as he carries out his ministry of compassion (Matthew 4:18–25). Eventually Jesus sends his disciples out to teach, preach, and heal, to practice the ministry of compassion in which he earlier trained them as apprentices (Matthew 10). In sending them, Jesus says, "A disciple is not above his teacher, nor a servant above his master; it is enough for the disciple to be like his teacher, and the servant like his master" (10:24, 25). Besides discourse, lecture, dialogue, conversation, and storytelling, Jesus employs the pedagogical technique of apprenticeship. He apparently thinks that guided practice is indispensable for educating disciples in a ministry of compassion. For Jesus' disciples, Roy Zuck insists, "learning was living, living with and like Jesus."[1]

Contemporary philosophers and theologians have written a great deal, in recent years, about educating the heart. Cornel West, MacIntyre, and Nussbaum in philosophy, for example, and Delores Williams, Hauerwas, and Ronald Thiemann in theology argue that narrative is crucial not only for educating a community for a life of virtue but for "understanding issues of epistemology and methods of argument, depicting personal identity, and displaying the content of Christian convictions."[2] I agree. One aim of this chapter is to argue, however, that although necessary, narrative is insufficient in itself to fully and satisfactorily educate the heart for virtue in general and for compassion in particular. Part of the thesis I argue here is that if compassion is a common aim of public life and education, as argued in chapter 6, then apprenticeship must be a central pedagogical method of public education. This claim, of course, is nothing new. Paulo Freire most prominently and compellingly has insisted on this.[3] I will show, first, how compassion, as the moral aim of public education, is the point at which covenantal communities and secular societies interact. Second, I will show that in order to educate the public for compassion, schools must employ not only narrative and critical reflection but also apprenticeship. Finally, I show what a culture of compassion would look like in contrast to our current culture of self-fulfillment.

THE CULTURAL ROLE OF COMPASSION

Jesus' ministry can properly be seen as situated at the intersection of two families or communities, the family of faith and the family of humanity. On the one hand, Jesus dedicates a great deal of his ministry, as noted, calling and cultivating followers—cultivating a family of faith. To the question "Who is my mother, and who are my brothers?" Jesus gestures toward his gathered community of disciples and replies, "Here are my mother and my brothers. For whoever does the will of my Father in heaven is my brother, and sister, and mother" (Matthew 12:48–50). On the other hand, Jesus dedicates a great deal of his ministry to the family of humanity: those who fall outside the family of faith, the irreligious and self-righteously religious, the despised and marginalized, the wealthy and poor, the powerful and dispossessed. He ministers to the wealthy but despised tax collector Zacchaeus (Luke 19) as well as to prostitutes and irreverent sinners (Mark 2:15–17). In short, Jesus counts himself a member of a particular, local family of faith and at the same time a member of a universal, global family of humanity.[4] The question arises, then, How can one be a citizen of one's local community, as Nussbaum puts it, and at the same time a citizen of the world?[5]

I have already answered this question in chapter 6. My thesis is that compassion is that normative, moral experience in and through and by which both the particularity and the universality of faith is manifested. Admittedly, not all Christian theologians[6] have found compassion a compelling moral experience. Nevertheless, I am convinced, along with Nussbaum, that it is so, especially for those communities of faith that claim the biblical tradition.

My special focus here is to suggest ways that public schools can assume responsibility for educating students for a life of compassion. Nussbaum, in *Cultivating Humanity*, indicates how compassion functions as a common moral experience that links local and universal communities and establishes the possibility of citizenship in both. "The world citizen must develop sympathetic understanding of distant cultures and of ethnic, racial, and religious minorities within her own."[7] In other words, "[h]abits of empathy and conjecture conduce to a certain type of citizenship and a certain form of community: one that cultivates a sympathetic responsiveness to another's needs, and understands the way circumstances shape those needs, while respecting separateness and privacy."[8] The compassion cultivated in one's local community is precisely the experience that interconnects a person with the rest of humanity and establishes the possibility of moral citizenship in a global community. This fact does not elude Jesus; it is a central feature of his ministry and mission. He makes this very point poignantly in his parable of the good Samaritan and in his encounter with the Samaritan woman at the well. By showing compassion to the injured stranger, the Samaritan reveals that his local faith community has cultivated in him a "sympathetic responsiveness" to difference and otherness, so that his compassion makes that injured man, who was of an alien and hostile culture, his neighbor. Similarly, the compassion Jesus shows the Samaritan woman at the well is a particular instance of a common universal experience that makes it possible for peoples of all faiths to worship God, as Jesus puts it, in spirit and in truth.

Compassion is the practice of a normative, public virtue, in other words, whereby enemies are made neighbors and foreigners made friends, a practice in which all humans are empowered to participate locally in their family of faith and universally in the family of humanity. Jesus calls his disciples to be followers and not merely admirers by calling them to practice, as he did, this kind of compassion. But what does it take to educate a society for compassion and global citizenship? What pedagogical techniques are best suited to nourishing compassion as a public, even, global, virtue?

Educating for Compassion

One of the great moral, spiritual, and historical tasks of Christian communities is to educate their collective heart for compassion so that in concrete and specific ways they might prepare themselves to fulfill the ministry to which Jesus calls his people: namely, to preach good news to the poor, proclaim release to the captives, restore sight to the blind, liberate those who are oppressed, and proclaim the acceptable year of the Lord (Luke 4:18–19). This aim is neither restricted nor distinctive to convenantal communities. As I argued in chapter 6, compassion is a common, universal human experience, and educating for it can and should be an aim and responsibility of public education and life and not just of private, religious education. The question arises, then, What means and methods are conducive to nurturing compassion in public education and life?

The compassion required for global citizenship presupposes a mature moral character, one habituated already to such virtues as I have examined throughout this book, and entails the process of cultivating the obediential dispositions and empathetic emotions constituting them. This is to say that compassion, as a normative, public virtue, involves a considerable challenge to teacher and pupil alike and requires a remarkable measure of diligence and clear thinking on the part of any society interested in cultivating it. Just as educating for justice, in Plato's *Republic*, demands of the Athenians a collective and lifelong diligence, so does educating for compassion in our own place and time. This is because compassion requires not only strengthening moral character in the individual pupil but also nurturing a profound sense and practice of moral community, a sense of responsibility for and accountability not only to one's family of faith but ultimately to all humanity. This practice of global community, as we know, is often subverted by feelings of hatred, vengeance, fear, insecurity, greed, selfish pride, nationalism, racial prejudice, and the like. But we also know that these emotions are not simply raw, irrational physiological impulses. They are learned habits inspired by certain conventional attitudes and beliefs; as such they arise from complex social contexts yet fall within the power of humans to create and alter. What is needed, accordingly, are measures and methods whereby the formation of character for compassion becomes a central dimension of educating the heart for public life. Although these measures and methods must be the responsibility of home and houses of worship, I want to make the case here that they can and should be the responsibility of places of public education as well. Educating for compassion involves at least four pedagogical features.

Educating for Compassion Involves Narrative

Jesus is justly famous for his storytelling. Often, when questioned or challenged, he engages his listeners with stories, like the parable of the good Samaritan. For the Christian community, however, Jesus is not simply master storyteller; he is the story. His is not only the voice narrating the stories, he is the voice in the stories he is narrating. As incarnate Word, Jesus is not only principal character but author of the drama, who in his own concrete, historical acts creates the plot that he is also in the process of telling. Telling stories, in other words, is a primary way Jesus interprets the historical drama that he is creating. His discourses (such as the Sermon on the Mount), which themselves are part of the plot, provide further reflection on narrative, conferring additional layers and patterns of meaning on his story.

When it comes to storytelling, however, Jesus is not alone. He stands in a long line of Jewish rabbis for whom storytelling is central to their pedagogical enterprise. Indeed, all of the world's great religious founders were master storytellers, so much so that one wonders whether without this capacity their movements might not have withered and died. Why is this so? Why is narrative such a powerful tool for educating the heart? The answer lies partly in what I argued in chapter 2, that narrative provides access to our emotions. Nussbaum makes this point forcefully when she insists that emotions or virtues very often "are not taught to us directly through propositional claims about the world. . . . They are taught above all through stories. Stories express their structure and teach us their dynamics. These stories are constructed by others and, then taught and learned. But once internalized, they shape the way life looks and feels."[9] If compassion is to shape the way life looks and feels in public life, then, stories in general and stories of compassion in particular are crucial, especially for the moral development of childhood habits of heart.

Another related part of the answer is that narrative[10] not only provides access to the life of human emotions but touches and arouses the heart. It possesses a potency that animates the heart, inspiring it to practice habits of virtue. Narrative animates the emotions that are the soil in which virtue is rooted. Upon ending his parable of the Samaritan, Jesus enjoins his listeners to "Go and do" what the telling of the parable partly empowers them to do, that is, "likewise"; go and act compassionately toward all peoples, including enemies, go and become citizens of the world. So if a central task of public education is fostering compassion, then a central means for doing so is by and through what Nussbaum calls the "narrative imagination," which includes storytelling.[11] For Plato storytelling is unsurpassed in its power to shape the moral character of children; that is why he has Socrates set forth strict guidelines for censoring both the moral content of stories and the pedagogical method of teaching them.[12] For him stories do not merely transmit values and wisdom, they awaken and activate the heart; they possess power to shape for good or ill the very marrow of a person's and community's moral habits. Put another way, as does Mary Moore, "narratives are an important source of imagination,"[13] and, as I argued in chapter 6, imagination is a key dimension of a community's capacity for experiencing compassion. The capacity for great virtue and great vice lies dormant in the human heart. Stories possess an imaginative power capable of nurturing the greatest virtues and the greatest vices. Cultivating the capacity for compassion, accordingly, requires cultivating the power of imagination involved in narrative activity. When children hear tales in which vices are glorified, they tend to glorify them for themselves, or at least justify desiring them. If they hear tales glorifying virtue, then they glorify virtue. As Katherine Cather puts it, "[p]eople reared in lands whose national heroes are fierce, avenging heroes grow into men of fierceness. To them a show of mercy is a badge of weakness. Pity is something of which a strong man should be ashamed."[14] She goes on to say that the secret of the spoken or written tale and its power to shape moral character is the fact that a story "touches the heart. It arouses the emotions and makes people feel with the characters whose acts make the plot. Mirth, anger, pity, desire, disdain, approval, and dislike are aroused, because the characters who move through the tale experience these emotions."[15] Nussbaum concurs when she argues that "narrative imagination is an essential preparation for moral interaction. Habits of empathy and conjecture conduce to a certain type of citizenship and a certain form of community.... This is so because of the way in which literary imagining ... inspires intense concern with the fate of the characters."[16] Jesus' parable of the good Samaritan, for example, moves a child to disapprove of those in the story who are indifferent to the plight of the injured man and moves a child to pity him and to admire the Samaritan who cares for the injured. During the story, the listener, the child, "forgets himself and experiences, thinks and feels with the hero of the story."[17] The story's secret lies in the power of the narrative imagination "to make the characters of the story so alive and human that those who hear it live with them and enter into their experiences."[18] Similarly, when a drama invites the audience "to identify with the tragic hero" and portrays that "hero as a relatively good person, whose distress does not stem from deliberate wickedness," then, says Nussbaum, "the drama makes compassion for suffering seize the imagination. This emotion is built into the dramatic form."[19]

Educating for compassion must and can begin early in childhood, as soon as a child begins to listen to stories and to engage in storytelling herself. "The basis for civic imagining must be laid in early life," as Nussbaum says, for "as children explore stories, rhymes, and songs . . . they are led to notice the sufferings of other living creatures with a new keenness."[20] These activities educate the child's heart for compassion in several ways. First, many stories tell a tale of compassion as a desirable, noble habit of heart, stories in which the compassionate and just hero (or community) is praised and the mean and unforgiving antihero is condemned or punished. Jesus' parables very often include such a scenario, for example, the story of the unforgiving servant. Second, it is important that the child learns and tells stories of compassion that originate in traditions other than his own. In doing so, he learns compassion not only in the story's content, but also by entering into and empathizing with compassionate characters of other traditions. As Nussbaum suggests, "[a]s soon as children engage in storytelling, they can tell stories about other lands and other peoples,"[21] and this telling is itself an exercise in compassion. In hearing and telling compassionate stories from other traditions the pupil is vicariously expanding the range of her own capacity for compassion for the peoples among whom these other stories originate. Third, by engaging in the act of creating stories of compassion from his own imagination, the pupil begins to enter into the experience of compassion at a profoundly powerful and personal depth. Young pupils might tell stories, imagined or real, in which they help someone in need and try to imagine what would happen if help was unavailable or denied. More advanced students might reimagine actual historical events in such a way that reconciling compassion instead of hostile revenge is pivotal. Each of these narrative techniques possess a power to begin to habituate the child's heart to compassion as a virtue greatly to be desired, a virtue she must expect not only of herself but of other citizens as well.

The current focus on narrative, then, is well founded, I think, especially when the moral development of children is considered vital not only to the health of a specific society but also to global citizenship. Narrative is one pivotal, indispensable way in which educating the heart for compassion is rendered a practical possibility. A weakness plaguing the recommendations of many advocates of narrative education, however, is a tendency to think of narrative and critical reflection on narrative as somehow sufficient or at least singularly central for character development and moral education. They are not.

Educating for Compassion Involves Apprenticeship

Jesus taught his disciples as much by apprenticeship and association as by story and discourse. It is rapidly becoming a pedagogical truism that a teacher teaches moral character as much by who she is and what she does as by what she thinks and says. Jesus calls his disciples with "Follow me" rather than "Listen to me," not because he disparages listening but because following or practicing a particular pattern of life is of more profound significance for moral and spiritual formation than mere listening. He calls disciples so "they might first be 'with him,' " as H. H. Horne puts it, "and then that he might 'send them.' "[22] A central technique Jesus uses for training disciples, in short, is apprenticeship, on-site training in the art of compassionate, global citizenship. So although storytelling is necessary and essential to educating the heart, it is by itself insufficient. Rather, storytelling "feeds the desire for experience,"[23] argues Cather, the desire to participate in projects of compassion that stories and storytelling inspire but cannot themselves fulfill. Educating the heart for compassion naturally and logically embraces a kind of collective, pedagogical apprenticeship in which pupils, under supervision, engage in community projects involving experiences of compassion.

The fact that Jesus trains disciples as apprentices is continuous, of course, with the Christian understanding of incarnation. Moore makes this point in a chapter entitled "Incarnational Teaching." "Incarnation is God's enfleshment or presence in the world. [So incarnation] can be expected in the teacher–student relationship ... in acts of compassion and acts of anger toward injustice."[24] Incarnational teaching includes apprenticeship, because teaching God's presence in the world must involve actually "[c]aring for others [as] part of teaching" and not merely as "an extracurricular activity that some do because they are 'nice.' " Indeed, "caring for others is an important quality in the teaching-learning process and an important goal"[25] whereby teacher and student train together, participating in projects of compassionate service, as did Jesus and his disciples. Similarly, Freire seems to insist on the necessity of pedagogical apprenticeship when he speaks of "the word" as an event able to "transform the world." Within the word, he says, "we find two dimensions, reflection and action, in such radical interaction that if one is sacrificed—even in part—the other immediately suffers. There is no true word that is not at the same time a praxis."[26] When it comes to moral and spiritual pedagogy, accordingly, there is no true teaching and learning that does not at the same time include active apprenticeship. To make this claim is to imply at least to things; first, that any true word is at the same time communal, and second, that any true word is "not the privilege of some few men, but the right of every man." As Freire says, "no one can say a true word alone—nor can he say it for another, in a prescriptive act which robs others of their words."[27] The teacher's task, then, includes incarnational training, practicing with pupils the ancient art of acting compassionately in the world. In so doing not only pupils but also teacher and world are transformed.

This theology of incarnation helps clarify, I think, the relation between Jesus and his disciples as one of apprenticeship. "Jesus' actions are not just illustrations of his message," Graham Stanton insists, "they are his message,"[28] and his central message is the Kingdom of God. J. T. Dillon suggests that there are at least four categories of actions by which Jesus taught the Kingdom of God and, I might add, taught compassion as the central public virtue of that kingdom. These four kinds of actions are "feasting in fellowship . . . keeping bad company . . . breaking the law . . . [and] healing the distressed,"[29] all of which involve public acts of compassion. Because Jesus' pedagogical relationship with his disciples is primarily that of apprenticeship, his disciples learn what the Kingdom of God is by doing the very same things; feasting in fellowship, keeping bad company, breaking Sabbath laws, and healing the distressed—in short, acting compassionately. Yet apprenticeship, as a culminating stage in educating the heart for virtue, is almost entirely ignored by educators in home, church, and, until recently, public school.

The question arises whether I mean to imply by "apprenticeship" that one of Jesus' basic pedagogical methods is teaching by example, by embodying what he teaches? At first an answer would seem to be a simple and straightforward yes. But that is not quite adequate. I agree with Dillon when he argues that "Jesus was not a teacher who teaches by example. He does not practice what he preaches, he does not live what he teaches; more accurate to say that Jesus *preached what he practiced* and *taught what he lived*. Jesus taught by actions. His actions are what he teaches, not an example of something that he teaches."[30] This subtle but significant distinction points out the difference between demonstration and apprenticeship. Demonstration involves dramatization or role-playing as preparation for acting concretely and historically, as a kind of drill or rehearsal imitating what concrete, historical action might be like. Narrative acts of storytelling or role-playing are a species of demonstration and are significant preparation for apprenticeship; but they are not themselves apprenticeship. In contrast, apprenticeship is acting concretely and historically, so much so that what is done is what is spoken and what is spoken is what is done. It is the teacher and pupil together acting compassionately in the world that bears the potential of transforming it. What public school education (not to mention church and home) sorely lacks pedagogically is moral, spiritual apprenticeship. Unless a society is willing to undertake apprenticeship as a central pedagogical method, the quest for virtue in moral education and the quest for moral society will remain the inconsequential illusion it largely and currently is.

What would public education look like, then, if it included apprenticeship as a significant dimension of moral education? There are precedents for employing apprenticeship as a pivotal pedagogical technique, but generally it is employed when students are chronologically well along in their education and takes the form of internships in a chosen profession. Professional schools of social work, business, medicine, and divinity, for example, commonly require apprenticeship-like experiences as preparation for professional practice. These internships function as an occasion in which the student and teacher jointly practice certain skills requisite for professional success. The humanities, outside of seminary education, noticeably and ironically neglect apprenticeship as a means of moral education. Jesus' use of apprenticeship is for the sake of moral and spiritual development, for the sake of God's Kingdom, for the sake of learning how to practice compassion. My contention is that if compassion is to be an experience that draws people into and together in public life, as I have argued it should, then the technique of apprenticeship should be employed early, frequently, and deliberately. In natural science the laboratory provides pupils at a fairly early age with occasion to practice actual, if elementary, scientific experiments. A telescope and the night sky function as laboratory for astronomy students, and social service agencies do so for students of social work. Similarly, for students in the humanities, a local community should and can function as a laboratory for apprenticeship in compassion, beginning perhaps as early as middle school, if not earlier.

An example of community as laboratory, or what is referred to as "service learning" in educational circles,[31] is found in the Maryland public high school system, where students are required to perform seventy-five hours of community service toward graduation. In 1994 the Maryland Board of Education mandated community service in order to help students acquire a sense of citizenship and its responsibilities. The system is not without difficulties and abuses,[32] but apprenticeship endeavors such as this are what is required of public education if compassion as a public virtue is to become a reality.

Principles of good service learning programs are varied and at times fairly detailed.[33] James Youniss and Miranda Yates put it concisely: "Effective service programs give students the chance to do meaningful work . . . such as feeding the hungry or the homeless, or bringing comfort to the elderly." In addition to the service itself, however, critical reflection is required. "Group effort and shared reflection about the service experience are important parts of these programs, as are supportive teachers who assign readings that introduce students to the philosophical and political thinking about the conditions behind social problems."[34] From this wealth of research and practice, I am proposing that two things are crucial to educating the heart: compassion and global citizenship as the end, and apprenticeship as a necessary means. We learn from the world's great moral and religious leaders that compassion as public virtue and apprenticeship as pedagogical technique are interdependent and compelling. Moses, Confucius, Buddha, Jesus, Paul, Muhammed, Gandhi, and King all cultivate a group of disciples or "intimate learners" so that they might "learn not so much the lessons as the way of their teacher, so that by personal witnesses the blessed truth might be passed on to others and so on to others."[35] One dimension of this blessed truth, for each of these teachers, is compassion; and the possibility of teaching pupils compassion involves, for each of them, practicing projects of compassionate concern. Practicing compassion for global citizenship should be the fieldwork of the humanities.

Educating for Compassion Involves Unity in Plurality

Jesus was famous, or perhaps infamous, among his contemporaries for stories and projects that challenged beliefs and behaviors that were otherwise taken for granted as "neutral, necessary, and natural," as Nussbaum puts it.[36] Of course, Jesus is not challenging beliefs and behaviors simply to defy them but in order to teach what it means to love compassionately. In order to do so, Jesus confronts his disciples with difference. When he has the Jewish religious leaders pass by the injured man with apparent disregard and has a despised Samaritan show compassion, for example, Jesus challenges racial and religious and moral prejudices. Yet he also suggests in this story a way in which the many might be one, difference might generate identity, and plurality might generate unity. What challenges Jesus' listeners most profoundly in the parable is the realization that despite thinking of themselves as superior and privileged, foreigners may very well equal or exceed them morally and spiritually. Potential exists in the common experience of compassion for peoples of differing faiths and no faith to share moral ground, creating therein a unity in plurality. As argued in chapter 2, the nature of human emotions is that they can be shared transculturally and as such function as the basis for unity and universality. Especially the capacity for narrative imagination and emotion that constitute compassion (a capacity that lies in the heart of every human and every community) establishes the possibility of engendering unity in plurality. Compassion by its very nature as compassion presupposes identity in difference, unity in plurality. It presupposes, ironically, that wherever there is difference and diversity among humans there can and should be identity and unity. Its character is to preserve and perpetuate what is distinct and different while at the same time to mediate and harmonize.

Any community that deigns to call itself moral ought to be about the business of compassionate global citizenship; otherwise its status as a moral community can and should be questioned and its existence resisted. Any genuinely moral community, by its very nature as moral, accordingly will show compassion to communities distinct from itself. The most profound and permanent way of opposing immoral communities, like Fascists and Nazis, while still showing compassion toward them, is by educating the communal heart for compassionate global citizenship.

Questioning one's own tradition (Sabbath laws), appreciating the traditions of others (the good Samaritan), and socializing and caring for the despised and disinherited (publicans and sinners) often produces, as Nussbaum points out, "a widespread fear—reflected for example in the argument of Allan Bloom's book *The Closing of the American Mind*—that critical scrutiny of one's own tradition will automatically entail a form of cultural relativism."[37] No doubt such fear contributed considerably to the deaths of Socrates, Jesus, Gandhi, and Martin Luther King, Jr. But as I argued in chapter 2 and throughout this book, relativism is not the inevitable consequence of difference and plurality. Human emotions in general and compassion in particular possess the power of intersubjectivity, of traversing while yet preserving difference and of establishing the universal truths that are presupposed in the compassionate judgements we make and projects we undertake.

Educating the heart for compassion, for unity in plurality, requires that public education, along with private and parochial education, weave together a colorful variety of experiences. I have already examined some of these experiences. In *Cultivating Humanity*, Nussbaum makes a compelling case for teaching compassion by requiring students to study and understand non-Western cultures and the experiences of peoples (e.g., women, Native Americans) whose voices have been marginalized in Western culture. This kind of study needs to be supplemented with experiences of learning by apprenticeship, requiring students to practice compassion under the supervision of teachers who practice compassion. In his use of apprenticeship, Jesus frequently finds occasion to train his disciples in habits of compassion, occasions when they must practice unity in plurality. In chapter 3 I examined Jesus' encounter with the Samaritan woman at the well (John 4) as an instance in which Jesus demonstrates the obediential dispositions and empathetic emotions constituting love. This encounter can also be examined as an instance par excellence of compassion, of unity in plurality, of local and global citizenship. Jesus affirms and preserves the distinct difference represented by the Samaritan woman. He accepts her differences and affirms and loves her in her differences—her gender, religion, race, and class. Historically and universally these dimensions of life (gender, religion, race, and class) not only suggest difference (that Jesus is terribly different from and has little in common with the Samaritan woman), but they often engender a hostility and repudiation that are rationalized on the basis of social and cultural conventions. In the midst of radical difference and plurality Jesus practices compassion from which his disciples begin to learn the meaning of radical acceptance and unity. He does not deny but preserves the woman in her difference; yet by feeling compassion for her he is able to mediate a harmony in which those who truly worship God worship in spirit and in truth. Such compassion is radical in that it places on equal and common ground communities, cultures, and histories that are otherwise terribly different; in that it undermines the prejudices and privileges that are presupposed by the conventions of tradition; and in that it requires communities ultimately to envision themselves, in all their local and unique color, as common citizens of a global community.

Educating for Compassion Involves Reflection and Analysis

Woven throughout any durable fabric of moral education is the thread of critical reflection and analysis. Just as educating the heart for virtue cannot exist, let alone succeed, without narrative imagination and apprenticeship, so also it cannot flourish without reflection and analysis. Indeed, the denial of this fact is its own refutation. The function of reflection in educating the heart for compassion is twofold. First, by means of reflective analysis we are able to sort out and see patterns and layers of meaning without which story and practice make little sense. Second, by means of critical reflection we discover what story and experience call us to do, what the work of the heart should be. Nussbaum emphasizes the first of these functions, Freire the second.

First, reflection sees patterns of meaning in story and apprenticeship. "Reflection permits the critical assessment of impressions," says Nussbaum: permits the critical assessment of emotions, stories, experiences, permits us to see patterns of meaning and layers of significance, permits us to interpret story and experience and "their linking into an overall pattern, their classification and reclassification."[38] Reflective analysis of love and compassion, she goes on to say, "moves us from an unarticulated sympathy with this or that story to a reflective grasp of our own sympathies."[39] Jesus' telling of the story of the good Samaritan employs reflective analysis at a couple of levels. The story itself is an interpretation of what it means to "Love the Lord your God with all your heart, and with all your soul, and with all your strength, and with all your mind; and your neighbor as yourself" (Luke 10:27). After telling the story, Jesus then asks the lawyer a question whose posing requires an even higher level of reflective analysis: "Which of these three, do you think, proved neighbor to the man who fell among the robbers?" and whose answer requires perhaps an even higher level: "The one who showed mercy on him" (Luke 10:36–37). Jesus requires his disciples to reflect not only on the stories he tells them but also on their apprenticeship experiences. Before sending them out on an apprenticeship assignment, Jesus articulates certain guidelines and criteria on the basis of which his disciples are to proceed and to assess their experiences. Matthew records these guidelines and criteria (chapter 10) and throughout the remainder of his gospel assesses the performance of Jesus and his disciples on the basis of them. Educating the heart, then, will require students and teachers alike to analyze and interpret stories and apprenticeship experiences in a way that confers on those experiences patterns of moral significance capable of inspiring students to ever greater projects of compassion.

Second, critical reflection functions as a pivotal activity of mind whereby people discover what story and apprenticeship call them to do and be. Jesus responds to the lawyers correct answer with "Go and do likewise" (Luke 10:37). But how do we "go and do likewise" today; how do we make contemporary the compassion portrayed in an ancient parable? Freire insists that to "go and do likewise" entails the second dimension of praxis, namely, reflection or what he calls "critical consciousness" or "conscientization."[40] At least two dimensions of critical reflection, as set forth by Freire, are relevant to the aim of educating the heart for compassion. First, through critical reflection a community discovers who in society are in need of compassion and what conditions, what social structures, must be transformed in order to alleviate suffering. The results of such a critical analysis provides students and their community with the direction they need for such action. Second, any project of healing or liberation is always in need of reexamination and revision. The work of critical reflection, in other words, is never done. Student apprentices will not only be about the task of serving others compassionately but about the task of critically reassessing the success of that service.

These four pedagogical measures—narrative, plurality, apprenticeship, and critical reflection—are necessary for any society interested in educating its citizens in the practice of compassionate global citizenship.

Toward a Culture of Compassion

What would a covenantal community that practiced compassion as a public virtue look like? What priorities, assumptions, and values would a society that cultivates global citizenship practice? In what ways would contemporary Western societies change if they practiced compassionate citizenship as a fundamental public virtue? To what extent would cultivating compassion transform the character of covenantal communities and contemporary society? What must be done? What must change?

What is needed, what an ethic of Christian virtue demands, it seems to me, is a thorough renovation of the attitudes and social structures of modern society, beginning with the renovation of covenantal communities themselves. Covenantal communities must uproot the false idols of our age and sow in their place seeds that will root in the soil of compassion. Idols are false assumptions and prejudices on which are founded dogmatic beliefs and practices that prevent a community or society from seeing the possibilities of and potential for creating a culture of compassion. Each idol, in its religious manifestation, is a way of admiring Jesus, as did the Pharisee, instead of following him, as did the disreputable woman. There are at least five types of false idols in our own day that must be uprooted, purged, and replaced by five covenantal assumptions and practices. These assumptions and practices are rooted in compassion, in the obediential dispositions and empathetic emotions belonging to the virtues of love, peace, and justice examined in this book.[41] Together with compassion, covenantal love, peace, and justice constitute the rationale and justification for advocating these alternative assumptions. Nothing short of a radical transformation of social assumptions and structures is required if compassion is to shape the character of public life and realize the goal of global citizenship. If we accept compassion as a public virtue, then we shall find it undermining certain false idols that are peculiar to our American age. Educating the heart for compassion will aim at deconstructing these false idols and reconstructing in their place assumptions and practices consistent with and justified by the virtues of love, peace, and justice. What follows is a sketch of the kind of social transformation that must take place and not an exhaustive analysis. Yet I believe this sketch is sufficient to indicate the radical conversion that will occur if covenantal communities follow and not merely admire Jesus.

Idols of the Sacred: From Spirituality to Incarnation

Central to idols of the sacred is a view of spirituality in which a person's relationship to God is assumed to be primarily and fundamentally one of personal piety, devotion, and worship. Spirituality as idolatry encourages the devotee to undertake a regime aimed at deepening the relationship with God. Indeed, deepening one's relationship with God is the goal of piety, and certain spiritual exercises (prayer, Bible reading, worship, liturgy, hymnody) are the means of doing so. This idol of pious spirituality tends to promote religion as a kind of pop psychology, a religion of self-fulfillment, of each self preoccupied with maximizing its personal, private spiritual and moral condition, while often ignoring the physical, social, economic, and political welfare of others. Piety, of course, encourages a devotee's interest in and concern for others, perhaps even for their economic welfare, but largely in hope and for the sake of persuading them to become self-interestedly pious as well. Pious spirituality requires, for example, a hermeneutic in which a process of personalization imposes on certain passages of Scripture a spiritual, self-interested, nonliteral interpretation. Indeed, the idol of personal, privatized piety dictates the kind of spiritualized interpretation that may be necessary. So Jesus does not literally mean to say that one should take no oath of allegiance, for example, to one's nation-state, because swearing allegiance to one's country in no way jeopardizes, so it is thought, one's personal, devotional commitment to God. What does jeopardize one's personal devotion to God is to swear or curse in a way that dishonors God's name and undermines one's personal piety. Nor did Jesus mean, by "Turn the other cheek" and "Love your enemies," literally to exclude retaliating and going to war under the flag of the nation-state to which one has sworn allegiance. Instead, Jesus means to say that in our personal relationships with people we should not seek vengeance or take lives, for to do so would jeopardize piety, our personal devotion and commitment to live holy, godly lives. Ironically, personal, self-interested devotion such as this is a subtle and deceptive way of admiring instead of following Jesus. It permits Christians to invite Jesus into their homes and to their tables without requiring them to transform their lives in a way that challenges the self-interested individualism of American consumerism and the military defense of that idol.

In contrast to idols of the sacred, the Christian notion and practice of incarnation assumes a spirituality of material engagement that requires discipleship and not merely admiration. By this I mean a spirituality that inspires a community to enter, as Jesus did, into the lives of humans, engaging human life compassionately, suffering with those who suffer and rejoicing with those who rejoice. Genuine acts of worship and devotion inspire a community to undertake projects of incarnate love, actively and mercifully caring for the physical, emotional, economic, social, and political welfare of the family of humanity. There is no genuine faith, no genuine personal devotion that does not incarnate itself in concrete works of love, peace, justice, and compassion. As incarnate, a covenantal community does not practice what it preaches but like Jesus preaches what it practices. And what it practices is an ethic of Christian virtue that defines devotion and spirituality in terms of projects of compassionate global citizenship. Living incarnately manufactures no need to spiritualize and personalize biblical passages but requires only that the practice of love and compassion, as Jesus embodied them, constitute an interpretive key. So when Jesus commands "Swear no oaths," for example, he means to include no oaths of allegiance to nation-states. Only then can Christian communities fully obey subsequent commands to "Turn the other cheek" and "Love your enemies" without feeling compelled to support at the same time wars that reify others as enemies. Only then can Christian communities genuinely follow and not just admire Jesus.

Idols of the Self: From Instrumental to Eucharistic Worth

One way society idolizes the self is by its assumption that human worth is a matter of merit and not grace, a matter of what one achieves and not what one is. Instrumentalism, as one manifestation of this idol, is an attitude that pervades modern thinking, infusing itself into virtually all spheres of life. It is the common American assumption that, as Kysar puts it, "one's worth is a direct reflection of what one has been able to accomplish."[42] For example, whether and how much one deserves the benefits of society's goods depends on the extent of one's personal achievement measured in terms of one's material and cultural contribution to society, especially to the production and consumption of those goods. This assumption privileges the notion of justice as fairness (broad justice) and tends to minimize the notion of justice as equal mercy (deep justice)—minimizes the kind of merciful compassion implicit in God's incarnation and genuinely covenantal communities. This idol of instrumentalism implies several other characteristically American beliefs. Most obviously, it implies that personal, human worth is acquired and not intrinsic; that humans must merit and earn their worth. Second, this idol assumes that the individual precedes the community and that heroic, individual achievement endows a person with worth and value. One's acceptance by and status in the community, then, is largely proportionate to one's individual, personal achievement. Third, instrumentalism implies a particular notion and practice of liberal freedom that entails "being able to do as you please," as Daniel Migliore puts it, "and in particular, being free to possess and consume things limitlessly."[43] In this sort of liberal freedom, a community confers value on those who accumulate the greatest amounts of its goods for their own private, personal use. Immigrants are regarded suspiciously by societies that think instrumentally, because they absorb social goods (such as jobs and unemployment benefits) that might otherwise be possessed and consumed by residents who value humans for what they achieve. Such idols of the self permit a community to admire Jesus without following him. They provide a way of valuing humans insofar as they enhance the self's quest to achieve and acquire worth and valuing community insofar as it can enhance one's worth and status.

Although there is a place for thinking and judging instrumentally, it does not include the question of human worth and welfare. If compassion is to emerge as a public virtue, the idol of instrumentalism must be replaced with certain assumptions, beliefs, and practices implied by a eucharistic view of the self and its worth. Eucharistic remembrance of incarnation and atonement assumes, first of all, that each person is created in the image of God and as such is graciously endowed by God with intrinsic and irrevocable worth. Implied is the belief that human worth cannot be earned or reduced to merit but is a gift to which the only reasonable response is gratitude. Accordingly, covenantal communities should deliver in and to the family of humanity the kind of care and mercy to which the recipient's primary and natural response will be a sense of gratitude, not desert. Eucharistic worth also implies that between individual and community a mutuality exists in which responsibility and accountability are correlative and reciprocal. Rather than meeting human need conditionally because worth has been merited, eucharistic communities meet human need unconditionally, because of their gratitude for the unmerited mercy with which God in Christ has valued them and met their human need. In addition, eucharistic worth implies a particular notion of freedom that involves a single-minded purity of heart that practices a kind of unmerited, unconditional love, free of the constraints of human love that require the recipient to achieve some level of merit. "For freedom Christ has set us free," declares Paul. And what have we been set free to do? Paul continues, "You were called to freedom . . . only do not use your freedom as an opportunity for the flesh, but through love be servants of one another" (Galatians 5: 1, 13). The servant does not consider whether those he serves merit or deserve love. He is liberated from such conditions and constraints to love freely and graciously, just as God in Christ is liberated to love humans freely and graciously. Christians, in eucharistic remembrance, should commit themselves to love humans freely and graciously and not meritoriously. Idols of the self seduce Christians into admiring (insofar as Jesus enhances one's worth, reputation, and success) but not following Jesus. Presupposing the eucharistic worth of all humans requires that Christians follow the pattern of Jesus' life according to which the entire family of humanity is treated graciously and compassionately as of equal, intrinsic, and ultimate worth.

Idols of the Marketplace: From Free Enterprise to Stewardship

Valuing humans eucharistically implies a model of economic practice that differs dramatically from the dominant free-market model, presupposed by capitalism, that idolizes both individualism and liberal freedom. This model presupposes individualism insofar as it believes that the locus of economic power should be individual and private instead of communal and public, and it presupposes liberal freedom insofar as it believes that those private individuals should be permitted to do as they please, produce as they please and profit as they please, independent (as far as is possible) of public interest and interference. Free enterprise, in short, presupposes the idol of instrumentalism: that the value of humans is defined in terms of their economic achievements, power to produce goods, and concomitant power to consume goods. Those of lesser worth, that is, those whose power to produce and consume goods is diminished or diminutive, those who have not realized their true economic potential, are generally considered lazy and unresourceful and of diminished value in society. People with diminutive economic resources are not, however, without some benefit, at least to those who possess economic power, for they are an important occasion for a peculiarly Protestant indulgence. By giving a bit of their excess to the less fortunate the economically powerful not only demonstrate publicly their good will and generosity and value to society but also justify their excess and assuage the feelings of guilt they properly feel for maintaining an economic system that greatly privileges them and underprivileges others. Charity, as Kysar says, "is the sharing of my excess for the sake of another who has too little, while at the same time assuring my continued excess."[44] Indeed, the disparity between empowered and disempowered must be maintained if the empowered are to continue to secure enough of society's goods to feel charitable and of value to society in that way. Idols of the marketplace, then, permit a community to admire Jesus without following him. They allow it to feel as if it is giving generously to the needy. Such charity, however, generates a pseudofeeling of generosity, for the giving is only out of one's excess, an excess generated by an economic system that distributes the goods of society unequally, unfairly, and unmercifully.

By whatever name we call such an economic system and practice—free enterprise, laissez faire, or capitalism—it is manifestly not commensurate with a biblical notion of stewardship. Indeed, the idol of free enterprise is undermined by the biblical notion of stewardship insofar as the latter model presupposes eucharistic notions of community and freedom. Stewardship presupposes a curious convergence of grace and accountability. Grace in that the power to manage affairs is simply given to the servant by the lord; servants do not merit these powers, they are simply recipients of the Lord's word and the power embodied in that word. Accountability in that the servant recipients are accountable to the Lord for their use of the power they have received. They are expected to use the resources over which they are stewards with a mercy equal to that grace and mercy that endowed them with those resources in the first place. This understanding is consistent with the Old English roots of the word "stewardship." As Max Stackhouse points out, "stewardship" derives from the practice of appointing

> reliable workers to be wardens of the pig sty: sty-wards. These wardens, living under the 'word' of the 'lord' of the manor, were to become trust-worthy custodians of resources that remain the possession of the lord of the manor, possessions that were indispensable to the life and well-being of the whole community. They were to lovingly and prudently care for that over which they had authority.[45]

A fundamental shift in thinking and practice must take place, in other words: a shift from thinking in terms of "possessions" to thinking in terms of "authority." The Lord of creation does not parcel out the resources of creation as pieces of economic property to be possessed by human stewards but rather endows people with the authority and responsibility to distribute the resources of creation in a merciful way. As wardens of God's creation and society's goods, covenantal communities should work to restructure the economic institutions and forces of society in such a way that, when it comes to economics, the goods of creation are distributed not only fairly but mercifully. This is compelling for two reasons, one theological and one practical. First, since God has dealt fairly and mercifully with covenantal communities, they also should deal with others fairly and mercifully. Second, the practice of establishing social structures that distribute the goods of creation fairly and mercifully (as did ancient Israel) satisfies the "word" of the "lord" of the manor more effectively and efficiently than do systems of free enterprise that conspire to leave the "sty" to magically manage itself. In short, stewardship requires the practice of the ancient, public virtue of compassion. It requires that stewards aspire to be global citizens, imagining and implementing ways to distribute the goods of the earth fairly and mercifully to the whole human family. This is the nature of true, covenantal freedom—the freedom to love compassionately, caring for all human creatures as the neighbors we are commanded to make of them. Practicing such stewardship requires, then, that a community follow and not just admire Jesus. It requires a community to devote itself passionately and personally to the kind of love, peace, and justice that together yield public projects of economic compassion.

Idols of the Sword: From Retaliation to Peacemaking

Idols of the sword take many forms, not the least of which is an often unconscious or sublimated devotion to retaliation, vengeance, and coercive ways of securing peace. Underlying the worship of this family of idols is the belief that justice is primarily a matter of strict fairness, an eye for an eye, a tooth for a tooth, and that equal coercion (turn about is fair play instead of turn the other cheek) is the primary means of executing it. Justice as fairness, in other words, is the basis on which communities often rationalize acting on feelings of retaliation and vengeance. Yet the biblical tradition suggests that retaliation and vengeance, when idolized by humans, degenerates into intimidation, violence, and abuse of those God commands us to treat as neighbors. In international conflicts, both humans and nations are susceptible to the idolatry of and misuse of retaliation, much as children, if permitted by their parents to do so, are likely to abuse the power to discipline siblings by retaliation. Nations, like children, tend to retaliate for at least two reasons: first, as a kind of catharsis, a means of venting anger and frustration and satisfying a need for expressing feelings of vengeance. Second, nations may retaliate because the anger they feel is an anger of despair and not an anger of hope. Anger of despair is myopic, unable to envision any alternative ways of approaching conflict and redeeming the perceived offender. In both cases, retaliation tends to function as an end rather than properly as a discipline by means of which to achieve redemption and reconciliation. The propensity of nations and the church to indulge the idol of retaliatory warmaking is a way of admiring instead of following Jesus. The church and nations generally justify retaliatory war on the basis of justice as strict fairness, by appealing to classic just war criteria. These criteria and the wars they justify are false idols by which Jesus is admired but not followed. First, just war criteria allow the church to reject some warmaking opportunities and choose peace, thereby deceiving itself into thinking it is following Jesus while at the same time finding ways to justify swearing allegiance to nation-states and sanctioning some of their wars. Second, adhering to just war criteria allows the church to feel it is advocating justice in the world, while treating the retaliatory punishment and violence of war as nevertheless a way of securing a kind of peace. Third, just war persuades the church into thinking it is doing justice in the world, while at the same time it preserves as enemies those others (including Christian) whom war seeks to destroy and whom covenantal communities are otherwise commanded to love as neighbors.

Compassion, as a public virtue underlying global citizenship, qualifies what is and is not acceptable when it comes to solving international or domestic conflicts. This is more easily seen if we keep in view the parent-child model and the means and end of discipline. Both the end and means of conducting international affairs and resolving conflicts are properly shaped by compassion. The aim of discipline—of conflict resolution—should not be simply distributing just deserts, although they should be served. The aim of punishment should be to chastise and redeem, not retaliate and serve justice in the sense of getting even. Punishment, in other words, is properly a means and not an end. Just deserts elevated to the status of discipline's aim promptly descends to the level of condemnation, retaliation, and recrimination and initiates a vicious cycle in which the punished child or nation is likely to respond in turn by condemning and retaliating. In contrast, the proper aim of domestic and international discipline is not punishment but chastisement and reconciliation. This distinction makes all the difference in an ethic of Christian virtue. Whereas the idol of equal fairness tends to employ punishment as an end, despairing of any hope of peaceful resolution and reconciliation, peacemaking employs discipline as a means to the hopeful end of transformation and reconciliation. Just as God in Christ seeks not to punish and condemn but to redeem and reconcile, so covenantal communities should influence international affairs by calling nations to discipline and redeem and not punish and condemn (John 3:17; Luke 6:37). Compassion as the public premise of Christian peace guides parents and nations in the proper means by which to achieve the aim of reconciliation. Christian discipline, on the one hand, precludes the use of intimidation, exploitation, and violence in its efforts to achieve redemption; it inspires, on the other hand, activating projects that establish a foundation for mutual trust and cooperation in domestic and international affairs. Devotion to peacemaking instead of the sword requires a community to follow and not simply admire Jesus. Following requires that a community make the same commitment to peace and peacemaking that Jesus embodies. To do this requires that its heart be so thoroughly shaped by God's love, peace, and justice that compassion and not retaliation are its natural and justifiable modus operandi. The parent should discipline compassionately and not vengefully so that the spirit of the child is redeemed and not crushed by violence and pain. If crushed, then the child will probably retaliate in kind when he is able. Nations should discipline compassionately and not vengefully, so the spirit of the disciplined nation is redeemed and not vengefully punished and crushed; otherwise that punished nation (e.g., Germany) is likely to seek to retaliate in kind, seeking vengeance of its own in some great and violent conflagration (e.g., Nazi Germany).

Idols of the Law: From Fairness to Mercy

Very often covenantal communities presuppose that what is required of them politically and legally is that they uphold just and fair laws and alter those that are not. *Lex talionis* is the most elemental and ancient manifestation of the kind of just fairness that underwrites the legal framework of many societies, ancient and modern, including the framework of most modern nation-states in the Western tradition. When it comes to retributive justice for the person who steals from another, some comparable possession, like freedom (e.g., two years' incarceration), must be legally confiscated. Of one who takes a life a life is required or a life sentence, considered comparable to taking a life. When it comes to distributive justice, all deserve equal opportunity of education and employment, it is thought, regardless of gender or race, and comparable work deserves comparable pay. Just laws and the principle of just fairness they reflect are, of course, necessary and compelling as guides to what is minimally required of covenantal communities (families of faith) as well as nation-states (the family of humanity). But law and justice petrify into idols when the faithful begin to think of law and just fairness as sufficient manifestations of its covenantal commitments and traditions. Worshiping such idols requires that Christians admire Jesus but not follow him; that they commit themselves to justice as equal fairness but not to the kind of justice as equal mercy embodied by Jesus. The current trend toward trying adolescents charged with murder as adults is a natural and logical extension of idolizing just fairness. This trend so apotheosizes *lex talionis* it is able to justify exacting from some children an eye for an eye and reinforces the claim that the primary aim of law as just fairness tends toward punishment and reward and not toward redemption and restoration.

Regrettably, attitudes presupposing something like *lex talionis* dominate even the consciousness and beliefs of many communities whose covenantal raison d'être is rooted in a particular habit of heart (i.e., compassionate mercy) that far exceeds the requirements of just fairness. Indeed, when covenantal communities require of themselves no more than just fairness and neglect or disown those feelings of grateful mercy without which they would not exist, then they sadly deceive themselves and become susceptible to worshiping the idol of just fairness.

What vision of society would covenantal communities create, however, if they were to follow and not merely admire Jesus; if they were to remain faithful to compassion as a public virtue? The ultimate aim of "retributive" justice, first of all, would not be just deserts but redemption and restoration. Second, the means of reproof would not be punishment and reward but chastising discipline, the implementation of procedures whereby the offender is likely to learn those skills necessary to live compassionately as a global citizen. Third, emotions inspiring covenantal practice would not include feelings of just vengeance and retaliation (just fairness) but feelings of merciful generosity that lead to projects of peacemaking and reconciliation. For covenantal communities, the ultimate aim of distributive justice, accordingly, would not be strict and equal distribution of society's goods but a stewardly, compassionate distribution of goods based on need, so that all members of the human family are sufficiently sustained in life and health. Fourth, the compassionate means of distribution will not be charity, which guarantees the continued excess of the charitable giver, but social structures and institutions that guarantee a minimum distribution of society's goods according to need. Finally, the emotions properly guiding distributive justice will not be desire for just deserts but feelings of compassion whereby covenantal communities treat others by the same mercy with which God has treated and redeemed them.

Educating the heart for compassionate, global citizenship is as urgent and compelling as it is demanding. Covenantal communities, including Christian ones, are certainly called to do so. I have argued that it is also incumbent on public institutions, like the public schools, to participate in such a task. Not only is this public virtue the practical point at which families of faith and the family of humanity intersect but it is a common and universal human experience on the basis of which societies flourish morally and without which societies wither and die. All relevant institutions, religious and nonreligious, can and should contribute to educating the heart for compassion. But covenantal communities have a special obligation to do so because they uniformly believe that they have been called not only by the voice of reason but also by the voice of God to love others as they love themselves.

FROM ADMIRING TO FOLLOWING

Throughout this book I have addressed, directly and indirectly, the question, What does "fidelity of heart" mean? or, the same thing, What does it mean to be a follower and not merely an admirer of Jesus? At the same time I have acknowledged with Kierkegaard that the peculiar failure of modern Christianity is its susceptibility to self-deception regarding its own fidelity of heart; in admiring Jesus it falsely believes it is actually following him; by hosting Jesus at dinner and engaging him in lively conversation about eternal issues, like the Pharisee, it thinks it is somehow, like the disreputable woman, devoutly and passionately following him. A good deal of modern Christian theology and ethics, as a function of this sort of self-deception, are in truth theologies of admiration and, for me at least, lack the ring of authenticity. The decay of modern Western Christianity, as a function of these theologies of admiration, is not therefore primarily a matter of heterodoxy or immorality; its decay is not manifest most profoundly in errant beliefs or in widespread vice and corruption, as many theologies of admiration (whether liberal, conservative, or orthodox) presuppose. These are little more than smokescreens for self-absorbed, fainthearted grumblers eager to deflect especially their own attention from the self-deception on which they craft their theologies.

Contemporary Christianity has devised at least two ways of sublimating this self-deception. In chapter 1 I referred to these two ways as "faith as magic" and "faith as amusement."[46] Faith as magic manifests itself in at least a couple of ways.[47] The one I attend to here exploits faith as a means to the preconceived end of arousing certain desirable emotions. The means by which magical faith secures this end involves the use of a wide variety of ritual, habitual practices that are central and not merely peripheral to magical success. These practices include everything from high church liturgies (incense, gesticulations, art, dance, and common prayer) to low church worship (praise services, revivals, personal devotions, healings, and speaking in tongues). Such practices, of course, are not in themselves deceptive and misleading, but their use as magic is deceptive insofar as they are commonly employed in the service of arousing emotions as an end in themselves. How so? The aim of faith as magic to arouse emotions is not itself unique, for faith as amusement also aims at arousing emotions. What is unique is that the emotions aroused by magic are, as Collingwood puts it, "focused and crystallized, consolidated into effective agents in practical life." This is different from faith as amusement, for in amusement emotions are aroused for cathartic purposes, to discharge them so that they will "not interfere with practical life." With magic, emotions are "canalized and directed upon practical life." The primary function of faith's magical incantations is to generate in the agent or agents certain "emotions that are considered necessary or useful for the work of living."[48] Faith as magic involves, accordingly, the tendency of devotees to employ rituals and pious devotion as a means of invoking the presence of the divine—invoking the name of Jesus and the power associated with that name. By so doing certain emotions are aroused that are needed for protection, sanction, and blessing in carrying out even the smallest tasks of daily life. Yet the arousal of emotion by employing faith magically, truth be told, is not really to inspire adherents to "follow" Jesus, as the devotees themselves would believe. Rather it is to invite Jesus to follow them and be with them in the routines of daily living and ex post facto to sanction their chosen style of life. Such faith invites Jesus to defend, sanctify, and sanitize a worldly style of life already in place, a life of just vengeance and just war, for example, a lifestyle common to those in the world who live quite apart from Christian faith or any faith at all. Magical faith does not, as commonly believed, empower one to follow Jesus by living a transformed life of covenantal love, peace, justice, and compassion; rather it exploits Jesus as a way of sanitizing the life of convenience and comfort one is eagerly living or eager to live. For this reason faith as magic evokes emotions that, according to Collingwood, are "valued on account of [their] function in practical life, evoked in order to discharge that function."[49] Practicing magical faith becomes for Christians "a kind of dynamo supplying the mechanism of practical life with the emotional current that drives it."[50] Yet magical faith admits only of admirers of Jesus and not followers. It does not require transformation, it does not require covenantal love, peace, justice, and compassion as Jesus preached and practiced them. It is not difficult to see that faith as magic and its theologies of admiration do not therefore require a community to carefully and diligently educate its heart for virtue, for the arousal of the desired emotions requires only the immediacy of pious devotion and not the discipline of obediential dispositions. Faith as magic requires only adherents who believe in a power that, when invoked, will arouse in them certain cherished emotions that make them feel holy and wholly justified in living lives of comfort and convenience.

Faith as amusement is another version of admiring instead of following. Ritual techniques and habitual practices are employed as means to the preconceived end of arousing emotions. Unlike magical faith, however, faith as amusement arouses emotions not for the sake of discharging the affairs of practical life but rather for the sake of catharsis, so that the emotions aroused "shall not interfere with practical life."[51] The emotions aroused by amusement are not useful, as with magic, "but enjoyable. . . . The emotions generated by an amusement must be discharged, like any others; but they are discharged within the amusement itself."[52] Experiencing the emotions aroused by participation in ritualistic practice: liturgy, hymn singing, private or common prayer—the eucharist, for example—is valued in and of itself as enjoyable and sufficient for the action of faith. This is the peculiarity of faith as amusement. The buildings and institutions of a religion, its rituals and practices, its prayers and scriptures, create a kind of "make-believe situation," as Collingwood puts it, "in which deep emotions can be safely discharged and diffused"[53] without having them intrude on the affairs of one's practical and professional life. Religious emotions aroused for the sake of amusement are thereby discharged within the sanctuary of faith. Doing so permits a person to satisfy a desire for spirituality (e.g., to feel forgiven) without requiring a significant transformation of that person's life (e.g., offer forgiveness to enemies), without requiring daily life and thought to be radically transformed by the covenantal love, peace, justice, and compassion preached and practiced by Jesus. This is but another way of saying that faith as amusement allows one to admire without requiring one to follow Jesus. Like magic, faith as amusement does not require that Christian virtues be carefully and painstakingly cultivated, that the heart be educated for compassionate global citizenship. It requires only that the amusements that arouse emotions be appealing to the adherent and that adherents situate themselves in relation to certain amusements (rituals and practices) that arouse the desired cathartic feelings. It is not a matter of educating the heart so much as properly situating oneself so that desireable feelings might be aroused and safely discharged.

Faith as magic and amusement are corruptions of Christian faith. As modern forms of religious self-deception, they are relentlessly corrosive, undermining with devastating completeness Christianity's very foundations and its capacity to fulfill its own mission, namely, that of calling itself and others to a distinctive, difficult, and disciplined covenantal pattern of life, one like what I have sketched in this book. Faith as magic and amusement ultimately establishes a collection of Christians (Christendom) analogous to honorary pallbearers who assume the label but not the labor of actually bearing the bier. Or Christendom becomes, as Kierkegaard puts it, "a collection of what one might call honorary Christians, in the same sense as one speaks of honorary doctors who get their degree without having to take an examination."[54] To admire Jesus is not such a bad thing, unless, of course, one mistakenly believes that in doing so one is actually following him. To be so deceived is the death of the very faith one pretends to propound. With faith as magic and amusement all danger and provocation are sucked out of Christianity, but with faith as convenantal virtue they are reintroduced in the midst of Christendom itself. Christian communities are themselves those who are accused of coming to Jesus by night, under the cover of a dark self-deception in which the labor and pain of being born again are meaningless inconveniences. As covenantal, faith does not arouse emotions for the sake of magic or amusement. Instead it strives to "practice" them. By "practicing emotions" I mean that the emotions of genuine faith are to be expressed or embodied as concrete moral projects in and through which are manifest dispositions that foster love, peace, justice and compassion. As covenantal, the heart of faith constitutes itself, as I have shown, in terms of obediential dispositions and empathetic emotions. Emotions so constituted do not and cannot be aroused magically, nor are they in the least amusing. Christians who expect faith to arouse emotions that will sanitize a style of moral life (e.g., just war and just fairness) that many people live quite apart from God's grace and love and Christians who expect to be amused and entertained and left alone will be equally disappointed by the demands and disciplines of covenantal faith. But to those Christians who want not magic or amusement but the true, beating heart of Christian faith, fidelity of heart supplies an answer. I have already indicated throughout this book what that entails: a passionate, personal, covenantal commitment to following the way that Jesus practiced love, peace, justice, and compassion.

All religious and philosophical ways of life sponsor their own distinctive versions of admiring instead of following. All are susceptible, I think, to a self-deception paralleling that of Christianity. All, accordingly, must diligently take care to practice their versions of fidelity of heart. In so doing, we shall find that for all morally compelling traditions, practicing one's faith will converge with other faiths in the common project of educating the heart for compassionate, global citizenship. Practicing emotions like compassion requires that the heart be educated and virtue cultivated and not merely that certain feelings be aroused. I have tried to show in this chapter what educating such a heart entails. As we reflecting on that, we can recognize one more dimension Christian faith must exhibit if it is to forgo both amusement and magic and educate itself in the practice of compassion: it must be prophetic,[55] not in the sense of predicting things to come but in the sense of telling itself, at considerable risk, that many who loudly lay claim to Christian faith may very well be deceived about their faith, and acting in bad faith in relation to it. Christian faith must also be prophetic in acknowledging that alien Samaritans may very well be practicing, by God's grace, the compassionate, global citizenship that many in the Christian community claim but fail to practice. For the unfaithfulness that comes from self-deception there is only one remedy: fidelity of heart itself.

Notes

One. Matters of the Heart

1. All quotations from the Bible are from the Revised Standard Version.

2. The recent retrieval of the role of virtue in Kant's moral philosophy is a compelling corrective and perhaps indicative that Aristotelian and Kantian moral approaches are not as far apart as previously supposed. It turns out that they both tend to emphasize the importance of character ethics and virtue and even make a place for emotions. Mary Gregor's introduction, translation, and notes to Kant's *Metaphysics of Morals* (Cambridge, England: Cambridge University Press, 1991) is a good example of such a corrective.

3. Martha Nussbaum, *Love's Knowledge: Essays on Philosophy and Literature* (New York: Oxford University Press, 1990), 40–42.

4. *Ibid.*, 40.

5. See chapter 3 for a more detailed discussion of Fletcher's views.

6. Nussbaum, *Love's Knowledge*, 42.

7. Kierkegaard, *Training in Christianity and the Edifying Discourse Which "Accompanied" It*, trans. Walter Lowrie (Princeton: Princeton University Press, 1944), 234.

8. *Ibid.*, 232.

9. *Ibid.*, 237–38.

10. *Ibid.*, 231.

11. *Ibid.*, 236.

12. Edward Long, *To Liberate and Redeem: Moral Reflections on the Biblical Narrative* (Cleveland, Ohio: Pilgrim Press, 1997), 10.

13. National Conference of Catholic Bishops, *The Challenge of Peace: God's Promise and Our Response* (Washington, D.C., 1983).

Two. Reenfranchising the Heart

1. Jeffrey Stout, *Flight from Authority* (Notre Dame: University of Notre Dame Press, 1981), 97.

2. Paul Lauritzen, "Is 'Narrative' Really a Panacea? The Use of 'Narrative' in the Work of Metz and Hauerwas," *Journal of Religion* 67, 3(1987): 322–39; quotation on p. 324.

3. Gary Comstock, "Truth or Meaning: Ricoeur versus Frei on Biblical Narrative,"

Journal of Religion 66, 2 (1986): 117–41; quotation on p. 188. John Howard Yoder offers a similar analysis of theology's contemporary dilemma: theological knowledge is often seen as "a null-sum game in which we must choose between authenticity and intelligibility"; "On Not Being Ashamed of the Gospel: Particularity, Pluralism, and Validation," *Faith and Philosophy* 9, 3 (July 1992): 288.

4. Edward J. Oakes, "Apologetics and the Pathos of Narrative Theology," *Journal of Religion* 72, 1 (1992): 37–58; quotation on p. 38.

5. See especially Martha Nussbaum, "Narrative Emotions: Beckett's Genealogy of Love," *Ethics* 98, 2 (January 1988): 225–54, reprinted in *Love's Knowledge: Essays on Philosophy and Literature* (New York: Oxford University Press, 1990), 286–313.

6. Nussbaum, *Love's Knowledge,* 40–42. A similar discussion of classical and modern treatments of reason and emotion can be found in Sidney Callahan, *In Good Conscience: Reason and Emotion in Moral Decision Making* (San Francisco: Harper/Collins, 1991); see especially chapters 3 and 4. Callahan selects St. Ignatius in theology and Kant in philosophy as typical models of how classical and modern thinkers dismiss the emotions.

7. Callahan, *In Good Conscience*, 40. For a review of the literature on the psychology of cognitive emotions, see N. Frijda, *The Emotions* (New York: Cambridge University Press, 1987).

8. Andrew Ortony, Gerald Close, and Allen Collins, *The Cognitive Structure of Emotions* (New York: Cambridge University Press, 1988), 5. Roger Scruton similarly argues for a threefold understanding of emotions in "Emotion, Practical Knowledge and Common Culture," in *Explaining Emotions*, ed. Amelie Rorty (Berkeley: University of California Press, 1980), 519–36; see especially 524.

9. Robert Solomon, *The Passions* (Notre Dame, Ind.: University of Notre Dame Press, 1976), 251; see 262–67. See also Wayne Proudfoot, *Religious Experience* (Berkeley: University of California Press, 1985), especially chapter 3.

10. Aristotle, *Rhetoric,* trans. W. Rhys Roberts, in *Works of Aristotle Translated into English*, vol. 11 (Oxford: Clarendon Press, 1924), 1378a. Aristotle's theory of emotions is well known and much discussed. See, for example, Martha Nussbaum, *The Fragility of Goodness: Luck and Ethics in Ancient Greek Tragedy and Philosophy* (New York: Cambridge University Press, 1986) and *Love's Knowledge,* 40–44.

11. Jonathan Edwards, *Religious Affections* (Portland, Ore.: Multnomah Press, 1984), 5–7. Friedrich Schleiermacher, as is well known, likewise recognized the importance in religion of a "feeling of absolute dependence." The true character of religion is a spiritual phenomenon "in which the soul is dissolved in the immediate feeling of the infinite and Eternal"; see *On Religion: Speeches to Its Cultured Despisers* (New York: Harper and Row, 1958), 15–16. But for Schleiermacher this feeling "is opposing the assertions from other quarters that piety is a Knowing, or a Doing, or both"; see *The Christian Faith*, 2nd ed., trans. H. R. Mackintosh and J. S. Stewart (New York: Harper and Row, 1963), 9. See also Proudfoot's discussion of Schleiermacher's noncognitivist view of feeling, in *Religious Experience*, 1–23.

12. Edwards, *Religious Affections*, 108. For an analysis of Edwards's view of religious affections see William Wainwright, "Jonathan Edwards and the Sense of Heart," *Faith and Philosophy* 7, 1 (January 1990): 43–62.

13. Paul Lauritzen, "Emotions and Religious Ethics," *Journal of Religious Ethics* 16, 2 (1988):307–24; quotation on p. 312. Wayne Proudfoot is another recent thinker who de-

velops a cognitivist theory of emotions, especially as they have to do with religious experience. See his *Religious Experience*, chapter 3.

14. Nussbaum, *Love's Knowledge*, 291.

15. *Ibid.*

16. Nussbaum and Lauritzen assume that belief and judgment are identical and interchangeable. But they are not. Belief is generally understood as a mental act of assenting, whether consciously or not, to a proposition or collection of propositions. Judgment is a cognitive act whereby a person evaluates what the world is like in terms of the beliefs to which the mind assents. What I argue is that emotions are constituted by judgments; these emotional judgments are made on the basis of beliefs to which a person has given assent. See Lauritzen, "Emotions and Religious Ethics," 312.

17. Robert C. Roberts, "Emotions among the Virtues of the Christian Life," *Journal of Religious Ethics* 20, 1 (spring 1992): 43.

18. Roger Scruton, "Emotion, Practical Knowledge and Common Culture," in *Explaining Emotions*, ed. Amelie Rorty (Berkeley: University of California Press, 1980) 519–36; quotation on p. 529.

19. Ortony et al., *Cognitive Structure*, 1.

20. Edwards, *Religious Affections*, 5.

21. *Ibid.*, 9–10.

22. Lauritzen, "Emotions and Religious Ethics," 315. Lauritzen quotes here from Michelle Rosaldo, "Toward an Anthropology of Self and Feeling," in *Culture Theory*, ed. Richard A. Schwedeer and Robert E. LeVine (Cambridge, England: Cambridge University Press, 1984): 137–57, 143.

23. Solomon, *The Passions*, 212.

24. Scruton, "Emotions," 528.

25. Edwards, *Religious Affections*, 7. Edwards goes on to distinguish affection from passion in terms of intensity. A passion, he says is "sudden and more violent"; "[t]he mind is more overpowered and less in control."

26. See Aristotle, *Metaphysics*, trans. W. D. Ross, in *The Basic Works of Aristotle*, ed. Richard McKeon. New York: Random House, 1941. 1040–50.

27. Solomon, *The Passions*, 230.

28. Edwards, *Religious Affections*, 9.

29. These are terms used by Charles Allen in "The Primacy of Phronesis: A Proposal for Avoiding Frustrating Tendencies in Our Conceptions of Rationality," *Journal of Religion* 69, 3 (1989): 359–74; see especially 359–63.

30. Stephen Crites, "The Narrative Quality of Experience," in *Why Narrative? Readings in Narrative Theology*, ed. Stanley Hauerwas and L.Gregory Jones (Grand Rapids, Mich.: Eerdmans 1989), 65–88; quotation on p. 85.

31. Allen, "Primacy of Phronesis," 360.

32. Quoted in *Ibid.*

33. Quoted in William Placher, *Unapologetic Theology: A Christian Voice in a Pluralistic Conversation* (Louisville, Ky.: Westminster/John Knox Press, 1989), 157.

34. Paul Ricoeur, *The Rule of Metaphor*, 246 (Toronto: University of Toronto Press, 1977), 221.

35. *Ibid.*, 246. Ricoeur of course does not ignore emotions, for example, in *The Symbolism of Evil*; but his interest is more in the metaphorical-mythological forms emotions

take and not so much, as is mine here, with the structure and dynamics of emotions and how they are bearers of truth.

36. See especially Søren Kierkegaard, *Concluding Unscientific Postscript*, part II. Trans. David Swenson, Princeton, N.J.: Princeton University Press, 1944.

37. This idea of intersubjectivity is akin to R. G. Collingwood's notion of historical reenactment. Speaking of the inside of an event, he says that "an act of thought [e.g., an emotional judgment] in addition to actually happening, is capable of sustaining itself and being revived and repeated without loss of its identity." I argue that the judgments/projects of emotions can be revived and repeated without the loss of identity. *The Idea of History* (Oxford: Oxford University Press, 1960), 300.

38. Solomon, *The Passions*, 104.

39. Nussbaum, *Love's Knowledge*, 375–76.

40. William J. Prior, "Compassion: A Critique of Moral Rationalism," *Philosophy and Theology* 2, 2 (1987): 173.

41. Solomon, *The Passions*, 272.

42. Daniel Beaumont, "The Modality of Narrative: A Critique of Some Recent Views of Narrative in Theology," summarizes several uses of narrative in contemporary thought (Ricoeur, Crites, Hauerwas, MacIntyre) and for various reasons rejects them as inadequate. Beaumont does not undertake the more difficult task of setting forth his own view of narrative, except to suggest that what should be at stake "is not the narrative form in which experience is *already found* but rather the preconditions of narrative, the way in which the narrative arises for the subject." *Journal of the American Academy of Religion* 65, 1 (spring 1997): 138.

43. Allen, "Primacy of Phnoresis," 360.

44. George Lindbeck, *The Nature of Doctrine: Religion and Theology in a Postliberal Age* (Philadelphia: Westminster Press, 1984): 131.

45. Yoder, "On Not Being Ashamed of the Gospel," 287.

46. Howard Brody, *Stories of Sickness* (New Haven: Yale University Press, 1987), 5.

47. This is a point Comstock stresses in analyzing Ricoeur's theory of meaning, especially as Ricoeur develops this theory in *The Rule of Metaphor*. See Comstock, "Truth or Meaning," 132.

48. Crites, "The Narrative Quality of Experience," 67.

49. David Burrell and Stanley Hauerwas, "From System to Story," in *Why Narrative? Readings in Narrative Theology*, ed. Stanley Hauerwas and L.G. Jones (Grand Rapids, Mich.: Eerdmans, 1989), 168–190; quotation on pp. 177–78.

50. Hans Frei, *The Identity of Jesus Christ: The Hermeneutical Bases of Dogmatic Theology* (Philadelphia: Fortress Press, 1975), 170–71. See Comstock's discussion of Frei's theory of meaning in "Truth or Meaning," 122–30.

51. Although in "Emotions and Religious Ethics" Lauritzen at times seems to acknowledge the mutuality of emotion and narrative (e.g., 315), this line of thought is not pursued. In "Is 'Narrative' Really a Panacea? The Use of 'Narrative' in the Work of Metz and Hauerwas?" Lauritzen raises questions about the adequacy of these [Metz's and Hauerwas's] accounts of truth" (338) but misses an opportunity to advance the debate by incorporating into his discussion of narrative his insightful work on emotion; *Journal of Religion* 67, 3 (1987): 322–39.

52. These are familiar themes throughout Kierkegaard's thought. See especially chapters

1, 2, and 3 of *Philosophical Fragments*, and in *Training in Christianity* see "Blessed Is He Whosoever Is Not Offended in Me," especially sec. D.

53. Collingwood sets forth this analysis in *The Idea of History* (see especially part 5). H. Richard Niebuhr's examination of external and internal history parallel's Collingwood's quite closely; see *The Meaning of Revelation* (New York: Macmillan, 1960), especially chapters 2 and 3.

54. *The Idea of History*, 213.

55. Nussbaum, *Love's Knowledge*, 287.

56. Ibid., p. 40.

57. See Ludwig Wittgenstein, *Philosophical Fragments*, trans. G. E. M. Anscomb (New York: Macmillan, 1953), sects. 201–19, pp. 207–19.

58. A. C. Grayling, *Wittgenstein* (New York: Oxford University Press, 1987), 82.

59. Nussbaum, *Love's Knowledge*, 265–66.

60. Patricia Greenspan, *Emotions and Reasons: An Inquiry into Emotional Justification* (New York: Routledge, 1988), 3–5. Greenspan's entire book develops the notion of emotional justification in some detail and in a way with which I largely agree. I recommend it to those who would like to pursue in more depth the notion, only introduced here, of emotional justification. Robert C. Roberts makes the point about the self-referentiality of justifying emotions in "Emotions as Access to Religious Truths," *Faith and Philosophy* 9, 1 (January 1992): 83–94; see especially 90–92.

61. Stanley Hauerwas, *A Community of Character: Toward a Constructive Christian Social Ethic* (Notre Dame, Ind.: University of Notre Dame Press, 1981), 111.

62. Gilbert C. Meilaender, *The Theory and Practice of Virtue* (Notre Dame, Ind.: University of Notre Dame Press, 1984), 6.

63. Hauerwas, *A Community of Character*, 111.

64. Lisa Sowle Cahill, *Love Your Enemies: Discipleship, Pacifism, and Just War Theory* (Minneapolis: Fortress Press, 1994); see 149–52 and 236–37 for a discussion of the nature of these two traditions.

65. *Ibid.*, 236.

66. *Ibid.*, 236.

67. *Ibid.*, 151.

68. Meilaender *The Theory Practice of Virtue*, 7, 8, 28.

69. *Ibid.*, 5.

70. Cahill, *Love Your Enemies*, 236.

71. *Ibid.*, 236.

72. *Ibid.*, 149–50.

73. *Ibid.*, 236.

Three. Love as a Christian Virtue

1. All quotations of biblical passages are from the Revised Standard Version.

2. Martha Nussbaum, *Love's Knowledge: Essays on Philosophy and Literature* (New York: Oxford University Press, 1990), 261.

3. Stephen Pope, "Love in Contemporary Christian Ethics," *Journal of Religious Ethics* 23, 1 (spring 1995): 167.

4. Dana Radcliffe, "Compassion and Commanded Love," *Faith and Philosophy* 11, 2

(1994): 50–71. By the term "commanded love" Radcliffe refers to the Kantian tradition and its emphasis on love as duty to rational law so that love is a matter under a person's direct, voluntary control.

5. Immanual Kant, *Foundations of the Metaphysics of Morals*, trans. Lewis Beck White (Indianapolis: Bobbs-Merrill, 1959), 15–16.

6. Ronald Green, "Kant on Christian Love," in *The Love Commandments: Essays in Christian Ethics and Moral Philosophy*, ed. Edmund Santurri and William Werpehowski (Washington, D.C.: Georgetown University Press, 1990), 163.

7. Radcliffe, "Comparison and Commanded Love," 51.

8. Sally Purvis makes this point nicely in "Mother, Neighbors and Strangers," *Journal of Feminist Studies in Religion* 7 (spring 1991): 19–34. In *Works of Love* Kierkegaard recommends the unknown dead as exemplary objects of Christian love: "The work of love in remembering one who is dead is . . . a work of the most disinterested, the freest, the most faithful love. Therefore go out and practice it; remember one dead and learn in just this way to love the living disinterestedly, freely, faithfully. In the relationship to one dead you have the criterion whereby you can test yourself" as to Christian love, quoted by (Purvis, 21).

9. Joesph Fletcher, *Situation Ethics: The New Morality* (Philadelphia: Westminster Press, 1996), 108, 103. What is surprising is that Fletcher at times speaks of love in terms of specific emotions but not without any apparent sense of self-contradiction: "Make no mistake about it; love can not only make people angry, it can be angry too," 117.

10. Fletcher, *Situation Ethics*, 104, 119.

11. C. H. Dodd, *Gospel and Law* (New York: Columbia University Press, 1951), 42. See also Fletcher, *Situation Ethics*, 105.

12. Preston Williams and other prominent African-American theologians, notably Martin Luther King, Jr., have absorbed the Kantian tradition's understanding of love. Even though love as an intensely self-interested emotion plays a powerful role in the black community's quest for freedom and justice, Williams and King disown in theory love's affective power. Indeed, an apparent discrepancy obtains between what Williams claims in theory and what he proposes in practice. He denies love's emotional quality while invoking love's emotional power. An "ontological understanding of love means . . . that love cannot be defined as a sentiment or an emotion. To understand love in this way is not only to deprive love of its ontological status but also rob it of its ability to be commanded." Yet Williams can also claim that love is "a potent force for social change" with the ability "to create and sustain . . . cultural values, patterns, and norms, and social institutions. The task of love [is] to empower all beings to fulfill their form without harming or diminishing the existence of other beings." But the powerful passion that King denies of love in theory is precisely the power that allows him to speak of love as "a potent force for social change." See Preston Williams, "An Analysis of the Conception of Love and Its Influence on Justice in the Thought of Martin Luther King, Jr.," *Journal of Religious Ethics* 18 (fall 1990): 22, 24.

13. David Sanderlin, "Charity According to St. John of the Cross," *Journal of Religious Ethics* 21, 1 (1993): 87. Sanderlin's views on the nature of self-denying love are not straightforward and simple. He wants to argue, for example, that "disinterested charity requires only an interior loss of desires for friendships and other temporal goods" but "not the literal sacrifice of these goods."

14. *Ibid.*, 95, 96.

15. *Ibid.*, 98.

16. See Ronald Green, "Kant on Christian Love," and Dana Radcliffe, "Compassion and Commanded Love," in *Faith and Philosophy* 11, 2 (1994) especially pages 50–55.

17. Green, "Kant on Christian Love," 261–66. Green's argument is a persuasive antidote to the popular misconception that Kant's moral theory excludes human emotions entirely.

18. Immanuel Kant, *The Doctrine of Virtue*, trans. Mary J. Gregor (Philadelphia: University of Pennsylvania Press, 1964), 62.

19. *Ibid.*, 126.

20. See, for example, the first two chapters of Edward C. Vacek, *Love, Human and Divine: The Heart of Christian Ethics.* (Washington, D. C.: Georgetown University Press, 1994).

21. Radcliffe, "Compassion and Commanded Love." 53.

22. Robert C. Roberts, "Emotions among the Virtues of the Christian Life," *Journal of Religious Ethics* 20, 1 (spring 1992), 43.

23. Timothy Jackson, "Christian Love and Political Violence," in *The Love Commandments: Essays in Christian Ethics and Moral Philosophy*, ed. Edmund Santurri and William Werpehowski (Washington, D.C.: Georgetown University Press, 1989), 213.

24. Gilbert Meilaender, *The Limits of Love: Some Theological Explorations* (University Park: Pennsylvania State University Press, 1987), 21.

25. Roberta Bondi, *To Love as God Loves: Conversations with the Early Church* (Philadelphia: Fortress Press, 1987), 29,30.

26. Jonathan Edwards, *Charity and Its Fruits: Christian Love as Manifested in the Heart and Life* (Carlisle, Pa.: Banner of Truth Trust, 1969), 155.

27. Quoted from Augustine's *Confessions* in Anders Nygren, *Agape and Eros*, trans. Philip Watson (Philadelphia: Westminster Press, 1953), 472–75; emphasis added.

28. Nygren, *Agape and Eros*, 473.

29. Bondi, *To Love as God Loves*, 42.

30. Roberts, "Emotions among the Virtues," 60.

31. Jonathan Edwards, *Religious Affections* (Portland, Ore.: Multnomah Press, 1984), 130–31.

32. See *Ibid.*, 130–31.

33. *Ibid.*, 126–27.

34. *Ibid.*, 127.

35. *Ibid.*, 128.

36. *Ibid.*, 129–30.

37. *Ibid.*, 130.

38. Nygren distinguishes between "vulgar eros" and "heavenly eros." "Between vulgar eros and Christian agape," he says, "there is no relation at all . . . The heavenly Eros, however, in its most sublimated and spiritualized form, is the born rival of the idea of Agape"; 51; see *Agape and Eros*, chapters 3 and 4.

39. *Ibid.*, 90–102.

40. Bruce Birch, *To Love as We Are Loved: The Bible and Relationships* (Nashville, Tenn.: Abingdon Press, 1992), 35.

41. Edwards does not use the word *eros* but employs the Augustinian language of appetite, which is loaded with the sense and meaning of *eros* as desire and passion for a particular other. I am especially indebted in this discussion to Paula M. Cooey's analysis of Edwards's view on this matter in "Eros and Intimacy in Edwards," *Journal of Religion* 68 (October, 1989): 484–501.

42. *Ibid.*, 485–486. In this passage Cooey is explicating Edwards's conception of Christian love, virtue, and affections.

43. *Ibid.*, 490.

44. Edwards, *The Philosophy of Jonathan Edwards: From his private notebooks.* Ed. H. G. Townsend. Eugene, Ore.: University of Oregon Monographs, 1955, 204.

45. Vacek, *Love, Human, and Divine,*, 252.

46. Purvis, "Mother, Neighbors, and Strangers," 19–36.

47. Sanderlin suggests that humans quite properly possess a "rational appetite that is naturally directed towards universal, infinite good," and that "[w]e rightly desire God for our happiness, so our love for God includes an appropriate element of self-interested, possessive desire." But he goes on to insist with St. John of the Cross "that we should desire nothing but God" and love others without any desirous attachments to them for any qualities they may possess. For then we would be loving them out of possessive self-interest and not properly out of disinterestedness, for the sake of desiring God alone. Paul's "affectionate desire" for the Thessalonians, according to Sanderlin's restrictions, would seem to be inappropriately possessive and self-interested and hence not properly charity. See Sanderlin, "Charity According to St. John of the Cross," 90–95.

48. William Placher, *Narratives of a Vulnerable God: Christ, Theology, and Scripture* (Louisville, Ky.: Westminster/John Knox Press, 1994), 3.

49. *Ibid.*, 139.

50. *Ibid.*, 116; see a few passages that reflect this focus: p. xiii, xv, 6, 10, 15, 116, 138, 162. There are many more such passages.

51. Gabriel Marcel, *The Philosophy of Existentialism*, trans. Manya Harari (New York: Citadel Press, 1963), 39. Nel Noddings makes the same point about "presence" and "disposability" in *Caring: A Feminine Approach to Ethics and Moral Education* (Berkeley: University of California Press, 1984), 19.

52. Bondi, *To Love as God Loves*, 44–45.

53. Marcel, *Philosophy of Existentialism*, 40.

54. Robert Kysar, *Called to Care: Biblical Images for Social Ministry* (Minneapolis: Fortress Press, 1991), 109.

55. Cooey, "Eros and Intimacy in Edwards," 491.

56. Birch, *To Love as We Are Loved*, 31.

57. Radcliffe, "Compassion and Commanded Love," 50. Radcliffe points to such passages as Matthew 9:35–36, 14:13–14, 15:32, 20:29–34; Mark 1:40–45, 6:34; and Luke 7:11–17.

58. James Gustafson, *Can Ethics Be Christian?* (Chicago: University of Chicago Press, 1975), 72, quoted in Radcliffe, "Compassion and Commanded Love," 66.

59. David Steere, "Our Capacity for Sadness and Joy: An Essay on Life Before Death," in *Theology of Joy*, ed. Johanna Baptist Metz and Jean-Pierre Jossua (New York: Herder and Herder, 1974), 15.

60. Edwards, *Religious Affections*, 161–62.

61. Johanna Metz, "Joy and Grief, Cheerfulness, Melancholy, and Humour or 'the Difficulty of Saying Yes,'" in Metz and Jossua, *Theology of Joy*, 79.

62. Francis Fiorenza, "Joy and Pain as Paradigmatic for Language about God," in *Theology of Joy*, ed. Johanna Baptist Metz and Jean-Pierre Jossua (New York: Herder and Herder, 1974), 79.

63. Carroll E. Izard, *Human Emotions* (New York: Plenum Press, 1977), 303–4.

64. For a full analysis of compassion, see chapter 6, "Compassion and Public Covenant."

65. Maya Angelou, *All God's Children Need Traveling Shoes* (New York: Random House, 1986), 206–9.

66. Max Scheler, *The Nature of Sympathy*, trans. Peter Heath (Hamden, Conn.: Archon Books, 1970), 12–13.

67. *Ibid.*, 13.

68. National Conference of Catholic Bishops, *Economic Justice for All : Pastoral Letter on Catholic Social Teaching and the U. S. Economy* (Washington, D.C.: United States Catholic Conference, 1986), 33–34.

69. Soren Kierkegaard, *Works of Love: Some Christian Reflections in the Form of Discourses*, trans. Howard and Edna Hong (New York: Harper, 1962), 72.

70. *Ibid.*, 249.

71. *Ibid.*, 255–256.

72. *Ibid.*, 259.

73. National Conference of Catholic Bishops, *Economic Justice for All*, 15.

74. *Ibid.*, 28.

75. *Ibid.*, 93.

76. Kysar, *Called to Care*, 109.

77. National Conference of Catholic Bishops, *Economic Justice for All*, 29–40.

78. Kysar, *Called to Care*, 109.

79. See Kysar's discussion of Israel's socioeconomic structures in *Called to Care*, chapter 1. My suggestion that covenantal economics implies a radical restructuring and redistribution of economic forces is in keeping with recommendations made by Daniel Finn and Prentiss Pemberton in *Toward a Christian Economic Ethic: Stewardship and Social Power* (Minneapolis: Winston Press, 1985); see especially chapter 8.

80. Kysar, *Called to Care*, 47.

81. Stanley Hauerwas, *The Peaceable Kingdom* (Notre Dame, Ind. University of Notre Dame Press, 1983), 19.

82. *Ibid.*, 24.

83. By emphasizing that commanded love must remain embedded in the particularity of Christian history and tradition, I do not mean to suggest that Christian ethics is irreversibly sectarian, with nothing to contribute to public morality and political life. Instead, as I argue in chapter 6, Christian love as compassion, as shared emotions, makes possible a basis for a plurality of religious and secular traditions to participate in a shared public morality.

Four. Peace as a Christian Virtue

1. Lisa Sowle Cahill, *Love Your Enemies: Discipleship, Pacifism, and Just War Theory* (Minneapolis: Fortress Press, 1994), 2.

2. Walter Wink, "Neither Passivity nor Violence: Jesus' Third Way," *Forum* 7, 1–2 (March–June 1991): 5–6.

3. Richard B. Hays, *The Moral Vision of the New Testament: Community, Cross, and New Creation* (San Francisco Harper, 1996), 321.

4. For discussions of these varieties of interpretations, see Julian Carron, "The Second

Commandment in the New Testament: Your Yes Is Yes and Your No Is No," *Communio* 20 (spring 1993): 5–25, and Dennis C. Duling, "Against Oaths: Crossan Sayings Parallels 59," *Forum* 6,2 (June 1990): 99–138.

5. See Corron, "The Second Commandment," 20; see also 38–40.

6. Katherine Sakenfeld, *Faithfulness in Action: Loyalty in Biblical Perspective* (Philadelphia: Fortress Press, 1985), 137.

7. Tertullian, "The Soldier's Chaplet," in *War and the Christian Conscience: From Augustine to Martin Luther King, Jr.*, ed. by Albert Marrin (Chicago: Henry Regnery 1971), 52–53.

8. This account of the trial and death of Saint Marcellus is included in Marrin, *War and the Christian Conscience*, 47–49.

9. Michael Sattler, "Schleitheim Confession," in *Sources of Protestant Theology*, ed. by William A. Scott (New York: Bruce 1971), 18–24.

10. Victor Paul Furnish, *The Moral Teaching of Paul: Selected Issues* (Nashville: Abingdon Press, 1985), 126.

11. I am in agreement with Yoder's discussion at this point when he says that "the text [Romans 13] cannot mean that Christians are called to do military or policy service" (205). See Yoder's discussion of Romans 13 in *The Politics of Jesus* (Grand Rapids, Mich.: B. Eerdmans, 1972), a discussion to which I am indebted and with which I am in general agreement.

12. Yoder, *The Politics of Jesus*, 205.

13. I agree with Yoder that chapters 12 and 13 of Romans form a single literary and theological unit and that chapter 13 should be interpreted in light of chapter 12. *Ibid.*, 197–200.

14. Furnish, *The Moral Teaching of Paul*, 127–28.

15. Yoder, *The Politics of Jesus*, 199.

16. Furnish, *The Moral Teaching of Paul*, 122–23.

17. Yoder, *The Politics of Jesus*, 194–95.

18. *Ibid.*, 207–8. Yoder's emphasis.

19. Katie Cannon, *Katie's Canon: Womanism and the Soul of the Black Community* (New York: Continuum, 1995), 94.

20. Canon, *Katie's Canon*, 92. "Unctuousness" is a quality of moral agency that Canon acknowledges she derives from the work of Alice Walker. For Canon, Zora Neale Hurston and many of the female characters in her novels embody unctuousness as the central and supreme moral quality for black women who had to "establish a relationship with suffering in their lives in order to survive," 91. Hurston herself, notes Canon, "repeatedly had to act sincere in the most insincere situations" in order to survive, thereby drawing on that quality of shrewd wisdom that Jesus praises in his parable of the unrighteous steward (Luke 16:1–8).

21. Walter Wink, "Neither Passivity nor Violence," 6.

22. *Ibid.*, 16.

23. Dietrich Bonhoeffer, *The Cost of Discipleship* (New York: Macmillan, 1959), 158–59.

24. Jonathan Edwards, *Religious Affections* (Portland, Ore: Multnomah Press, 1984), 147.

25. *Ibid.*, 148.

26. See Hays, *The Moral Vision of the New Testament*, 333–37.

27. Bonhoeffer, *Cost of Discipleship*, 164.

28. Gene Outka, "Universal Love and Impartiality," in *The Love Commandment: Essays*

in Christian Ethics and Moral Philosophy, ed. Edmund Santurri and William Werpenowski (Washington, D.C.: Georgetown University Press, 1989), 38–39.

29. Wink, "Neither Passivity nor Violence," 12, 16.

30. *Ibid.*, 19.

31. *Ibid.*, 17.

32. Bonhoeffer, *Cost of Discipleship*, 164.

33. Anders Nygren, *Agape and Eros*, trans. Philip S. Watson (Philadelphia: Westminster Press, 1953), 102.

34. *Ibid.*, 102.

35. *Ibid.*, 101.

36. See Richard Hays's discussion, *The Moral Vision of the New Testament*, 319–27.

37. Vincent Taylor, *Forgiveness and Reconciliation: A Study in New Testament Theology* (London: Macmillan, 1956).

38. *Ibid.*, 72.

39. Taylor, *Forgiveness and Reconciliation*, 85.

40. Mary Sherrill Durham, "The Therapist and the Concept of Revenge: The Law of Talion," *Journal of Pastoral Care* 44, 2 (summer 1990): 135.

41. *Ibid.*, 134.

42. See my discussion of vengeance as a legitimate moral feeling in the next section.

43. Richard Stith, "Generosity: A Duty without a Right," *Journal of Value Inquiry* 25, 3 (1991): 203–16.

44. *Ibid.*, 203.

45. *Ibid.*, 208.

46. *Ibid.*, 206.

47. Craig L. Blomberg, *Matthew*, in *The New American Commentary* series (Nashville, Tenn.: Broadman Press), vol. 22 (1992), compare I13; Exodus 22:26–27.

48. Blomberg, *Matthew*, 113.

49. Solomon, *A Passion for Justice: Emotions and the Origins of the Social Contract* (New York: Addison-Wesley, 1990), 272.

50. Solomon, *A Passion for Justice*, 274.

51. For example, just war theory includes "the just cause requirement": one nation (A) is justified in waging war with another nation (B) if and only if A is attacked by B or is attempting to help another nation (C) that is attacked by B. "Justified," in this criterion, presupposes a notion of justice that is rooted in the ancient law of talion and its feelings of vengeance. By attacking C, nation B has upset the just equilibrium among nations. A's sense of justice, feelings of unfairness, and desire for vengeance inspire it to respond to B's unfair attack on C and to reestablish the proper equilibrium among nations required by justice. All of the other criteria identified by just war theories (e.g., proportionality of just cause to means requirement, good intentions requirement) presuppose this most basic criterion of just war, which in turn arises from feelings of vengeance and fair retribution.

52. John Howard Yoder, *Nevertheless: The Varieties and Shortcomings of Religious Pacifism* (Scottsdale, Pa.: Herald Press, 1971), 111.

53. *Ibid.*

54. Because "holy war" is a notion so loaded with negative and, perhaps for some, positive connotations, I use the term "eschatological war" instead.

55. Reuven Firestone, "Conceptions of Holy War in Biblical and Qur'anic Tradition," *Journal of Religious Ethics* 24, 1 (spring 1996): 102. Firestone notes that "most scholars agree

that the book of Deuteronomy represents the most fully developed and theologically 'canonized' expression of holy war in ancient Israel," 104.

56. *Ibid.*, 103.

57. *Ibid.*, 103.

58. *Ibid.*, 102.

59. *Ibid.*, 105.

60. *Ibid.*

61. This exchange of views took place in the pages of the *Christian Century* in March 1932. H. Richard Niebuhr's article, "The Grace to Do Nothing," 49, 12 (March 23, 1932): 378–380, was rejoined by Rienhold Niebuhr's article, "Must We Do Nothing?" 49, 13 (March 30, 1932): 415–17.

62. H. R. Niebuhr, "The Grace to Do Nothing," 379.

63. *Ibid.*, 379.

64. Ulrich Mauser, *The Gospel of Peace: A Scriptural Messge for Today's World* (Louisville, Ky.: Westminster/John Knox Press, 1992), 187.

65. Clara Barton, *The Red Cross: In Peace and War* (Washington, D.C.: American Historical Press, 1906), 46.

66. I do not mean to suggest here that Professor Niebuhr would go as far as I in advocating a Red Cross model for the church, although I find that model consistent with the spirit of much of what he has to say about war and peace. See "The Relation of Christianity and Democracy," Earl Lecture, Berkeley Divinity School, October 1940, H. R. Niebuhr Papers, Harvard Divinity School; referred to by Joe Diefenthaler, *H. Richard Niebuhr: A Lifetime of Reflection on the Church and the World* (Macon, Ga.: Mercer Univeristy Press, 1986), 56.

67. Jesus at times does judge and condemn, of course. But the groups of people he targets for condemnation are ironically those hypocritically religious who are quick to condemn others (Matthew 23) and those who neglect the neglected (Matthew 25).

68. Mary Elsbernd, *A Theology of Peacemaking: A Vision, A Road, A Task* (Lanham, Md.: University Press of America, 1989), 77.

69. H. R. Niebuhr, "The Grace to Do Nothing," 380.

70. National Conference of Catholic Bishops, *The Challenge of Peace: God's Promise and Our Response*. Washington, D.C.: United States Catholic Conference, 1983), vii.

71. Eileen Egan, "Peacemaking in the Post–Just War Age," in *Studying War No More?* ed. Brian Wicker (Grand Rapids, Mich.: Eerdmans, 1994), 62.

72. Wink, "Neither Passivity nor Violence," 18.

73. *Ibid.*, 12–14.

74. *Ibid.*, 16.

75. *Ibid.*, 17.

76. *Ibid.*, 24.

77. Hays, *The Moral Vision of the New Testament*, 343.

78. R. G. Collingwood, *The Principles of Art* (Oxford: Clarendon Press, 1938), 336.

79. Cahill, *Love Your Enemies*, 246.

Five. Justice as a Christian Virtue

1. A Turkish tale; adapted from a retelling by Paul Jordan-Smith, "Man's Justice and God's Justice," *Parabola* 16, 4 (1991): 71–72.

2. Uma Narayan, "Colonialism and Its Others: Consideration on Rights and Care Discourses," *Hypatia* (spring 1995): 133. This essay is one among several that constituted the Symposium on Care and Justice held at the annual meeting of the American Political Science Association, New York City, September 2, 1994.

3. John Rawls, in *A Theory of Justice* (Oxford: Oxford University Press, 1971), sets forth a contemporary philosophical version of this tradition, while Harlan Beckley set forth a theological version; see Beckley, "A Christian Affirmation of Rawls's Idea of Justice as Fairness," parts 1 and 2, *Journal of Religious Ethics* 13 and 14 (Fall 1985 and Fall 1986): My concern in this chapter is not to undertake an analysis and critique of these two versions of liberal justice; I undertake that discussion in the chapter 6. My present focus is on the dispositions or habits of heart that are essential to the concerns of the liberal justice tradition.

4. Roberta Bondi, *To Love as God Loves: Conversations with the Early Church Fathers* (Philadelphia: Fortress Press, 1987), 29–30.

5. Carol Gilligan, "Justice and Responsibility: Thinking about Real Dilemmas of Moral Conflict and Choice," in *Toward Moral and Religious Maturity*, ed. C. Brusselmans (Morristown, N.J.: Silver Burdett, 1980), see 230–35.

6. See H. Richard Niebuhr, *The Responsible Self: An Essay in Christian Moral Philosophy* (New York: Harper and Row, 1963), especially chapters 2 and 3.

7. Darlene Ehinger, "Toward an Ethic of Mutuality: An Integrated Concept of Justice," *Sewanee Theological Review* 36, 3 (1993): 403.

8. *Ibid.*, 404.

9. Niebuhr, *The Responsible Self*, 60–61; see also 164–66.

10. *Ibid.*, 64.

11. *Ibid.*, 165–66.

12. *Ibid.*, 166.

13. *Ibid.*, 63.

14. Johann B. Metz, *Faith in History and Society: Toward a Practical Fundamental Theology*, trans. David Smith (New York: Seabury Press, 1980), 88–99.

15. Russell Butkus, "Dangerous Memory and Social Justice Education," *Religious Education* 82 (summer 1987): 427. See also K. Brynolf Lyon, "The Unwelcome Presence: The Practical Moral Intention of Remembering," *Encounter* 48, 1 (winter 1987): 144.

16. Hans-George Gadamer, *Truth and Method*, 2nd rev. ed. (New York: Crossroads Press, 1989): 15–16.

17. K. Brynolf Lyon, "The Unwelcome Presence, 139–40.

18. Ernest G. Schactel, *Metamorphosis* (New York: Basic Books, 1959): 284.

19. Brevard S. Childs, *Memory and Tradition in Israel* (New York: Alec R. Allanson, 1962): 51.

20. Lyon, "The Unwelcome Presence," 142.

21. *Ibid.*, 147.

22. Childs, *Memory and Tradition*, 34.

23. As Childs points out, "Nehemiah requests that God 'remember for good' all that he has done (5:19). The Psalmist pleads that God credit to David's account all his suffering (132:1). Similarly, Yahweh remembers in Israel's favour the devotion of her youth (Jeremiah 2:2). . . . Conversely, God can also remember in one's disfavour. It is accredited against Edom that it participated in the destruction of Jerusalem (Psalm 137:7)." *Memory and Tradition*, 32.

24. *Ibid.*, 33.

25. See *Ibid.*, 38–39.

26. Butkus, "Dangerous Memory," referring to the political theology of Johann B. Metz, 438.

27. James T. Morgan, "Memory, Land, and Pilgrimage: Roots of Spirituality," *Religious Education* 87, 4 (fall 1992): 536.

28. *Ibid.*, 563.

29. Lyon, "The Unwelcome Presence," 144.

30. *Ibid.* 143.

31. See Norman Fiering, "Irresistible Compassion: An Aspect of Eighteenth-Century Sympathy and Humanitarianism," *Journal of the History of Ideas* 37 (1976): 195–218.

32. Robert Solomon, *A Passion for Justice: Emotions and the Origins of the Social Contract* (New York: Addison-Wesley, 1990), 225.

33. Jonathan Edwards, *The Nature of True Virtue* (Ann Arbor: University of Michigan Press, 1960), 51.

34. Edwards, *True Virtue*, 52. Edwards is careful to qualify this claim by properly insisting that he does not mean to say that any experience of anger or gratitude presupposes moral virtue or justice or public benevolence. The most that can be claimed is that justice, as an act of public benevolence, involves gratitude and anger.

35. Solomon, *The Passions*, 284.

36. Carroll Saussy, *The Gift of Anger: A Call to Faithful Action* (Louisville, Ky.: Westminster/John Knox Press, 1995), 17–18.

37. William Temple, *Readings in St. John's Gospel* (London: Macmillan, 1963): 38–39.

38. *Ibid.*, 39.

39. Saussy, *The Gift of Anger*, 115.

40. *Ibid.*, 103.

41. William Werpehowski, "Do You Do Well to Be Angry?" *Annual of the Society of Christian Ethics* (1996): 74. Werpehowski refers here to Jonathan Edward, *Ethical Writings*, ed. Paul Ramsey (New Haven: Yale University Press, 1989): 272–82.

42. Werpehowski, "Do You Do Well to Be Angry?" 68.

43. Werpehowski, "Do You Do Well to Be Angry?" speaking of Jonathan Edward's treatment of anger, 68.

44. *Nicomachdean Ethics* 1126a2–3, quoted in Martha Nussbaum, "Equity and Mercy," *Journal of Philosophy and Public Affairs* 22,2 (1993): 97.

45. Nussbaum, "Equity and Mercy," 101.

46. Saussy, *The Gift of Anger*, 16.

47. *Ibid.*, 115.

48. Werpehowski, "Do You Do Well to Be Angry?" 68.

49. Joseph Fletcher, *Situation Ethics: The New Morality* (Philadelphia: Westminster Press, 1966), 156. Indeed, it seems to me that the entire range of holy affections and Christian virtues is properly understood in the context of eucharistic gratitude.

50. Paul F. Camenisch, "Gift and Gratitude in Ethics," *Journal of Religious Ethics* 9 (spring 1981): 1–34.

51. *Ibid.*, 2.

52. Besides the eucharist, there are, of course, other sacred occasions through which the divine proffers unearned gifts to humans, occasions that therefore properly inspire gratitude in the recipients.

53. Camenisch, "Gift and Gratitude," 4–11.

54. *Ibid.*, 3.

55. *Ibid.*, 2.

56. *Ibid.*, 9.

57. Archibald M. Hunter, *The Parables Then and Now* (Philadelphia: Westminster Press, 1971), 69.

58. *Ibid.*

59. James Gustafson, *Can Ethics Be Christian?* (Chicago: University of Chicago Press, 1975), 101.

60. Camenisch, "Gift and Gratitude," 23.

61. Quoted in *ibid.*, 25.

62. In the notion of transcendence I happily acknowledge that many who do not believe in God nevertheless experience feelings of "natural piety." These feelings arise for them out of a sense of awe and reverence and gratitude for life, beauty, health, and happiness that seems to them to originate from powers beyond themselves.

63. Nussbaum, in "Equity and Mercy," 87n, discusses Supreme Court justice Anthony Scalia as advocating, in *Walton v. Arizona*, a perspective exemplifying what I refer to here as "strict equity."

64. I examine and critique these sophisticated philosophical and theological versions of liberal justice in chapter 6.

65. Nussbaum, "Equity and Mercy," 87.

66. Although Euro-American males of the current generation may properly feel that they personally are not responsible for the gender injustices of the past, they are, I would argue, by implication nevertheless socially accountable to society for seeing to it that proactive steps are taken to rectify past offenses. Affirmative action attempts to do exactly that.

67. *Ibid.*, 98–104.

68. Oliver Sacks, *The Man Who Mistook His Wife for a Hat and Other Clinical Tales* (New York: Summit Books, 1987), 104.

69. *Ibid.*, 105–6.

70. *Ibid.*, 106.

71. *Ibid.*

Six. Compassion as Public Covenant

1. Robin Lovin uses this phrase to refer to the role of the church in public life. See "Social Contract or Public Covenant?" in *Religion and American Public Life: Interpretations and Explorations*, ed. Robin Lovin (New York: Paulist Press, 1986), 142–44.

2. William Rehg, "Discourse Ethics and the Communitarian Critique of Neo-Kantianism," *Philosophical Forum*, 22, 2 (winter 1991): 120.

3. Attempts at reconciling liberal and communitarian concerns by making incremental adjustment to one or the other or both sides of the conflict are many, and include William Rehg, "Discourse Ethics and the Communitarian Critique of Neo-Kantianism," *Philosophical Forum* 22, 2 (winter 1991): 120–38; Ralph Ellis, "Toward a Reconciliation of Liberalism and Communitarianism," *Journal of Value Inquiry* 25 (1991):55–64; William Galston, *Liberal Purposes: Goods, Virtues, and Diversity in the Liberal State* (Cambridge, England: Cambridge University Press, 1991); and Gerald Doppelt, "Beyond Liberalism and Communitarianism: Towards a Critical Theory of Social Justice," in *Universalism versus*

Communitarianism: Contemporary Debates in Ethics, ed. David Rasmussen (Cambridge: MIT Press, 1990), 39–60. Both Galston's and Doppelt's treatments of liberal and communitarian concerns are especially helpful. Galston's revision of liberalism, however, remains (as he himself admits) firmly within the liberal tradition. Doppelt, I think, is more successful in his attempt to find a rapprochement between liberal and communitarian concerns.

4. John Cobb, "Christianity, Political Theology, and the Economic Future," *Civil Religion and Political Theology*, ed. Leroy S. Rouner (South Bend, Ind.: University of Notre Dame Press, 1986), 215. I do not here condone the hostility often directed toward the kind of individualism alleged of John Locke and the contractarian tradition. I largely agree with Richard Mouw's "modest defense" of Locke's individualism as at least partly affirming the dignity and sacredness of the individual. See Mouw, "John Locke's Christian Individualism," *Faith and Philosophy* 8, 4 (October 1991): 453–54.

5. Nancy E. Snow, "Compassion," *American Philosophical Quarterly* 28, 3 (July 1991): 202.

6. Cobb, "Christianity, Political Theologuy and the Economic Future," 215–16. Cobb goes on to note that even though "socialist theory criticizes . . . it does not clearly affirm the alternative ontology of internal relations Instead it relocates the substantive individuals at the level of classes. Individual persons cease to be significant agents in their own right, and their fate has importance only as representative of the class. Between classes, on the other hand, relations are external."

7. Harlan Beckley, "A Christian Affirmation of Rawls's Idea of Justice as Fairness," part 2, *Journal of Religious Ethics*, 14, 2 (fall 1986): 229.

8. Harlan Beckley, "A Christian Affirmation of Rawls's Idea of Justice as Fairness," part 1, *Journal of Religious Ethics* 13, 2 (fall 1985): 234.

9. *Ibid.*, 226.

10. Quototation from Rawls in Beckley, "A Christian Affirmation," part 2, 243.

11. Cobb, "Christianity, Political Theology, and the Economic Future," 216–17.

12. Michael Sandel, "Justice and the Good," in *Liberalism and Its Critics*, ed. Michael Sandel (New York: New York University Press, 1984): 172.

13. *Ibid.*, 172–73.

14. Stanley Hauerwas, *Resident Aliens* (Nashville, Tenn.: Abingdon Press, 1989): 43.

15. See John Howard Yoder, "A People in the World: Theological Interpretation," in *The Concept of the Believer's Church*, ed. James Leo Garrett, Jr. (Scottsdale, Pa.: Herald Press, 1969).

16. Hauerwas, *Resident Aliens*, 45.

17. *Ibid.*, 46.

18. *Ibid.*, 94.

19. Stanley Hauerwas, *Against the Nations: War and Survival in a Liberal Society* (Notrre Dame, Ind.: University of Notre Dame Press, 1992): 1.

20. Lovin, "Social Contract or Public Covenant," 135.

21. Norman Fiering, "Irresistible Compassion: An Aspect of Eighteenth-Century Sympathy and Humanitarianism," *Journal of the History of Ideas* 37, 2 (1976) 198.

22. For example, the optimistic eighteenth-century view of human nature inspired many philosophers and theologians to view compassion or sympathy as a natureal passion and, as such, an inevitable human reaction to the suffering of others. Today, however, most would consider compassion to be a voluntary act or a habit that is socially and culturally

nurtured. In addition, most eighteenth-century thinkers tended to juxtapose the passions and reason, whereas among most contemporary thinkers there is a consensus that emotions are cognitive experiences and not necessarily at odds with reason.

23. William J. Prior, "Compassion: A Critique of Moral Rationalism," *Philosophy and Theology* 2, 2 (winter, 1987): 173.

24. Quoted in Stanley Hauerwas, *Dispatches from the Front* (Durham, N.C.: Duke University Press, 1994): 166.

25. Hauerwas, *Dispatches*, 166.

26. Nussbaum, *Love's Knowledge: Essays on Philosophy and Literature* (New York: Oxford University Press, 1990), 375–376.

27. *Ibid.*

28. I need not belabor here what many have noted, namely, that compassion is part of an emotional terrain closely related to but distinguishable from other similar experiences. Gregory Pence's brief comparison of compassion with related experiences indicates an emotional landscape crowded with a variety of kindred experiences. "Like compassion, pity can be aroused by suffering, but may contain condescension and interpersonal distance absent in compassion. [Love], benevolence and altruism carry much broader meanings than compassion and aren't [uniquely] focused on suffering." See "Can Compassion be Taught?" *"Journal of Medical Ethics* 9 (1983): 189–91. See also Nancy Snow's dicussion in "Compassion," 195–197.

29. Lawrence Blum, "Compassion," in *Explaining Emotions*, ed. Amelie O. Rorty (Berkeley: University of California Press, 1980): 508. Of course when a person is in a positive condition of joy and pleasure we likewise exult with that person Blum points out; but this condition of joy is not negative and thus not an occasion for compassion.

30. Solomon, *A Passion for Justice: Emotions and the Origins of the Social Contract* (New York: Addison-Wesley, 1990), 225.

31. Blum, "Compassion," 508.

32. *Ibid.*, 509–10.

33. Adrian M. S. Piper, "Impartiality, Compassion, and Imagination," *Ethics* 101 (July 1991): 737–38.

34. Toni Morrison, *Beloved* (New York: Penguin Books, 1988) 67–68.

35. Max Scheler, *The Nature of Sympathy* (Hamden, Conn.: Archon Books, 1970): 13.

36. Blum, "Compassion," 509–10.

37. *Ibid.*, 510.

38. Snow, "Compassion," 198.

39. *Ibid.*, 198.

40. *Ibid.*, 199.

41. Solomon, *The Passions*, 171.

42. Blum, "Compassion," 511.

43. "Engrossment" is a word Nel Noddings employs to describe the profundity of emotional intersubjectivity required between the one caring and the one-cared-for. See *Caring: A Feminine Approach to Ethics and Moral Education* (Berkeley: University of California Press, 1984): 19.

44. Jean Grimshaw, *Philosophy and Feminist Thinking* (Minneapolis: Univeristy of Minnesota Press, 1986): 216.

45. Blum, "Compassion," 512.

46. Snow, "Compassion," 197.

47. Piper, "Impartiality, Compassion, and Imagination," 743.

48. Blum, "Compassion," 511; see also 513.

49. See Mary Ann Glendon, *Rights Talk: The Impoverishment of Political Discourse* (New York: Free Press, 1990): 171.

50. See chapter 9 of Galston, *Liberal Purposes.*

51. *Ibid.,* 191.

52. Nussbaum, *Love's Knowledge,* 375. She makes this claim in the curious context of explaining how the Homeric gods are distinguishable from humans. Humans "prize compassion," so "we have to say that in their [the gods'] dealings in our realm, the gods are not just different, they are worse," for the gods do not prize compassion.

53. Michael Sandel, *Liberalism and the Limits of Justice* (Cambridge: University of Cambridge Press, 1982), 172.

54. I take the phrases "self-absorption" (here) and "vicarious possession" (later) from Adrian Piper, but I give them meanings quite different from his meanings in "Impartiality, Compassion, and Imagination," 732–737.

55. John Rawls, *A Theory of Justice* (Oxford: Oxford University Press, 1971), 178.

56. Beckley, "A Christian Affirmation," part 2, 243.

57. Rawls, *Theory of Justice,* 178. In "Kantian Constructivism in Moral Theory," *Journal of Philosophy* 77 (1980): 515–72, Rawls similarly argues that "citizens in their personal affairs ... have attachments and loves that they believe would not, or could not, stand apart from"; but in public life, Rawls goes on to say, no such attachments are demanded or desired if justice is to be served. See Michael Sandel's related discussion in *Liberalism and the Limits of Justice,* 181–83.

58. Sandel, "Justice and the Good," 179.

59. See Stanley Hauerwas, *After Christendom* (Nashville, Tenn.: Abingdon Press, 1991); see especially chapter 2 "The Politics of Justice."

60. Hauerwas, *After Christendom,* 46.

61. *Ibid.,* 68.

62. See note 54 of this chapter.

63. Sandel, "Justice and the Good," 182.

64. See *Church and State in American History,* eds. John F. Wilson and Donald L. Drakeman (Boston: Beacon Press, 1987): 182.

65. This principle avoids merely begging the question when it is recalled, from earlier in this chapter, the three conditions (relatively central, involuntary, and social suffering) that together define the nature and occasion for compassionate public participation in suffering.

66. As noted earlier in this chapter, one criterion for judging when the suffering of a person is a legitimate object for public compassion is the centrality of that suffering to the person's life and well-being. Combining the relative centrality of suffering with the principle of minimum suffering, suffering loss of life is both more central and less minimal than the suffering the mother experiences in waiving her right to an abortion.

67. Several questions might be raised here. First, can virtues like courage or compassion be taught? Plato has Socrates and Protagoras argue this question in *Meno.* Socrates argues no, Protagoras yes. The contemporary consensus is that Protagoras is correct and that emotions and virtues are cultural, social constructions over which humans have a great deal of control. Only Platonic or antiquated eighteenth-century views (that emotions and virtues are somehow natural, noncognitive experiences) would deny that teach-

ing and learning emotional habits has any relevance to enfranchising compassion in public life.

68. Stephen Carter, *The Culture of Disbelief: How American Law and Politics Trivialize Religious Devotion* (New York: Basic Books, 1993:) 105–6.

69. *Lemon v. Kurtzman*, 1971, 403 U.S. 602 (1971).

70. William J. Prior, "Compassion," 174.

Seven. Educating the Heart for Compassion

1. Roy B. Zuck, *Teaching as Jesus Taught* (Grand Rapids, Mich.: Baker Books, 1995), 108.

2. Stanley Hauerwas and L. Gregory Jones, eds., *Why Narrative? Readings in Narrative Theology* (Grand Rapids, Mich.: Eerdmans, 1989), 5.

3. See especially *Pedagogy of the Oppressed*, trans. Myra B. Ramos (New York: Continuum, 1990), *Education for Critical Consciousness*, trans. Myra B. Ramos (New York: Continuum, 1973), and *Pedagogy of the Heart*. trans. Donaldo Marcedo and Alexandre Oliveira (New York: Continuum, 1998).

4. This awareness of being a citizen of two different families is similar to the Stoic view, articulated by Nussbaum, that "education should make us aware that each of us is a member of two communities: one that is truly great and truly common . . . in which we look neither to this corner nor to that, but measure the boundaries of our nation by the sun; the other, the one to which we have been assigned by birth." *Cultivating Humanity: A Classical Defense of Reform in Liberal Education* (Cambridge: Harvard University Press, 1997), 58.

5. See Nussbaum, *Cultivating Humanity,* chapter 2.

6. I have already noted in chapter 6 that Hauerwas rejects compassion as a category of moral reflection for Christians.

7. Nussbaum, *Cultivating Humanity*, 69.

8. *Ibid.*, 90.

9. Nussbaum, *Love's Knowledge: Essays on Philosophy and Literature* (New York: Oxford University Press, 1990), 287.

10. I use the term "narrative" here, as I use it throughout this book, to refer to "a twofold activity by which the imaginative mind first discovers in experience a plot constituted by characters, events, and temporal sequence . . . [and] secondly . . . to the susceptibility of plot to a community discovering in it some pattern of meaning" (chapter 2, third section, "Emotions and Truth." Clearly I do not mean by "narrative" what Freire, in *Pedagogy of the Oppressed*, means by it, namely, a relationship in which a teacher passively narrates subject matter and a student passively listens (see chapter 2).

11. Nussbaum, *Cultivating Humanity*, chapter 3.

12. See books 2 and 3 of the *Republic*.

13. Mary E. M. Moore, *Teaching form the Heart: Theology and Educational Method* (Minneapolis: Fortress Press, 1991), 139.

14. Katherine Cather, *Religious Education through Story-Telling* (New York: Abingdon Press, 1925): 24.

15. *Ibid.*, 25.

16. Nussbaum, *Cultivating Humanity*, 90.

17. Cather, *Religious Education*, 25.

18. *Ibid.*, 26.

19. Nussbaum, *Cultivating Humanity*, 93.

20. *Ibid.*, 93.

21. *Ibid.*, 69.

22. Herman Harrell Horne, *The Teaching Techniques of Jesus* (Grand Rapids, Mich.: Kregel, 1920), 143–44.

23. Cather, *Religious Education*, 25.

24. Moore, *Teaching form the Heart*, 92.

25. *Ibid.*, 93.

26. Freire, *Pedagogy of the Oppressed*, 75–76. Freire states in a note that sacrifice of action equals "verbalism" or "idle chatter" and that sacrifice of reflection equals "activism" or an unwillingness to engage in genuine dialogue.

27. *Ibid.*, 76.

28. Quoted in J. T. Dillon, *Jesus as Teacher: A Multidisciplinary Case Study* (New York: International Scholars, 1995), 67.

29. Dillon, *Jesus as Teacher*, 54; for Dillon's more detailed discussion of these four actions, see 54–68.

30. *Ibid.*, 68.

31. A great deal is being written these days about "service learning." The following books introduce some of the basic principles of service learning: D. Giles, E. Honnet Porter, and S. Migliore, *Research Agenda for Combining Service and Learning in the 1990s.* (Raleigh, N.C.: National Society for Experimental Education, 1991); Honnet E. Porter and S. J. Poulsen, *Principles of Good Practice for Combining Service and Learning* (Racine, Wis.: Johnson Foundation, 1989); Barbara Jacoby et al., *Service-Learning in Higher Education: Concepts and Practices* (San Francisco: Jossey-Bass, 1996); Carl Fertman, George White, and Louis White, *Service Learning in the Middle School: Building a Culture of Service* (Columbus, Ohio: National Middle School Association, 1996).

32. See James Youniss and Miranda Yates, "A Community Disservice," *Washington Post*, Sunday, June 14, 1998, C1; they discusses some of the difficulties the Maryland experiment is encountering.

33. One example is the Wingspread Principles, which is the result of an experiment published by Porter and Poulsen as *Principles of Good Practice*. The Wingspread Principles function as criteria for establishing a successful service-learning program. Such a program:

1. Engages people in responsible and challenging actions for the common good.
2. Provides structured opportunities for people to reflect critically on their service experience.
3. Articulates clear service and learning goals.
4. Allows those with needs to define those needs.
5. Clarifies the responsibilities of each person and organization.
6. Matches service providers and service needs in a way that accounts for changing conditions.
7. Requires active and sustained organizational commitment.
8. Includes training, supervision, support, and evaluation in order to meet goals.
9. Insures that time commitment is flexible and appropriate for those involved.
10. Involves program participation by and with diverse populations.

34. Youniss and Yates, "A Community Disservice," C4.

35. Horne, *The Teaching Techniques of Jesus*, 143.

36. Nussbaum, *Cultivating Humanity*, 32.

37. *Ibid.*, 33.

38. Nussbaum, *Love's Knowledge*, 273.

39. *Ibid.*, 282.

40. The discussion of conscientization and critical consciousness that follows has its roots in of Freire, *Pedagogy of the Oppressed*, chapter 4, and *Education for Critical Consciousness*, 41–58.

41. I have been inspired and guided in the following discussion by Robert Kysar's provocative discussion in the chapter "Changing the Popular Consciouness" in *Called to Care: Biblical Images for Social Ministry* (Minneapolis: Fortress Press, 1991), 99–119.

42. Kysar, *Called to Care*, 109–10.

43. Daniel Migliore, *Called to Freedom: Liberation Theology and the Future of Christian Doctrine* (Philadelphia: Westminster Press, 1980).16.

44. Kysar, *Called to Care*, 109.

45. Max L. Stackhouse, *Public Theology and Political Economy: Christian Stewardship in Modern Society* (Grand Rapids, Mich.: Eerdmans 1987), xiii.

46. These two categories are inspired by R.G. Collingwood's analysis of art as "magic" and "amusement," in chapters 4 and 5 of *The Principles of Art* (Oxford: Clarendon Press, 1938).

47. A way not directly relevant here is when a community exploits faith as a means of convenience, a means of avoiding the discipline and difficult task of following Jesus. Prayer very often is exploited, for example, as a means of trying to avoid discipline and secure convenience for oneself, as when one calls on God to supernaturally intervene in life so that the struggle of discipline can be preempted and a life of convenience and comfort magically secured.

48. Collingwood, *The Principles of Art*, 66.

49. *Ibid.*, 68.

50. *Ibid.*, 69.

51. *Ibid.*, 66.

52. *Ibid.*, 78.

53. *Ibid.*, 79.

54. Kierkegaard, *Training in Christianity. And the Edifying Discourse Which "Accompanied" It*, trans. Walter Lowrie (Princeton: Princeton University Press, 1944), 246.

55. The remainder of this chapter parallels and is inspired by Collingwood's great concluding paragraph of *The Principles of Art*, 335–36.

Bibliography

Allen, Charles. "The Primacy of Phronesis: A Proposal for Avoiding Frustrating Tendencies in Our Conceptions of Rationality." *Journal of Religion* 69, 3 (1989): 359–374.

Angelou, Maya. *All God's Children Need Traveling Shoes*. New York: Random House, 1986.

Aristotle. *Metaphysics*. Trans. W. D. Ross in *The Basic Works of Aristotle*. Ed. Richard McKeon. New York: Random House, 1941.

Aristotle. *Rhetoric*. Trans. W. Rhys Roberts. *Works of Aristotle Translated into English*. Vol. 2. Oxford: Clarendon Press, 1924.

Barton, Clara. *The Red Cross: In Peace and War*. Washington, D.C.: American Historical Press, 1906.

Beaumont, Daniel. "The Modality of Narrative: A Critique of Some Recent Views of Narrative Theology." *Journal of the American Academy of Religion* 65, 1 (spring 1997): 125–39.

Beckley, Harlan. "A Christian Affirmation of Rawls's Idea of Justice as Fairness." parts 1 and 2. *Journal of Religious Ethics* 13 and 14 (fall 1985 and fall 1986): 210–242; 229–246.

Birch, Bruce. *To Love as We Are Loved: The Bible and Relationships*. Nashville, Tenn.: Abingdon Press, 1992.

Blomberg, Craig. *Matthew*. In New American Commentary series. Vol. 22. Nashville, Tenn.: Broadman Press, 1992.

Blum, Lawrence. "Compassion," In *Explaining Emotions*, ed. Amelie Rorty. Berkeley: University of California Press, 1980: 507–17.

Bondi, Roberta *To Love as God Loves: Conversations with the Early Church*. Philadelphia: Fortress Press, 1987.

Bonhoeffer, Dietrich, *The Cost of Discipleship*. New York: Macmillan, 1959.

Brody, Howard. *Stories of Sickness*. New Haven: Yale University Press, 1987.

Burrell, David, and Stanley Hauerwas. "From System to Story." In *Why Narrative? Readings in Narrative Theology*, ed. Stanley Hauerwas and L. G. Jones. Grand Rapids, Mich.: Eerdmans, 1989.

Butkus, Russell. "Dangerous Memory and Social Justice Eduction." *Religious Education* 82 (summer 1987): 426–46.

Cahill, Lisa Sowle. *Love Your Enemies: Discipleship, Pacifism, and Just War Theory*. Minneapolis: Fortress Press, 1994.

Callahan, Sidney. *In Good Conscience: Reason and Emotion in Moral Decision Making*. San Francisco: Harper/Collins, 1991.

Camenisch, Paul F. "Gift and Gratitude in Ethics." *Journal of Religious Ethics* 9 (spring 1981): 1–34.

Cannon, Katie. *Katie's Cannon: Womanism and the Soul of the Black Community*. New York: Continuum, 1995.

Carron, Julian. "The Second Commandment in the New Testament: Your Yes Is Yes, Your No Is No." *Communio* 20 (spring 1993): 5–25.

Carter, Stephen. *The Culture of Disbelief: How American Law and Politics Trivialize Religious Devotion*. New York: Basic Books, 1993.

Cather, Katherine. *Religious Education through Story-telling*. New York: Abingdon Press, 1925.

Childs, Brevard S. *Memory and Tradition in Israel*. New York: Alec R. Allanson, 1962.

Cobb, John. "Christianity, Political Theology, and the Economic Future." In *Civil Religion and Political Theology*, ed. Leroy S. Rouner. South Bend, Ind.: University of Notre Dame Press, 1986: 207–23.

Collingwood, R. G. *The Idea of History*. Oxford: Oxford University Press, 1960.

———. *The Principles of Art*. Oxford: Clarendon Press, 1938.

Comstock, Gary. "Truth or Meaning: Ricoeur Versus Frei on Biblical Narrative." *Journal of Religion* 66, 2 (1986): 117–41.

Cooey, Paula. "Eros and Intimacy in Edwards." *Journal of Religion* 69 (October 1989): 484–501.

Crites, Stephen. "The Narrative Quality of Experience." In *Why Narrative? Readings in Narrative Theology*, ed. Stanley Hauerwas and L. G. Jones. Grand Rapids, Mich.: Eerdmans, 1989: 65–88.

Diefenthaler, Joe. *H. Richard Niebuhr: A Lifetime of Reflection on the Church and The World*. Macon, Ga.: Mercer University Press, 1986.

Dillon, J. T. *Jesus as Teacher: A Multidisciplinary Case Study*. New York: International Scholars, 1995.

Dodd, C. H. *Gospel and Law*. New York: Columbia University Press, 1951.

Doppelt, Gerald. "Beyond Liberalism and Communitarianism: Towards a Critical Theory of Social Justice." In *Universalism versus Communitarianism: Contemporary Debates in Ethics*, ed. David Rasmussen. Cambridge: MIT Press, 1990: 39–60.

Duling, Dennis D. "Against Oaths: Crossan Sayings Parallels 59." ⟨Forum⟩ 6, 2 (June 1990): 99–138.

Durham, Mary Sherrill. "The Therapist and the Concept of Revenge: The Law of Talion." *Journal of Pastoral Care*. 44, 2 (summer 1990): 131–37.

Edwards, Jonathan. *Charity and Its Fruits: Christian Love as Manifested in the Heart and Life*. Carlisle, Pa.: Banner of Truth Trust, 1969.

———. *The Nature of True Virtue*. AnnArbor: University of Michigan Press, 1960.

———. *The Philosophy of Jonathan Edwards: From His Private Notebooks*. Ed. H. G. Townsend. Eugene, Oregon: University of Oregon Monographs, 1955.

———. *Religious Affections*. Portland, Ore.: Multnomah Press, 1984.

Egan, Eileen. "Peacemaking in the Post–Just War Age." In *Studying War No More?* ed. Brian Wicker. Grand Rapids, Mich.: Eerdmans, 1994: 59–63.

Ehinger, Darlene. "Toward an Ethic of Mutuality: An Integrated Concept of Justice." *Sewanee Theological Review* 36, 3 (1993): 396–415.

Ellis, Ralph. "Toward a Reconciliation of Liberalism and Communitarianism." *Journal of Value Inquiry* 25 (1991): 55–64.

Elsbernd, Mary. *A Theology of Peacemaking: A Vision, a Road, a Task.* Lanham, Md.: University Press of America, 1989.

Fertman, Carl, George White, and Louis White. *Service Learning in the Middle School: Building a Culture of Service.* Columbus, Ohio: National Middle School Association, 1996.

Fiering, Norman. "Irresistible Compassion: An Aspect of Eighteenth-Century Sympathy and Humanitarianism." *Journal of the History of Ideas* 37, 2 (1976): 195–218.

Finn, Daniel, and Prentiss Pemberton, *Toward a Christian Economic Ethic: Stewardship and Social Power.* Minneapolis: Winston Press, 1985.

Fiorenza, Frances. "Joy and Pain as Paradigmatic for Language about God." In *Theology of Joy,* ed. Johanna Baptist Metz and Jean-Pierre Jossua. New York: Herder and Herder, 1974.

Firestone, Reuven. "Conceptions of Holy War in Biblical and Qur'anic Tradition." *Journal of Religious Ethics* 24, 1 (spring, 1996): 99–123.

Fletcher, Joseph. *Situation Ethics: The New Morality.* Philadelphia: Westminster Press, 1996.

Frei, Hans. *The Identity of Jesus Christ: The Hermeneutical basis of Dogmatic Theology.* Philadelphia: Fortress Press, 1975.

Freire, Paulo. *Education for Critical Consciousness.* Trans. Myra B. Ramos. New York: Continuum, 1973.

———. *Pedagogy of the Heart.* Trans. Donaldo Marcedo and Alexandre Oliveira. New York: Continuum, 1998.

———. *Pedagogy of the Oppressed.* Trans. Myra B. Ramos. New York: Continuum, 1990

Frijda, N. *The Emotions.* New York: Cambridge University Press, 1987.

Furnish, Victor Paul. *The Moral Teaching of Paul: Selected Issues.* Nashville, Tenn.: Abingdon Press, 1985.

Gadamer, Hans-George. *Truth and Method.* 2nd ed. New York: Crossroads Press, 1989.

Galston, William. *Liberal Purposes: Goods, Virtues, and Diversity in the Liberal State.* Cambridge, England: Cambridge University Press, 1991.

Giles, D., E. Honnet Porter, and S. Migliore. ⟨Research Agenda for Combining Service and Learning in the 1990s.⟩ Raleigh, N.C.: National Society for Experimental Education, 1991.

Gilligan, Carol. "Justice and Responsibility: Thinking about Real Dilemmas of Moral Conflict and Choice." In *Toward Moral and Religious Maturity,* ed. C. Brusselmans. Morristown, N.J.: Silver Burdett, 1980: 230–35.

Glendon, Marry Ann. *Rights Talk: The Impoverishment of Political Discourse.* New York: Free Press, 1990.

Grayling, A. C. *Wittgenstein.* New York: Oxford University Press, 1987.

Green, Ronald. "Kant on Christian Love." In *The Love Commandments: Essays in Christian Ethics and Moral Philosophy,* ed. Edmund Santurri and William Werpehowski. Washington, D.C.: Georgetown University Press, 1990: 261–80.

Greenspan, Patricia. *Emotions and Reasons: An Inquiry into Emotional Justification.* New York: Routledge, 1988.

Grimshaw, Jean. *Philosophy and Feminist Thinking.* Minneapolis: University of Minnesota Press, 1986.

Gustafson, James. *Can Ethics Be Christian?* Chicago: University of Chicago Press, 1975.

Hauerwas, Stanley. *After Christendom.*Nashville, Tenn.: Abingdon Press, 1991.

————*Against the Nations.: War and Survival in a Liberal Society.* Notre Dame, Ind.: University of Notre Dame Press, 1992.

————. *A Community of Character: Toward a Constructive Christian Social Ethic.* Notre Dame, Ind.: University of Notre Dame Press, 1981.

————. *Dispatches from the Front.* Durham, N.C.: Duke University Press, 1994.

————. *The Peaceable Kingdom.* Notre Dame, Ind.: University of Notre Dame Press, 1983.

————. *Resident Aliens.* Nashville, Tenn.: Abingdon Press, 1989.

Hauerwas, Stanley, and L. Gregory Jones, eds. *Why Narrative? Readings in Narrative Theology.* Grand Rapids, Mich.: Eerdmans, 1989.

Hays, Richard B. *The Moral Vision of the New Testament: Community, Cross, and New Creation.* San Francisco: Harper, 1996.

Horne, Herman Harrell. *The Teaching Techniques of Jesus.* Grand Rapids, Mich.: Kregel, 1920.

Hunter, Archibald M. *The Parables Then and Now.* Philadelphia: Westminster Press, 1971.

Izard, Carroll E. *Human Emotions.* New York: Plenum Press, 1977.

Jackson, Timothy. "Christian Love and Political Violence." In *The Love Commandments: Essays in Christian Ethics and Moral Philosophy,* ed. Edmund Santurri and William Werpehowski. Washington, D.C.: Georgetown University Press, 1989: 182–220.

Jacoby, Barbara, et al. ⟨Service-Learning in Higher Education: Concepts and Practices.⟩ San Francisco: Jossey-Bass, 1996.

Jordon-Smith, Paul. "Man's Justice and God's Justice." *Parabola* 16, 4 (1991): 71–72.

Kant, Immanuel. *The Doctrine of Virtue.* Trans. Mary J. Gregor. Philadelphia: University of Pennsylvania Press, 1964.

————. *Foundations of the Metaphysics of Morals.* Trans. Lewis Beck White. Indinapolis: Bobbs-Merrill, 1959.

————*The Metaphysics of Morals.* Trans. Mary Gregor. Cambridge, England: Cambridge University Press, 1991.

Kierkegaard, Søren. *Concluding Unscientific Postscript.* Trans. David Swenson Princeton, NJ: Princeton University Press, 1944.

————. *Philosophical Fragments.* Trans David Swenson. Princeton: Princeton University Press, 1962.

————. *Training in Christianity. And the Edifying Discourse Which "Accompanied' It.* Trans. Walter Lowrie. Princetion: Princetion University Press, 1944.

————. *Works of Love: Some Christian Reflections in the Form of Discourses.* Trans. Howard and Edna Hong. New York: Harper, 1962.

Kysar, Robert. *Called to Care: Biblical Images for Social Ministry.* Minneapolis: Fortress Press, 1991.

Lauritzen, Paul. "Emotions and Religious Ethics." *Journal of Religious Ethics* 16, 2 (198) 307–24.

————"Is Narrative Really a Panacea? The Use of "Narrative" in the Work of Metz and Hauerwas." *Journal of Religion* 67, 3 (1987): 322–39.

Lindbeck, George. *The Nature of Doctrine: Religion and Theology in a Postliberal Age.* Philadelphia: Westminster Press, 1984.

Long, Edward. *To Liberate and Redeem: Moral Reflections on the Biblical Narrative.* Cleveland, Ohio: Pilgrim Press, 1997.

Lovin, Robin. "Social Contract or Public Covenant?" In *Religion and American Public Life: Interpretations and Explorations,* ed. Robin Lovin. New York: Paulist Press, 1986.

Lyon, K. Brynolf. "The Unwelcome Presence: The Practical Moral Intention of Remembering." *Encounter* 48, 1 (winter 1987): 139–48.

Marcel, Gabriel. *The Philosophy of Existentialism.* Trans. Manya Harari. New York: Citadel Press, 1963.

Mauser, Ulrich. *The Gospel of Peace: A Scriptural Message for Today's World.* Louisville, Ky.: Westminster/John Knox Press, 1992.

Meilaender, Gilbert. *The Limits of Love: Some Theological Explorations.* University Park: Pennsylvania State University Press, 1987.

————*The Theory and Practice of Virtue.* Notre Dame, Ind.: University of Notre Dame Press, 1984.

Metz, Johanna. *Faith in History and Society: Toward a Practical Fundamental Theology.* Trans. David Smith. New York: Seabury Press, 1980.

————. "Joy and Grief, Cheerfulness, Melancholy, and Humour or the Difficulty of Saying Yes." *Theology of Joy,* ed. Johanna Baptist Metz and Jean-Pierre Jossua. New York: Herder and Herder, 1974.

Migliore, Daniel. *Called to Freedom: Liberation Theology and the Future of Christian Doctrine.* Philadelphia: Westminster Press, 1980.

Morgan, James T. "Memory, Land, and Pilgrimage: Roots of Spirituality." *Religious Education* 87, 4 (fall 1992): 558–68.

Moore, Mary E. M. *Teaching from the Heart: Theology and Educational Method.* Minneapolis: Fortress Press, 1991.

Morrison, Toni. *Beloved.* New York: Penguin Books, 1988.

Mouw, Richard. "John Locke's Christian Individualism." *Faith and Philosophy* 8, 4 (October 1991): 448–60.

Narayan, Uma. "Colonialism and Its Other: Considerations on Rights and Care Discourses." *Hypatia* (spring 1995): 133–45.

National Conference of Catholic Bishops. *The Challenge of Peace: God's Promise and Our Response.* Washington, D.C., United States Catholic Conference, 1983.

————. *Economic Justice for All: Pastoral Letter on Catholic Social Teaching and the U. S. Economy.* United States Catholic Conference, Washington, D.C.: 1986.

Niebuhr, H. Richard. "The Grace to Do Nothing." *Christian Century* 49, 12 (March 23, 1932): 378–80.

————. *The Meaning of Revelation.* New York: Macmillan, 1960.

————. *The Responsible Self: An Essay in Christian Moral Philosophy.* New York: Harper, 1963.

Niebuhr, Reinhold. "Must We Do Nothing?" *Christian Century* 49, 13 (March 30, 1932): 415–17.

Noddings, Nel. *Caring: A Feminine Approach to Ethics and Moral Education.* Berkeley: University of California Press, 1984.

Nussbaum, Martha. *Cultivating Humanity: A Classical Defense of Reform in Liberal Education.* Cambridge: Harvard university Press, 1997.

———. "Equity and Mercy." *Journal of Philosophy and Public Affairs* 22, 2 (1993): 83–125.

———*The Fragility of Goodness: Luck and Ethics in Greek Tragedy and Philosophy,* New York: Cambridge University Press, 1986.

———. *Love's Knowledge: Essays on Philosophy and Literature.* New York: Oxford University Press, 1990.

Nygrne, Anders. *Agape and Eros.* Trans. Philip Watson. Philadelphia: Westminster Press, 1953.

Oakes, Edward J., "Apologetics and the Pathos of Narrative Theology." *Journal of Religion* 72, 1 (1992): 37–58.

Ortony, Andrew, Gerald Close, and Allen Collins. *The Cognitive Structure of Emotions.* New York: Cambridge University Press, 1988.

Outka, Gene. "Universal Love and Impartiality." In *The Love Commandments: Essays in Christian Ethics and Moral Philosophy,* ed. Edmund Santurri and William Werpehowski. Washington, D.C.: Georgetown University Press, 1989: 1–103.

Pence, Gregory. "Can Compassion be Taught?" *Journal of Medical Ethics* 9 (1983): 189–91.

Piper, Adrian M. S. "Impartiality, Compassion, and Imagination." *Ethics* 101 (July 1991): 726–57.

Placher, William. *Narratives of a Vulnerable God: Christ, Theology, and Scripture.* Louisville, Ky.: Westminster/John Knox Press, 1994.

———. *Unapologetic Theology: A Christian Voice in a Pluralistic Conversation.* Louisville, Ky.: Westminster/John Knox Press, 1989.

Pope, Stephen. "Love in Contemporary Christian Ethics." *Journal of Religious Ethics* 23, 1 (apring 1995): 167–97.

Porter, Honnet E, and S. J. Poulsen. *Principles of Good Practice for Combining Service and Learning.* Racine, Wis.: Johnson Foundation, 1989.

Prior, William J. "Compassion: A Critique of Moral Rationalism." *Philosophy and Theology* 2, 2 (1987): 173–91.

Proudfoot, Wayne. *Religious Experience.* Berkeley: University of California Press, 1985.

Purvis, Sally. "Mother, Neighbors and Strangers." *Journal of Feminist Studies in Religion* 7 (spring 1991): 19–36.

Radcliffe, Dana. "Compassion and Commanded Love." *Faith and Philosophy* 11, 2 (1994): 50–71.

Rawls, John. "Kantian Constructivism in Moral Theory." *Journal of Philosophy* 77 (1980): 515–72.

———. *A Theory of Justice.* Oxford: Oxford University Press, 1971.

Rehg, William. "Discourse Ethics and the Communitarian Critique of Neo-Kantianism." *Philosophical Forum* 22, 2 (winter 1991): 120–38.

Ricoeur, Paul. *The Rule of Metaphor.* Toronto: University of Toronto Press, 1977.

———. *The Symbolism of Evil.* Trans. E. Buchanan. Boston, Mass.: Beacon Press, 1967.

Roberts, Robert C. "Emotions among the Virtues of the Christian Life." *Journal of Religious Ethics* 20, 1 (spring 1992): 37–68.

———. "Emotions as Access to Religious Truths," *Faith and Philosophy* 9, 1 (January 1992): 83–94.

Rosaldo, Michelle. "Toward an Anthropology of Self and Feeling." In *Culture Theory*, ed. Richard A. Schwedeer and Robert E. LeVine. Cambridge, England: Cambridge University Press, 1984.

Sacks, Oliver. *The Man Who Mistook His Wife for a Hat and Other Clinical Tales*. New York: Summit Books, 1987.

Sakenfield, Katherine D. *Faithfulness in Action: Loyalty in Biblical Perspective*. Philadelphia: Fortress Press, 1985.

Sandel, Michael. "Justice and the Good." In *Liberalism and Its Critics*, ed. Michael Sandel. New York: New York University Press, 1984.

———. *Liberalism and the Limits of Justice*. Cambridge. England: Cambridge University Press, 1982.

Sanderlin, David. "Charity According to St. John of the Cross," *Journal of Religious Ethics* 21, 1 (spring 1993): 87–115.

Sattler, "Schleitheim Confession." In *Sources of Protestant Theology*, ed. William A. Scott. New York: Bruce, 1971.

Saussy, Carroll. *The Gift of Anger: A Call to Faithful Action*. Louisville, Ky.: Westminster/John Knox Press, 1995.

Schactel, Ernest G. *Metamorphosis*. New York: Basic Books, 1959.

Scheler, Max. *The Nature of Sympathy*. Trans. Peter Heath. Hamden, Conn.: Archon Books, 1970.

Schleiermacher, Friedrich. *The Christian Faith*. 2nd ed. Trans. H. R. Mackintosh and J. S. Stewart. New York: Harper and Row, 1963.

———. *On Religion: Speeches to Its Cultural Despisers*. New York: Harper and Row, 1958.

Scruton, Roger. "Emotion, Practical Knowledge and Common Culture." In *Explaining Emotions*, ed. Amelie Rorty. Berkeley: University of California Press, 1980: 519–36.

Snow, Nancy. "Compassion." *American Philosophical Quarterly* 28, 3 (July 1991): 195–205.

Solomon, Robert. *A Passion for Justice: Emotions and the Origins of the Social Contract*. New York: Addison-Wesley, 1990.

———. *The Passions*. Notre Dame, Ind.: University of Notre Dame Press, 1976.

Stackhouse, Max L. *Public Theology and Political Economy: Christian Stewardship in Modern Society*. Grand Rapids, Mich.: Eerdmans 1987.

Steere, David. "Our Capacity for Sadness and Joy: An Essay on Life Before Death." In *Theology of Joy*, ed. Johanna Baptist Metz and Jean-Pierre Jossua. New York: Herder and Herder, 1974.

Stith, Richard. "Generosity: A Duty without a Right." *Journal of Value Inquiry* 25, 3 (1991): 203–16.

Stout, Jeffrey. *Flight from Authority*. Notre Dame, Ind.: University of Notre Dame Press, 1981.

Taylor, Vincent. *Forgiveness and Reconciliation: A Study in New Testament Theology*. London: Macmillan, 1956.

Temple, William. *Readings in St. John's Gospel*. London: Macmillan, 1963.

Tertullian. "The Soldier's Chaplet." In *War and the Christian Conscience: From Augustine to Martin Luther King Jr.*, Ed. Albert Marrin. Chicago: Henry Regnery, 1971.

Vacek, Edward C. *Love, Human and Divine: The Heart of Christian Ethics*. Washington, D.C.: Georgetown University Press, 1994.

Wainwright, William. "Jonathan Edwards and the Sense of Heart." *Faith and Philosophy* 7, 1 (January 1990): 43–62.

Werpehowski, William. "Do You Do Well to Be Angry?" *Annual of the Society of Christian Ethics* (1996): 59–77.

Williams, Preston. "An Analysis of the Conception of Love and Its Influence on Jutice in the Thought of Martin Luther King, Jr." *Journal of Religious Ethics* 18 (fall 1990): 15–31.

Wilson, John F., and Donald L. Drakeman, eds. *Church and State in American History*. Boston: Beacon Press, 1987.

Wink, Walter. "Neither Passivity nor Violence: Jesus' Third Way." *Forum* 7, 1–2 (March-June 1991): 5–28.

Wittgenstein, Ludwig. *Philosophical Investigations*. Trans. G. E. M. Anscombe. New York: Macmillan, 1953.

Yoder, John Howard. *Nevertheless: The Varieties and Shortcomings of Religious Pacifism*. Scottsdale, Pa.: Herald Press, 1971.

———. "On Not Being Ashamed of the Gospel: Particularity, Pluralism, and Validation." *Faith and Philosophy* 9, 3 (July 1992): 285–300.

"A People in the World: Theological Interpretation." *The Concept of the Believer's Church*, ed. James Leo Garrett, Jr. Scottsdale, Pa.: Herald Press, 1969.

———. *The Politics of Jesus*. Grand Rapids, Mich.: Eerdmans, 1972.

Zuck, Roy B. *Teaching as Jesus Taught*. Grand Rapids, Mich.: Baker Books, 1995.

Index